# CRO...

# The Spiritual Universe of an Irish Village

## Marella Hoffman

Featuring folk historian Norma Buckley

In association with the Avondhu Blackwater Partnership

Published by Cambridge Editions, in association with the Avondhu Blackwater Partnership

A CIP catalogue record for this book is available from the British Library.

ISBN 9798690973063

Cambridge Editions, Bath House, Cambridge, CB1 2BD, United Kingdom
Printed and bound by CPI Books, Chatham, ME58TD, UK

Crow photography on cover and inside, Kevin Egan, email kevinegan06@gmail.com
Drone-photo of Doon Holy Well, Liam O' Brien, email liamob1986@gmail.com
Maps, Marella Hoffman

Other books
by Marella Hoffman

*Oral History to Assist Refugees and Host Communities,*
Sustainable Development Goals Collection, Taylor & Francis for the United Nations,
2020 (2nd edition)

*Practicing Oral History with Refugees and Host Communities,* Routledge, 2019 (1st edition)

*Practicing Oral History to Improve Public Policies and Programmes,* Routledge, 2017

*Asylum under Dreaming Spires - Refugees' Lives in Cambridge Today,*
with the Living Refugee Archive, University of East London, 2017

*Savoir-Faire des Anciens - Un Village des Corbières Maritimes, Hier et Demain,*
La Sorbonne University with Onslaught Press, 2017 (2nd edition)

*Savoir-Faire des Anciens - Un Village des Corbières Maritimes, Hier et Demain,*
Cahiers de la Salce, 2016 (1st edition)

*Magnets,* Cambridge Editions with Cambridge University Press, 2007

*The Fleurs Trilogy,* Cambridge Editions, 2020

Vol I, *Que J'aime Voir ~ Eyes and Gazes in Baudelaire's Les Fleurs du Mal*
Vol II, *Battant les Murs ~ Spaces and Places in Baudelaire's Les Fleurs du Mal*
Vol III, *Son Mouchoir et ses Gants ~ Objects, Collections and Commodities in Baudelaire's Les Fleurs du Mal*

Forthcoming

*Ancestral Ways for the Future ~ Eco-Knowledge in the French Mediterranean Hills,* 2021
(English translation of Hoffman's *Savoir-Faire des Anciens,* first published in 2016)

*The Eagle's Eye ~ Stories Told by the Land in a South of France Village,* 2022

For Pat and Johanna Carney
and for my great-grandparents Michael Sweeney and Hanora Martin,
all from Doon, Gleann an Phréacháin

Published on the day of Samhain 2020,

festival of the ancestors

## Thanks to institutions and experts

This book is produced in association with North Cork's *Avondhu Blackwater Partnership*. Reflecting their decades of hands-on support for the heritage and development of Gleann an Phréacháin or Glenville, they gave the project warm encouragement, and the local home that it was looking for.

The University of Cambridge and the University of Notre Dame in the USA jointly funded a summer fellowship for me to work on this project while hosted at Boston College, USA. University of Cambridge also funded a summer fellowship for me to work on it in Ireland, based at University College Dublin. Beaufort College at the University of Cambridge provided hospitality, library facilities and moral support.

Norma Buckley speaks Chapters 2, 4, 7 and 11. As a well-known folk historian in Crow Glen, she gave me over 50 hours of interviews for the book. She is also a core character threading through other chapters, and was a long-term associate of the *Avondhu Blackwater Patnership*. Her biography is inside.

Crow Glen Parish Priest Fr Donal Cotter and his colleague Rev Dr Noel O' Sullivan at University of Maynooth's Theology Faculty both gave open-minded encouragement for the project, and trusted me not to make a mess of it.

As well as contributing a Foreword, War of Independence author and historian Diarmuid Grainger encouraged and advised me by correspondence, and corrected the manuscript.


## Thanks to individuals

Thanks to all the individuals across the centuries, known about and unknown, who risked or gave their lives to create for us the democratic Republic that we have inherited from them today.

To so many of the older generation in the Glen of the Crow for being unique, quirky characters with the profound gentleness that is the mark of truly spiritual people. To name just a few - there are many others: Johnny Riordan, Jim Barry, Rita Healy, Norah and Jim O' Mahoney, Eily Gowen, Beena O' Callaghan who gave me kind encouragement as a young writer, and May Herlihy, whose soul passed on while I was finishing the book.

To the remarkable Carney family in America, whom I had never heard of. They irrupted politely into my life bringing with them unknown chunks of village history. Without them, more than half of this book would never have been written. Special thanks to Keith Carney of Washington, DC, originally, like all of them, a Glen of the Crow boy from Doon. He's the great instigator.

To my brother, Bernard Buckley from Glen of the Crow townland Glenagoul (site of a famous hurling match in 1741, as you can read inside). He improved the book with his close reading of the manuscript and many helpful corrections.

*As far as I'm concerned, I walk with God.*

~ Mary Carney,
great-grand-daughter of Johanna Carney of Doon, Crow Glen

*You're not meant to bother Saint Michael the Archangel with day to day stuff. But I do.*

~ Norma Buckley,
Crow Glen

# Gleann an Phréacháin Village

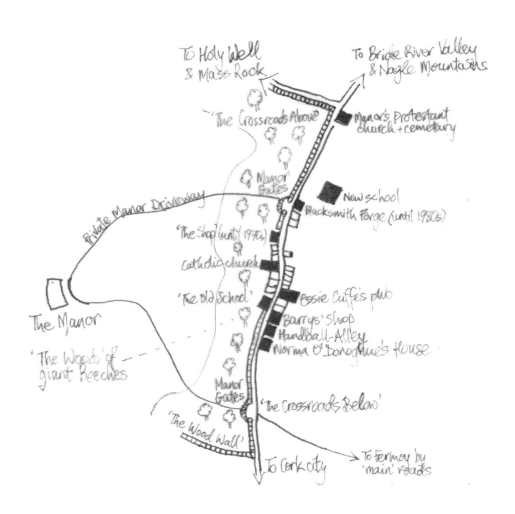

To Holy Well & Mass Rock

To Bride River Valley & Nagle Mountains

'The Crossroads Above'

Manor's Protestant church + cemetery

Private Manor Driveway

Manor Gates

New school

Blacksmith Forge (until 1980s)

'The Shop (until 1970s)

Catholic church

'The Old School'

Essie Cuffe's pub

Barrys' Shop

Handball-Alley

Norma O'Donoghue's House

The Manor

'The Wood' of giant Beeches

Manor Gates

'The Crossroads Below'

'The Wood Wall'

To Cork city

To Fermoy by 'main' roads

# The Bride River Valley

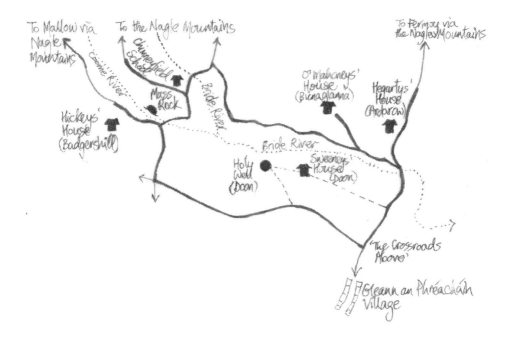

The BRIDE Project (short for *Biodiversity Regeneration In a Dairying Environment*), based in nearby Castlelyons, pays local farmers to do some agro-ecological farming profitably, in the areas that the River Bride flows through. Their free 85-page book, *Farm Habitat Management Guidelines,* gives step by step guidance to get started on even a smaller patch of ground, and apply for funding. Download it for free at www.thebrideproject.ie/wp-content/uploads/2020/04/BRIDE-Project-Farm-Habitat-Management-Guidlines.pdf

# pReface

## by the Avondhu Blackwater Partnership

The *Avondhu Blackwater Partnership* is a public service organisation dedicated to rural development and enterprise in the North Cork area. [1] In recent decades, we have drawn into the area and helped to deliver 45 million euros of grants and investments. We are very pleased to be partners in the publication of this book about the heritage of Glenville and its hinterlands in the Nagle Mountains. *Avondhu Blackwater* has long supported Glenville's heritage activities and Norma Buckley, a speaker in the book, was an active community representative on our board for many years.

The land here in our area is rich, fertile and beautiful, with a temperate climate. As we see in these chapters, it has been prized and sought-after for centuries, by invaders and settlers as well as by our own local farmers. If we manage it well, it is a land capable of supporting prosperous, diverse communities in a sustainable way into the far future.

The book glances back over past centuries of inequality and social injustice here - times when there was extreme prosperity for the few, while the majority were kept in poverty. A core mission for us at *Avondhu Blackwater* today is the opposite - **equality** - the commitment that prosperity and progress be shared out evenly across communities, leaving no-one behind.

Another part of our mission is of course **environment**: if we don't protect and preserve our natural environment, we won't have a future in it. But at *Avondhu Blackwater*, we also address environment in its wider, social sense. This is what the world-famous geographer from Glenville, Prof Anne Buttimer, called 'a sense of place' - the sense of belonging to, participating in, and taking shared responsibility for this rich place that we all live in together. [2]

---

1 *Avondhu* is an old, picturesque term for the Blackwater Valley and its hinterlands (from 'Abhainn Dubh' in Irish, meaning 'Black River'). *The Avondhu* is also the name of the thriving regional newspaper that covers events in the area.
2 Prof. Anne Buttimer, 'Home, Reach and the Sense of Place' in *The Human Experience of Space and Place,* Anne Buttimer & David Seamon (eds.), Routledge, 1980

Young and old, newcomers and families who have been here for centuries, we can all participate in this sense of **belonging**. And having a shared knowledge of the heritage that unfolded here in the past can help us chart our way towards a shared future.

This book explores too some of the specific **strengths and skills** that we can inherit from our ancestors: it shows us their sense of long-term vision, their courage and commitment in taking action to develop that vision, their humour and resourcefulness, their solidarity and enjoyment of life... The book invites readers to look into the many admirable activities of our ancestors and to sift through them for ourselves, noting those qualities that we might like to carry forward today.

This book is full of local voices so it is fitting that Barry Kennedy, whose family have run Essie Cuffe's pub at the heart of the village for nearly two centuries, gives its *Afterword*. The book is offered as another tool for use by the already active volunteer groups who look after Glenville's heritage sites, and the thriving local associations who meet in its community rooms and in Barry's pub facilities.

The book retrieves for the community yet more swathes of local history and **heritage** that risked being forgotten. Bringing them together in one publication like this opens up so many avenues for further **local development**. There are many threads here that others can pick up and develop further: recording oral history and folklore; mapping out the meanings of our original placenames in Irish; mapping international links and exchanges with the descendants of our local emigrants; studying our old farming methods, and developing future ones that fully respect nature and the environment...

For instance, **food** is one of the many themes threading through the book, where food is as much a key to our future, as it was to our past. Food quality, food equality and sustainability are all part of our mission here at *Avondhu Blackwater*, through programmes like our *Community Food Initiative*, which promotes a healthy, balanced, sustainable diet for all.

Producing food through the rich agriculture of this area will of course continue to be a core strength for our farmers. But as climate change threatens food supplies internationally, the book urges us to further develop this food self-sufficiency or 'food sovereignty' for which Ireland is already reputed. Citing a prize-winning farm in the Bride River Valley as an example, the book reminds us that this can be done in ecological ways that will make our farming, natural resources and communities truly sustainable for the long term ahead.

**Migrations** and returns are another core theme of the book. The chapters remind us that not all emigrants from our area get to come back home. But wherever they are - making their contributions to world society elsewhere - they can still *belong* here. The book shows that through our shared ancestry and love for this land, we can have many creative, productive connections with Irish descendants abroad, in the future as we have done in the past. This is what Prof. Anne Buttimer calls our '*reach*' - our contacts, exchanges and influence with the outside world. For instance, the author of this book returns to Glenville to re-invest there some of the research skills she has built up elsewhere. And the Irish American Carney family return with such affection for our land, that it makes us look at it afresh ourselves and redouble our efforts to protect and appreciate it.

Our area has of course long been appreciated by **visitors** from abroad, especially Americans enjoying the fishing, golfing, scenery and heritage along our beautiful *Blackwater Way*. And here at *Avondhu Blackwater* we have for decades been involved in deep collaborations with the European Union. The chapters of this book remind us that links and **exchanges** with the continent were already central to the life of the Gaelic clans in the Blackwater Valley and Nagle Mountains as far back as the fourteenth century, when they often spoke French and Latin here, as well as Irish and English!

Equality, rural development, partnerships, community, producing quality food, the environment… You can see how many themes in this book mirror our own values and commitments at *Avondhu Blackwater*. That is why we are so pleased to welcome this book project into our culture and communities.


Valerie Murphy
CEO, Avondhu Blackwater Partnership


www.avondhublackwater.com
Instagram@avondhublackwater

# foreword

by Diarmuid Grainger, historian and author [3]

Marella Hoffman has written an intimate book about her native place. In Ireland, that sense of place is seamlessly associated with history and folklore. From Antrim to Kerry, from Donegal to Wexford, and everywhere in between, that feeling for *dinnseanchas* - defined by the Reverend Patrick S. Dinneen, in his dictionary, as 'legends about and explanations of the names of places' - is ever present.

We sometimes need to leave a place for a period of time in order to stand back and look at it with fresh eyes; and this is exactly what Marella Hoffman has done. She records the speech patterns, hardships, doubts, fears and joys that are intrinsic to the human condition. It is, in my opinion, doubtful if the worldview she has formed of her homeplace would be so sharp, so comprehensive if she had not left her native village at the age of nineteen; nor, indeed, if she had not become an ethnographer, studying and lecturing for many years at Cambridge and other centres of academia.

Her natural inquisitiveness ranges over many centuries, encompassing, in no particular order, the old bardic school system, the coming of the Normans, the penal times, the War of Independence and Civil War, the hedge school system. But the episode to the forefront, the great national physical and mental scar that some argue has yet to be healed, is the Famine. Many have commented on how difficult it is, on observing Irish society and the Irish landscape in the present day, to imagine the scenes recorded by government officials, travellers from abroad in Ireland, members of the Society of Friends and others who, because of their privileged access to formal education, were able to write about what they had witnessed. Their accounts, written in the pedantic and stilted language of the day, provide a vivid word picture of the awful suffering behind the dry statistics of the formal history books: one million dead, one million

---

3  From the village of Cloughduv, south-west of Crow Glen, Diarmuid Grainger is the author of the 2019 book *Witnesses to Freedom: A Day by Day Account of The War of Independence in Cork*, available on www.amazon.co.uk   His forthcoming book is on his ancestors' role in the eighteenth-century Whiteboys movement that resisted British rule in Ireland, paving the way for the subsequent War of Independence.

fleeing to North America in the immediate aftermath, and emigration becoming part and parcel of the Irish psyche.

The 'silver bus', in which the descendants of those who emigrated in the 1840s travel around County Cork, becomes a metaphor for the resilience of the human spirit. They come from all walks of life in the United States, and their shared high spirits, and the depth of their emotions on coming 'home', are one of the highlights of the book.

The star performer is Norma Buckley. To those who think that a Catholic upbringing in rural Ireland was an endless series of rituals which sapped the human energy and spirit, her recollections as related to Marella Hoffman prove otherwise. A woman like her who prompts such mirth in her advanced years cannot but have been a howl in her youth; the reader will feel he is part of the action, sitting in and joining the show with two fun-filled women and a greyhound in the front room of a cosy home in the barony of Barrymore.

Hoffman's account of the War of Independence springs from a throwaway remark regarding her family's involvement in it, something of which she was totally unaware. Her book now takes an unexpected turn, a desire by the author to delve into the history behind the foundation of the State and the part played by the men and women of her area in achieving that aim. As she says herself, 'Those were things worth knowing, things that - once I started to hear about them - I couldn't let go of'.

She points out and delves into some of the contradictions that are part of the make-up of Ireland. The book contains a landlord who immerses himself in the music and native language of the peasant, yet is indifferent to their plight as they are forced to emigrate during the Famine. There is the bright light of poetry in the Irish language, fostered and encouraged through the patronage of the de Barras, de Nóglas and de Róistes, all of whom were new to this country after 1170 and whose people before them were of French and Welsh Norman stock. And there are the men who brought freedom to this country in the second decade of the twentieth century, but ended their lives in loneliness and social obscurity in New York, Boston and Chicago.

To this list of cultural and historical contradictions we may add the Americans' visit in this book to the Manor, a place to which their ancestors had no chance of ever entering - and the great dignity and self-possession shown by Keith Carney at the Manor dinner when he refuses to summon another human being by ringing a bell. It was an act of supreme elegance and dignity which said, 'Sorry, Sunshine. Those days are gone'.

There are Crow Glens everywhere, spread across five continents and two hemispheres, small and not so small, where people live out their lives as best they can, sometimes in trying circumstances. It was Daniel Corkery, man of letters and professor of English in University College Cork, who said that there are people who travelled the whole world who don't know their own backyard. Marella Hoffman, in writing this wonderful book, has described her own backyard of Crow Glen/ Glenville/ Gleann an Phréacháin in a way that is both local and universal.


Diarmuid Grainger

Author of *Witnesses to Freedom: A Day by Day Account of The War of Independence in Cork*

# Introduction

Images at the opening of this chapter:

~ Saint Brigid's cross, handwoven from local rushes by Norma Buckley of Gleann
~ Holy Water font to hang inside the front door of the home
~ This book's signal for when interviewees are speaking
~ This book's signal for the author's commentary on what they have said

# What this book is about, and who it's for

The Irish name of the village featured in this book is *Gleann an Phréacháin*, meaning *Glen of the Crow*. The place is twelve miles due north of Cork city, which is on Ireland's south coast. I grew up in a traditional household in the village before emigrating to work abroad at nineteen.

The book is not just about the village itself, but also its surrounding hinterlands. It uses the original names for the place: the Irish-language *Gleann an Phréacháin* or *Gleann* for short, and *Glen of the Crow* or *Crow Glen* in English. Colonisers anglicised the name to 'Glenville' and it's still called Glenville today. But that anglicisation wasn't a *translation*, in the way that 'Glen of the Crow' is the accurate translation for *Gleann an Phréacháin*. Translation is a respectful carrying over of a word's meaning from one language into another. Instead, the colonisers just flattened down the placename in Irish, and pasted over it any term they fancied in English. There was no attempt to retrieve or carry forward the original meaning. This wisdom and meaning that lie hidden in our old placenames is a rich subject: we'll return to it when we go up into the hills above the Bride River Valley later on.

As well as using the older names for the village, I've also used, with capital letters, the handful of ultra-local terms that we villagers used for naming our immediate surroundings. *The Village, The Street, The Crossroads Below, The Crossroads Above, The Wood, The Wood Wall* - we who lived in the village had our own little mini-language of place-naming made up of these terms.[4]

I wrote this book for two main audiences. One is the local people in Glenville and the surrounding area in North Cork. I hope they will read, enjoy, discuss and debate the book, and make it their own in whatever ways they wish. The other audience I had in mind is the diaspora abroad - people who, or whose ancestors, emigrated from Ireland and especially from this North Cork area, like the Irish-American Carney family through whose eyes we see some of the chapters of this book.

Chapters 2, 4, 7 and 11 are about religious traditions in the Glen of the Crow, told entirely in a local speaker's words. All the other chapters are

---

4 Automatically familiar to locals, placenames like *The New Line, Leary's Cross, The Mallow Road, Norry Roche's Cross, The Terrace, The Cover Road* and *Keame Hill* are other examples of this very local lingo that you won't find on any map.

about historical events there. Readers can navigate between these two main themes of the book, depending on which interests them most.

I've spent my career as a university academic abroad, moving across disciplines and then working extensively for government with communities, before ending up as an ethnographer. As a branch of anthropology, ethnography is about spending long periods in specific places listening to how the people there see their own world and - with their permission - writing up their worldview in book form.

As a Fellow of the Royal Anthropological Institute, my books examine the differing lifestyles and worldviews of people in specific places and times. I've written books about the attitudes of the permanently unemployed White underclass in an English town; about refugees' experiences of nationality and identity in their adopted homeland; about the rural practices and ecological lifestyle of an 87-year-old hermit shepherd in the French Mediterranean mountains…

Now I wanted to turn that lens back onto the culture I grew up in. This book was originally going to be just about religious practices in the Glen of the Crow, past and present, because our religion was such an intense, all-encompassing activity when I was growing up there.

But once I arrived on the terrain, the interviews I was recording quickly started to stumble onto other things - historical facts that I had never known about Gleann an Phréacháin and about my own family's role in its history. These were things worth knowing, things that - once I started to hear about them - I couldn't let go of.

I had made the cardinal mistake, unforgivable in an ethnographer, of believing I knew Gleann inside out. Ethnographers must approach every site of study with fresh eyes, assuming they know nothing about it and letting local people initiate them with their local knowledge.

I quickly discovered that there was much, much more to be known about Gleann. Historical facts to be proud of, things that shouldn't be forgotten. The telling of those histories doubled the size of the book I had intended to write. Now the religious practices and the historical events twine around each other in alternating chapters.

It was the eruption into my life of the Carney family - originally from Doon in Crow Glen and now from America - that gave this book its other half. I'll let the chapters tell you their story. The Carneys led me to stumble upon acts of breath-taking heroism and altruism done here in

Gleann an Phréacháin by people of such calibre that I couldn't bear for their stories not be told out loud, right here and now.

The revealed facts of those heroes' lives also shifted my own identity and my sense of what my own history was, like an earthquake lifting up great chucks of the ground beneath you. It was dramatic, but what lay beneath was much richer, more valuable and more inspiring than the covering that had lain over it. I had to see these people's stories told.

I considered doing two separate books - one on the religious practices and another on the historical events. But you will see as you read this book that in Ireland in particular, history cannot be separated from spiritual life. Across the centuries in Crow Glen they interwove, like branches growing out of the same trunk. Any initial efforts I made to separate them seemed as artificial as if I were trying to cut them apart with scissors.

So the two threads now alternate through the chapters like a braided plait. The historical chapters are full of escapades and lively derring-do. There are misplaced bodies, secret hide-outs, kidnaps, miracles, daring escapes and rescues. They alternate, thankfully, with chapters of quieter reflection on spiritual matters over cups of tea by the fire.

In those quieter chapters, a local person tells the long story of the spiritual practices of the community in the Glen of the Crow. But while the tape recorder listened, her casual revelations of dramatic historical secrets regularly sent me running back into the archives again, to uncover and verify the next layer of exploits by the village's amazing ancestors.

At the beginning of each chapter, photos that are captioned on the ensuing page show key people, places or objects from that chapter. Sections that are marked with a microphone show where my interviewees are speaking, and the pages where I comment briefly on their interviews are marked with a photo of my own clipboard.

## Research methods used

You'll see in the course of the book that I spent a lot of time researching it in libraries and archives. That's a strange lifestyle: sitting for days on end in one far-off place (for instance, in the library of the Royal Anthropological Institute at the British Museum in London) in order to find out about another place hundreds of miles away (my own parish of Gleann an Phréacháin in Ireland). But I was richly rewarded by those dusty old papers. I was amazed to discover how many layers of important *writings* and literature had already been laid down in Crow Glen centuries before I ever thought of writing about the place myself. I was mainly amazed that I had never been taught about any of them in the course of my own schooling and living there.

Like an archaeologist carefully lifting away layers of soil to reveal hidden treasures, I found now that the lands of Crow Glen conceal layers of intensely *local* writings that reach back over centuries, and even millennia. This book introduces them for your entertainment. For instance, there's a 234-page manuscript, handwritten in beautiful calligraphy and partly in Irish, from a hundred years ago. There's an important anonymous letter sent from Crow Glen to the British government in the 1920s, with one strategic mis-spelling in it. There are songs and poems of love, revenge and landscape composed and sung by Gleann farmers in the nineteenth century. There are beautiful, moving poems in Irish by famous Crow Glen Bards of the thirteenth, seventeenth and eighteenth centuries. And there are exciting oral sagas that historians date back to the third century AD.

In Chapter 8, 'The Bards of Crow Glen and the Nagle Mountains', the landscape itself will speak to us like a freshly opened book. It will walk you through its small roads and boreens, in places like *Lyrenavarrig, Lyrenamon, Mullanabowree, Toorgariffe*... These extraordinary placenames are like exotic jewels that stud our landscape. But here they will get up out of their rich soil and speak their native Irish meanings back to us, handing over the messages they contain about how our ancestors lived in those places.

For the chapters on the War of Independence too, I did a lot of research in academic libraries and archives. The works I consulted are listed in the chapters' footnotes and in the bibliography at the back of the book. It was important that all those historical events be verifiable as documented facts, especially as some may be news to some readers who think, like I did, that they already know the Glen of the Crow in full. (But I suspect that few of the 'secrets' revealed between these covers will actually be news to real Crow Glenners - it's just that they wouldn't tell you about them! I had to go and find out them out for myself.)

Those dangerous, dramatic events actually happened for real in the lives of hundreds of people around the Glen of the Crow, and many who were later dispersed abroad by emigration. Shards of these events remained, of course, in the memories of the people but they almost never spoke about them afterwards. It was as if a pact of silence had been agreed.

Once, in the 1990s, a researcher made an appointment to come and see my grandmother Nell in our house in the village, when she was in her late 80s. Tea was laid out beside the fire, ready for his visit. But after leaving them alone, my mother was surprised to see the researcher drive away in his car three minutes later. It turned out that he was writing about the War of Independence in County Cork and had wanted to interview Nell about events in Gleann an Phréacháin. '*It's too soon*', was all Nell would say about it when my mother asked her why she had sent him away.

Almost thirty years later, this book is timed to honour the centenary anniversary of those events. I believe that the story of the War of Independence in the Glen of the Crow is being published here for the first time. And I hope that now, at the centenary, even Nell would agree that it is right that those people's incredible, selfless deeds on our behalf be told. With amazing modesty, the families involved never spoke about it again. Many local families fought or took serious risks on behalf of the armed Irish effort but this book focuses around the Bride River Valley where three families - the Hickeys, the Hegartys and my own ancestors, the Sweeneys - organised for the IRA to have their main headquarters, strategy meetings and weapons store. Before publication, I asked Hickeys and Hegartys for permission to publish their grandparents' stories, and to publicly celebrate their bravery for the first time. They happily gave it. As the present-day Willy Hegarty put it, standing in the doorway of Teresa Barry's shop in the village: '*It's time*. It's time now to honour those good people, and the way they stuck their necks out for us.'

I hope that this book will raise at least as many questions as it answers, and I really hope that others in the Glen of the Crow - families, school groups, associations - will pick up and pursue the very many threads of history that are still lying around there waiting to be told. There is much more yet to be unfolded out of Gleann about all the layers of history addressed in this book - more about the oral sagas on Fionn Mac Cumhaill, the archaeology of our sacred sites, the details of the War of Independence, the Irish-language names of all our townlands... It's not difficult to do what I have done, and I will always be happy to advise anyone who's interested in doing more.

For the chapters on spirituality, I used only oral history interviews that I recorded locally in Gleann an Phréacháin. I wanted to hear practitioners' own spiritual experiences directly, without them being framed or defined in any way by the Church or by me or anyone else. So those interview chapters on spirituality involved no archives or libraries: the local speaker is the only expert there, and I only listen and record.

Whether you are a local or an outsider, there are two different ways that you can read the chapters on religion. If you feel, as I do, that life does have a spiritual dimension, you can appreciate those chapters as the efforts of one culture to step forward and engage directly with those spiritual realms. Or if you have a purely secular view of life, you can stand back like my anthropologist colleagues would and just appreciate the sheer complexity of the symbols, rituals and practices that people developed in this culture that was otherwise, in material terms, quite simple.

Perhaps other young people disliked it all but as a child, I really appreciated the material beauty of those ritual practices and objects: the pictures and statues and stained glass windows, the candles and red lamps, the singing and chanting and processing, the incense and flowers, the special outfits, the coloured glass Rosary beads, the lace cloths, the hand gestures, the sky-blue of Our Lady's cape, the gold chalices and silver candlesticks, the polished dark timber seats… I could go on and on. It was all very lush and elaborate compared to the simplicity of our homes, clothes and possessions at that time. At the very least, I wanted in this book to celebrate those elaborate aesthetics of rural Irish Catholicism that I had found so magical as a child.

There is a significant lack of ethnographic writing on rural Irish Catholicism, and I wanted to contribute to filling that gap. In 1995, Lawrence Taylor of Maynooth University wrote *Occasions of Faith: An Anthropology of Irish Catholics*, a study of Catholic practices at that time in a Donegal village. [5] But it is very much a book for academics only. In 1998, an academic PhD thesis was written at University College Cork on Catholic folk practices in Cork city, but it was never published. [6] I believe that *Crow Glen - The Spiritual Universe of an Irish Village* is the only ethnographically-minded book for a broad audience that listens to rural Irish Catholic practices as they are done today in 2020.

Many who live in Gleann an Phréacháin now are secular people who either no longer, or never did, practice the religion. A few may practice other religions, as was always the case in Gleann. But I hope that all will

---

5 Lawrence Taylor, *Occasions of Faith: An Anthropology of Irish Catholics*, Pennsylvania University Press, 1995

6 Joseph Feller, *Roots and Wings: Orthodoxy, Tradition, and Creativity in Irish Folk Catholicism*, unpublished PhD thesis, University College Cork, 1998

find it of some interest to overview in this book this aspect of Gleann's traditions. Catholicism is certainly not all that went on there, and it's not all that's going on in this book, but it is one of the deep threads of the locality's history. And I hope it will be interesting to hear it told in a new way - from practitioners' own viewpoint rather than from the perspective of the Church or the media.

I had intended to do shorter interviews on religion with a wider range of people in Crow Glen. But I ended up instead doing a series of long interviews with just one. Once or twice in their career, an ethnographer may be lucky enough to stumble upon what is called in the trade an 'ideal anthropological speaker'. This is a grassroots individual who has a rare eloquence for and interest in describing the society that they are a part of. If you find one of them, you stick with them and let them narrate a whole book to you. So that is what I did with my Crow Glen informant on spiritual matters.

But good ethnographers always add that 'Further research is needed'. The best ethnographies open up a whole world to explore in one small locality, where people may not have noticed before that there are such treasures lying around waiting to be examined. And once the treasure chest is opened, it can seem that lifetimes wouldn't be long enough to get to the bottom of exploring it. After reading this book, I invite you to imagine how rich it would be to also interview many other practitioners of the religion in Crow Glen, setting their diverse accounts and experiences into dialogue with each other and with the ones told here.

The only thing I have added to the chapters on spirituality is a *Glossary* at the back of the book explaining about fifty technical terms that the interviewee uses to describe the spiritual practices done in the Glen of the Crow. This specialised vocabulary or mini-language of Irish Catholicism is of course second nature to practitioners. But to non-Catholics, some of it would be as obscure as medieval Gaelic. The *monstrance, special intentions, favours granted, plenary indulgences, the Communion of Saints...* Like any other language, it's easy when you know how, but double Dutch if you're not initiated.

That language was as intense as the incense and the stained glass artworks in the windows: '*Turn then most gracious advocate thine eyes of mercy towards us and after this our exile, show unto us the blessed fruit of thy womb, Jesus. Oh clement, oh loving, oh sweet Virgin Mary*'. As a small child I burbled away, reciting that whole prayer with enthusiasm while understanding as yet only four words of it: 'eyes', 'fruit', 'loving' and 'sweet'. The rest - 'advocate', 'mercy', 'exile', 'womb', 'clement' and 'virgin' - were words I didn't know yet even in ordinary English, not to mind in their specifically Catholic meanings.

Young people today may have heard the Glossary's terms before, but how many really know what a *plenary indulgence* is, or how their ancestors went about getting one? Or what a *scapular* does? Or what exactly *First Fridays* are?

Even to those for whom that spiritual tongue holds no secrets, I make no apology for including a Glossary, if only for the sheer enjoyment of it. Standing back and seeing those fifty technical spiritual terms listed together can help us to view our own culture from a distance, as if we were studying the culture of a Vietnamese hill-tribe, or that of a laboratory of computer programmers in California's Silicon Valley.

The Glossary reminds us just how complex, intricate and learned this particular set of religious practices was and is. And that it is a universe away from the secular, scientific-materialist worldview that's mainstreamed in the Western world today.

I wanted to hold up a mirror to the sheer complexity of that spiritual universe that I was raised in until I emigrated at nineteen, in the late 1980s. For me, stepping from that worldview into the secular worldview of the universities where I worked abroad was a leap like growing up in an Amazonian river-tribe and being dropped into the Chinese Imperial Court of the fifteenth century.

That is why Crow Glen's religious practices seemed to me a genuinely fascinating story in anthropological terms. They are as dense and complex a religious culture as any you could seek to study anywhere on earth. Now I finally had the time to go and use the tools of my trade on my own people. I would go back to Gleann and research this matter on the ground, by listening at length to people's local accounts of their own spiritual practices.


## Spirituality

I've just described my intellectual motivation. But I had also felt for some time that there may be more *spiritual* truth - more spiritual accuracy and reality - to the traditional Gleann practices than they tend to be given credit for nowadays.

Today, Ireland's ordinary secular culture is comfortable with 'New Age' practices and ideas. Notions like personal development, inner relaxation, healing vibes, attuning to one's higher self, listening to one's inner life and intuitions... Even angels or spirit guides may be acceptable along with your acupuncture or Pilates. Those things are casually fashionable at the moment, an easy-going norm. But the notion of *novenas, transubstantiation, the Glorious Mysteries* and *mantillas* - maybe not so much! Although they're still practiced by many, these symbols and practices are not 'fashionable' right now.

But my studies around the world had shown me two things. Firstly, that the various maps of the spirit world, worked out separately by people on different continents in different eras, are in fact remarkably similar. And secondly, that the differences lie mostly in each religion's degree of sophistication and maturity. At one end of the spectrum there are rigid, dogmatic religions that offer primarily *group* activity and identity. They have a narrow code of group practices that are policed with severity and punishments, both on earth and in heaven. They tend to rule most brutally of all over the two aspects of human life that seem to haunt them the most - sexuality and freedom of speech. Extreme examples would be the cruel 'Spanish Inquisition' run by the Catholic Church from the fifteenth century, or the present-day religious fanatics issuing a death-sentence against a British author for writing a novel.[7]

By contrast, spiritual activity at the other end of the spectrum tends to emphasise the *inner* prayer life of diverse, thoughtful individuals. That tends to yield *direct* personal experience of spiritual beings. And they in turn - when encountered - tend to communicate above all compassion, forgiveness and kindness, not condemnation. Genuine familiarity with these spiritual beings tends to yield a religion that offers a wide diversity of practices, and a palette of gentle wisdoms and insights rather than one severe truth laid down by the religion's *'one book, one law'*.

Of course, even individual religions - Christianity, Islam, Judaism, Buddhism - can and do contain within them these two extremes. They have all at times been expressed as militant, aggressive, repressive regimes, while at other moments producing gentle mystical traditions that encounter spirit directly and welcome the diversity of life.

---

7 This death sentence was issued against novelist Salman Rushdie in 1998 in response to his novel *The Satanic Verses*. He was moved around the world in hiding under international police protection for the next 20 years, with regular attempts on his life.

For some reason, it seems that religious systems that encourage individuals to cultivate their own direct, inner experience of the spirit world tend to yield a very diverse set of spiritual practices, like the different plants growing in a wildflower meadow. *Inner* seems to equate with or yield diversity. Whereas more 'outward-focused' religions, where mobs shout out the supremacy of their *one god*, seem allergic to diversity.

Over the years, when I used to weigh up my memory of the Gleann an Phréacháin practitioners against this spectrum of world religions that I met during my work abroad, it always niggled at the back of my mind that the practices that I remembered Crow Glenners doing seemed quite sophisticated on all the counts described above. [8] Yet that was not how I saw rural Irish Catholics depicted in the media or in literature, where they seemed more like a flock of naïve victims led around passively by dominant priests.

Far from being passive or nostalgic, the local speaker in this book, unprompted by me, stands back and points out many ways that the religion practiced in Gleann has evolved and matured over time, partly through the influence of practitioners themselves. She sees it as having changed in many ways for the better, even over the last couple of decades.

Another criterion for assessing the maturity of a religious practice is to what extent its forms and symbols are just empty material habits. Many religions use statues, sacred objects and images, chants and recitations. But there is a spectrum of spiritual maturity around these too. On the one hand are people of any religion who, even if they hardly realise it themselves, are just 'going through the motions' as they mutter prayers absentmindedly and bow to statues.

But on the other hand, there are people for whom prayers and sacred objects are just triggers or trampolines that catapult them into intense inner experiences of spiritual energies, or encounters with higher spiritual beings. The Crow Glen speaker herself evokes this perennial 'problem' with religion - how it can veer between those two extremes even for an individual practitioner at different moments. Few human beings in any culture can maintain a state of mystic exaltation the whole time. Striving to keep one's practices fresh must surely be a daily task for even the most accomplished practitioners - even for the Pope or the Dalai Lama.

---

8 This book doesn't discuss the Irish Catholic Church as an institution at all. That is a different matter outside the scope of the book. I'm talking here about the actual spiritual life that I saw Crow Glen practitioners elaborating for themselves, albeit within the Catholic Church.

But in my opinion, there is another, even higher, measure of a religion's maturity. That is whether its practitioners can tolerate a degree of gentle humour around it, whether generated by themselves or by others. I was not prepared for how much we laughed during the time that I spent working with my Crow Glen interviewee on this book's spiritual chapters. The recordings are peppered with moments where she has us both creased with laughter while she talks about her own sincere religious practices and the doing of them. [9] Some of that humour you'll see in her chapters. But some of it was so witty, and told in such an *Irish* way, that I was unable to squeeze it down into words on the page afterwards. No-one will doubt the depth or sincerity of the speaker's spiritual practice, but she was so funny about it. To me that is a rare and unfakeable sign of a mature spiritual practice.

## Different worlds

Whether we're talking about local religion or local history, the fact will always remain that I don't and can't ever really know *your* Crow Glen, and you can't ever know mine. There *is* no 'one' Crow Glen, just as there is no 'one' New York and no 'one' London. That is the rich mystery of place.

A place is a prism. Every individual who is living out their life in it is having a different view, experience and perspective on it. Even if they live in the place in the same era, right next door to each other, one person may be the most privileged, dominant individual benefitting from all of the place's resources while their neighbour may be entirely dominated, exploited or enslaved.

Even in one village at any given era, people can have radically different experiences of poverty and of privilege, as we will see in this book. Some will have right-wing, and some left-wing, politics. Some will decide to take

---

9  This is a rare and special quality, but unfortunately the opposite is not so rare. An extreme example in recent years was when religious fundamentalists broke into the offices of the humourist Parisian newspaper *Charlie Hebdo* and executed 12 journalists at their desks, as well as injuring 11. It was because they had drawn cartoons that the attackers found disrespectful towards their religion. That event may seem almost laughably extreme but it had the desired effect. Since then, such gestures of terror have successfully narrowed the scope of freedom of speech, debate and satire even in Western democracies (Sam Berkhead, 'How the *Charlie Hebdo* attack has changed free speech in France and the US', *International Journalists' Network*, 8-1-2016).

direct political action to try to bring change, and others will keep their head down hoping that the winds of history will blow over them. Across the chapters and centuries in this book, we will see all these dynamics playing out in Crow Glen.

Like a honeycomb, a place contains as many versions of itself as there are people who have ever lived in it. Each has experienced it uniquely through their own eyes and circumstances. Each person holds inside themselves a microcosm that is *their* version of the place, at their unique moment in time. For some, it's a lovely place where they had a great time. For others, they had a terrible time there that they want to forget. As you will see repeatedly in this book, those two people may have lived in the same place 300 years apart, or they may have rubbed shoulders there at the same time. (So there is, of course, no one '*Spiritual Universe of Crow Glen*', as this book's title goes. There are as many 'spiritual universes' in Crow Glen as people who have ever lived there.)

A recent philosophy called postmodernism claims that all versions of places and everyone's account of their experiences are equally valid. But in today's climate of dangerous fake news, we've learned that we can and must also safeguard any verifiable facts that are available.

Proper historians stick with the facts. Forensically, like police detectives, they try to record: what actually happened here for certain, regardless of what anyone thought or felt about it? It's those kind of facts in the Glen of the Crow that the chapters of this book retrieve from under the blanket of forgetfulness.

But remember, it's still true that one person's Gleann an Phréacháin will never be another's. Yours is your own to tell. And my precise, personal version of the religion will never be the same as your version of it. But what we can do is to build bridges across those distances by being interested in each other. We can listen to each other's descriptions of how we see the world.

Reperences

Berkhead, Sam, 'How the *Charlie Hebdo* attack has changed free speech in France and the US', *International Journalists' Network*, 8-1-2016

Feller, Joseph, *Roots and Wings: Orthodoxy, Tradition, and Creativity in Irish Folk Catholicism* by, unpublished PhD thesis, University College Cork, 1998

Taylor, Lawrence, *Occasions of Faith: An Anthropology of Irish Catholics*, University of Pennsylvania Press, 1995

# Crow Flies in

Crow flies in and settles with a little jump onto his nest in the Beech canopy that runs the length of Crow Glen Village. Crow and his people have lived up here since time began, in the ancient forest, long before the two-leggeds moved in.

His black liquid eye is ringed with yellow. On its shiny surface are reflected two dozen centuries that have played out down below, where the two-leggeds live their days. Things forgotten, things remembered, things much sung about, things never yet told. Sitting above them, Crow has witnessed it all.

Today, Crow senses that someone is coming from the South. Crow knows these things, as sure as wind and rain. A returner, someone who's been away a long time. A listener. One who stirs the pots of stories.

And he sees that others are coming too - from the West, from farther away. A dozen other returners.

Things are going to happen because of these returns. Layers of time are going to be stirred up.

Crow will keep one eye half-open tonight, looking on.

Chapter **1**

# Return to Crow Glen

Images at the opening of this chapter:

~ Crow of Gleann an Phréacháin, the Glen of the Crow (photo by Kevin Egan)
~ The Manor Gates at the Crossroads Below
~ Entrance to Gleann Village, beside the Wood Wall
~ Norma Buckley, folklorist in Gleann an Phréacháin

# Returners

The figure of *Crow* has hovered over this village for centuries, if not millennia, like a living icon or totem. In this book you will see how the place took on his name. Records show that it was already called Gleann an Phréacháin by 1599, when English colonisers clumsily wrote the term down in their own registers as '*Glana Frehan*', before later giving up even trying to retain the sound and just calling the place 'Glenville'. [10]

To approach Crow Glen from the south, you arrive along the road from Cork, the city twelve miles away on Ireland's south coast. First, you hit *The Wood*, gateway to *The Village*. It's a dense, dark barrier of exceptionally tall trees wrapped around the Village. The Wood looms overhead, enfolding you. Protectively? Menacingly? Whatever you like. The Wood gives the Village a *Sleeping Beauty* feel as if, like the princess in the story, the Village exists in a slightly other dimension. A zone where things happen differently, and time runs at its own pace.

You move forward and step in under the canopy of the Wood. Now you meet *The Crossroads*, where you must pause. To your left: the baronial, white pillars and black, wrought-iron gates of the Manor, the estate from which the elites of the British colonial system ran life in Gleann for centuries.

Straight ahead, a wide, inviting road will sweep you up the gentle slope into the Village. The trees crowding in over this road are so vast that their canopies soar fully from one side of it to the other, like a cathedral. They gently darken this roadway, no matter what the light is like outside.

These are giant, 250-year-old Beeches: serried masses of them, still standing like a redundant army since the colonisers planted them long ago. They loom out over *The Wood Wall*. This old dry-stone wall, nine feet high, runs along like a ribbon at their feet for half a mile, right through the Village and beyond. Measuring up to three yards round their trunks, these Beeches are as high as six-storey houses. But if you know them well and intimately - up-close at ground-level inside the Wood Wall - each at its base has a ring of overground roots that form mossy indentations. These gothic arches recede back into the trunk, forming green caves a foot high and a foot deep, where little fairy-like plants live and thrive.

---

10   This was in their *Calendar to Fiants of the Reign of Henry VIII, 1510-47, & Queen Elizabeth, 1558-1603*, London, 1601

Moving on up the slope into the Village, two rows of neat, brightly painted houses open like an embrace along either side of *The Street*. It is broad and bright enough to have hosted a big outdoor farmers' market in previous centuries. Here the Beeches stand back a little, peering down into *the Street* without darkening it. The houses are pink. Yellow. Tortoise-shell blue. Mauve. Like a photo from the tourist board. And dotted up along the two sides of the Street are a country shop, a pub, a church, a school.

Though the Village was just one street lined with a handful of houses, its farmers' market was disproportionately large until well into the nineteenth century. Wilson's *Directory of Ireland, 1834* lists Gleann an Phréacháin as one of Ireland's important 'Fair Towns'. It says: 'The Fair Towns were very important… people walked for miles on a fair day to go to sell their produce. Until the Fair Day, people would have no money and so once the produce or the animals were sold, then the bills would be paid.' [11] Before researching this book, I had never heard of this thriving market of food and produce in Gleann. And I didn't know either that food, hunger and the trading of produce would be a theme that twines through this book from beginning to end.

But this discovery in the archives about Gleann's nineteenth-century market did provoke one forgotten memory of my own. I suddenly recalled that livestock gatherings still happened there once or twice a year when I was a child in the 1970s. Farmers would park their trucks the length of the Village, and stand their bulls out beside the trucks to be examined by the local vet. It was a strange scene - to see standing around loose and casual in our Street those big, dangerous bulls whom no-one would normally go near on a farm. After those events, bulls would come into my dreams at night, nosing at the front door of our house, trying to get in.

If you keep on going up to the top of the Village, you'll meet *The Crossroads Above*. It will take you out of the Village towards the north mountains. Its sits five hundred yards from *The Crossroads Below* where you came in. When I was a child and until I emigrated at nineteen, this was my world and it felt like a big world.

The Village has been called the Glen of the Crow for many centuries. When I was a child, a thousand navy-black crows lived in the canopies of the giant Beeches that loomed across the road from our house. The crows each stand a foot tall on the ground, with broad, triangular beaks the

11 'Fair Towns of Ireland', *Wilson's Directory of Ireland, 1834*, available at www.from-ireland.net/category/miscellaneous/cork-miscellaneous/page/3

colour of sea-rocks. When the Beeches are in leaf, their interlocked canopies form a dark green, bouncy cloud that runs the length of the Village. The crows' homes sit on top, dotted a few yards from each other. Their heavy nests are three feet wide and a foot deep, thick and solid-woven, the edges left untidy. This strip of high-rise real estate for crows runs well beyond both the Crossroads Above and the one Below.

Mysteriously, the Crows have always flown away together in unison every morning, and returned at dusk. I have never known where they go or why. When they come drifting back in on the twilight, their hundreds of black, outstretched bodies block out the Village sky. They circle in big, slow, overlapping wheels. This circling is smooth and lazy but they make thousands of screeching *Caws* that sound urgent, contradictory, deafening.

All this lasts for about fifteen minutes until each has relocated their own nest and sat down heavily into it, jabbering angrily at their neighbours. Those in adjoining trees continue to pass comment loudly to each other for another five or ten minutes until dusk folds over them like a cloak, settling them into an invisible group silence.

To us, this drama was as normal as the sun going down. As a small child, I assumed this happened at every village in the wider world. I thought this vast, black, squawking sky-event was just part of the day, like washing your face. But for visitors who witnessed it unwarned, it was terrifying. As a teen, when I saw the horror-scenes where crows attack people in the Hitchcock film *The Birds*, I understood how visitors perceived ours.

Ours were exactly like the crows in the film - just as big, black, loud, flapping, soaring and numerous. But they never swooped down on us. Busy occupying their own stratum of the air, they seemed hardly to notice us at all, down below.

As a child, all I knew was that the crows' return told you it was time to stop playing and start making your way back to your family's house for your supper. That was also the time of day when the children's television programme *Wanderly Wagon* came on our only TV channel. *Wanderly Wagon* was a sweet and clever show about a bunch of rag-tag individuals, some animal and some human, who lived a caring, cooperative life together in a little flying house on wheels.

When I was very young, I assumed it was the crows' return that made the TV programme come on. Both the crows and *Wanderly Wagon* were mysterious and strange, and both came flying in punctually on the twilight sky. And one of the puppet characters in *Wanderly Wagon* happened to be the wise and kindly 'Mister Crow', who lived in the Wagon's cuckoo clock.

I grew up in a traditional, multi-generational household in the Village. [12] As newly-weds, my parents had moved in with my mother's parents and sister. Over the years my father extended the house. And in old age, my grandparents took up their station in armchairs at either side of the fire. Like statues of lions guarding a cosy castle door.

At that time, we villagers believed that many spirits, saints and angels lived in our houses with us. We believed that each of us also had a personal angel who moved everywhere with us, throughout the day and the night. As best they could, they protected us individually from accident, illness and spiritual problems.

When I was nineteen, shortly before I emigrated to work abroad, I asked my grandmother what she really, honestly, secretly - in her own heart of hearts - thought about religion. When no-one was looking, away from any keeping up appearances or pressure from priests, what did she really think? She said: 'I believe the air is full of spirits.'

This Village capped with Crows was our epicentre but connected away from it, unfolding out across the landscape like a treasure-map, were other focal places that gave the Village its flavour and made life there an adventure. The midsummer pilgrimage to the Holy Well, a couple of miles away. The Mass Rock, half a mile further on as Crow flies. These were hidden places that for us, glowed with animation but for passers-by, could not be seen. Our ancestors had sited them in folds in the landscape that disappear when you look out across it from a distance or from roads. Often protected by lookouts historically, those places couldn't be spotted or accessed without invitation. Those were the magical, outlier places that gave us our festivals.

But in early summer, the Village itself too had its Procession, which saw hundreds of us parishioners processing the Virgin Mary up and down the length of the Street, and beyond the perimeters of the Crossroads. She was (and still is) carried aloft on a platform on the shoulders of a guild of sash-wearing local men dedicated to her, who sing hymns to her as they bear her along. We children used to run ahead strewing flowers on the ground in front of the Procession. Petals, hymns, incense, flags, the life-size statue of Our Lady and us parishioners singing in our Sunday best - all of it

---

12  My European surname Hoffman is from my marriage abroad.

snaked along like one living carnival thing, streaming colours and perfumes and music. On that day, as well as on midsummer night for *The Bonfire*, the Village itself got to be one of our sacred spaces too, like those further out on the landscape. It got the power to make festival, make *frisson*, like the sacred sites out in the land did all year.

And I am going back now. I'm *Back from Abroad*. I'm pausing at the Crossroads Below and I'm walking back up into the Village. Like many others from the Village before me, I've spent my adult life working in other countries. And like they all eventually do, I'm coming back. To see the old places. To try to recall for myself how the old places and the old ways felt back then. And to see how they feel today.

I walk slowly up the Road, the Beech canopy arching over me. Countless other returners have made this journey that I'm making. And often much longer journeys, stretched painfully - like skin - across the centuries. They come back to the Village from the USA. From Canada. From Australia. From South Africa. Some left the Village themselves, as I did. But mostly, their grand-parents or great-grand-parents left it for them. In the 1920s, heading to Sydney. In the 1890s, to New York. Or most common of all, in the mid-nineteenth century when the Famine starved to death large swathes of the Village population. Survivors were sent on 'coffin ships' to places they'd never heard of with names like '*New-found-land*', on the frozen iceberg shores of Canada.

There is an appointed person in the Village to welcome returners, a local folklorist or folk historian. They go into the shop or the pub asking for memories of their family name, and they are sent to her. Both on paper and in her memory, she holds the tangled threads of the records that remain, and she has the time and the interest and the talent for it. So returners knock at her door, go in to her little side room. And after consulting her records, both the inner and outer, she can tell them which cottage or smallholding in the parish their people came from.

Then they drive there together. The returners walk those fields and weep. She has many accounts of six-foot-two American millionaires on their knees in the deep pastures around the Village, sobbing long wet tears into the muddy grass. Eventually, they all go back to her house. The returners are shaken, giddy with emotion. She gives them tea and home-made scones by the fire. Calms them down. The worst is over now. They have found the old home - they have stood in it, like in a new home - and now they can come back any time.

And they do come back, regularly. Often bringing other relatives, always calling to see her before going on to 'the old place'. Her Facebook friends include CEOs from across the English-speaking world. In her house on the right as you go up the slope into the Village, she waits for others. She is the rememberer, the welcomer. Her name is Norma Buckley. I want to ask her to help me to recall precisely how we did things back when I lived here. She knows me, knows my people. A small child in the 1970s, I left shortly before the Celtic Tiger boom made the whole country so much richer. I'm just a Village girl who's been away for a few decades. Most of her returners are making exotic journeys much more far-flung than mine. They come from Tasmania, or from the 1840s.

## Tree-Life

My own most vivid and tactile memory of the Village - pervading everything else like a perfume - is of the trees. The touch, feel, smell and mood of specific, individual trees. Each had its own personality. An ambiance, shape and texture - an overall feel like a house or a person has. First, each species of tree had its own character. An hour playing under any Sycamore was very different from an afternoon among the Blackthorns. And then each individual tree of that species had its own unique flavour too, composed like a recipe from the site where it was growing, what was around it, the way the weather hit it, the shape its branches had grown into...

In those days, children spent all their free time outdoors and we unthinkingly, automatically, used trees as our buildings. They were our private dwelling-spaces away from the adults. I realise now that trees did the babysitting - the equivalent of paid nannies today. We spent entire weeks playing in the canopy of the big Horse Chestnut tree at the end of my family's backyard. Or trespassing on the dry, sweet-scented circle of ground under the giant Sequoia in the priest's garden. Or - with even less likelihood of detection - clambering around inside the towering cliffs of Rhododendrons that are dotted like small mountains around the estate of the colonial Manor.

The most intimate of these spaces was the little house that a group of us small girls made for ourselves in the middle of *The Ball-Alley Wood*. We were three pairs of sisters from the Village houses, all matched in age. The Ball-Alley Wood was an unvisited half-acre of high, impenetrable shrubbery behind a very old stone hand-ball alley in the Village. It was an immense thicket of Blackthorn, guarded by a perimeter of gnarled, entangled Laurel that we loved. The Laurel leaves were long, fresh oblongs twice the length of your little hand, of an impossibly glossy green. Like a beautiful object that you might receive for your birthday or for Christmas.

Blackthorn sits low on the ground forming a cloud of spindly, thin branches with dark thorns over an inch long pointing in every direction. Being small and agile, we found the macabre thorns easy to avoid. We broke pathways through this Blackthorn and cleared a 3-D space in it, tall enough for us to stand up in and for it to be our *House*, once we had meticulously swept the earth in there with branches.

I can't explain it. There was nothing 'there' - not even a semblance of makeshift furniture or rugs or cups. But we must have furnished all that with our imagination. Because I remember our House in the Ball-Alley Wood as being vivid, palatial, private fun.

The one prop that we did use was the dried brown seeds of the dock plant, which we gathered to pretend it was tea. They looked like the brown-black tea leaves that our mothers bought in packets at the Village shop. Unseen at the heart of the Ball-Alley Wood, we served each other this tea in cups made from the shiny laurel leaves. There was no attempt to improvise any semblance of plates or trays of cakes and biscuits. Those were just 'there' - in full technicolour and flavour - hanging in the thick air of the game. Sitting on logs on the carefully swept earth, we sipped each other's tea and enjoyed those delicacies.

No-one else ever knew we were in there. Adults had no idea where you were when you were *Out Playing*. And if one of our Ball-Alley Wood tea parties was for a special occasion, we hooked fuchsia flowers over our ears as my grandmother had shown us how to do. Little chandeliers of scarlet and pink, those soft earrings glowed like fairy sculptures on our cheeks in the dark wood.

Children weren't a focal point of society then, as they are now: little queens whose every move is fascinating to their relatives. Adults saw us more as works in progress - larvae to be fed, watered and protected on our way to becoming full people. Adults never spent 'quality time' with children or questioned them about their thoughts or experiences. They felt no obligation to invent activities to keep us entertained. And that suited us fine, giving us a lot of physical and mental freedom.

I realise now that we experienced our chosen trees as friendly, care-taking adults. Adult relatives, neighbours, teachers and priests were more remote personages compared to those trees in whose arms - between whose feet - we spent our days. The Horse Chestnut at the end of our backyard was warm, ample, strong and welcoming. Arms open wide like a sunny day, like a muscular friend who would look after everything.

The giant Beeches in the Manor Wood - they were cool and aloof. Ancient and tall. Their thin skin is always cold to the touch. Slightly eerie, as if metallic or out of a fridge. Down at their roots were those caverns where fairies lived inside moist, mossy doors. Up above, the Beeches are beyond knowing. All we knew was that in Autumn, they threw down beautiful seeds that you could keep and play with for a long time. They look valuable, like things you would buy in shops. Crafted, chiselled, triangular objects, rigid and sharp-edged. They are shiny and lustrous. Rich, mahogany hues are burnished into their woodgrain when you look close-up.

The giant Sequoia in the priest's garden was quite the opposite of the Beeches. The floor around its base was always mysteriously dry - dryer than anywhere else in our wet Irish world. That Sequoia has a laughing, sunny energy as if it was still standing in a hot, dry country, enjoying itself. It's a self-contained microcosm of lazy, dry heat. The ground up to a yard out from its base is carpeted six inches deep with tiny, soft-but-firm catkins that the tree drops there each year. Green and scaly like little worms half an inch long, they turn orange-brown when they dry out. They build up a soft, bouncy cushion around the base of the Sequoia.

Bizarrely, the bark of that tree's vast trunk is soft too. It's much thicker and more fibrous than any other bark we knew. More like something from the jungle. Layered strips of it curl off spontaneously in great chunks, showing more underneath. And it's as soft as the cushion on a sofa. For fun, we would kneel down and bang our heads off it, just to feel how it didn't hurt. Your head bounced back off it with no sensation. The resinous, exotic perfume under that canopy was truly wonderful, like no other smell we knew except perhaps the incense in the church. But the Sequoia smelt sweeter and more airy, like a natural breeze.

Just a hundred yards away, our Blackthorns in the Ball-Alley Wood had a very different vibe. Blackthorn draws you in like a spell when it's a big, multi-dimensional bush or thicket like ours was. It gives a timeless, magical feeling of security, space and secret freedom once you get inside. Like a silent music playing. Very odd.

The Laurels in the Ball-Alley Wood - and all Laurels - felt to us loving, protective and comforting. And yet the front facade of a Laurel tree is glamorous, pert and shiny. Like a smart lady in her Sunday best heading off somewhere business-like. But inside its tangle of branches, Laurel is adult, responsible and safe, like a nice mother or teacher. It holds the space and boundary, so that you can play invisibly behind it.

The branches are only a couple of inches thick and they grow in every direction - up, down, out, sideways and around - not just straight up. Interlinked Laurel trees make a kind of spaghetti network that you can clamber around inside, or swing through like monkeys. The branches aren't very thick but they're smooth, welcoming, extremely strong and just slightly flexible. They don't mind you swinging off them and unless you choose one too young, they won't break. Their skin is warm to the touch, like on a slim, strong human arm. All this goes on behind the scenes while to the passing world, Laurel shows only its unmoving wall of long, rigid, glossy leaves.

Hawthorn: cute, diminutive trees no taller than a man. Attractive to children because as if scaled to their size. In May they produce exquisitely crafted, ivory-white roses no bigger than a child's fingernail, with little crimson-pink hearts that had a faint scent of honey. We associated them with Saint Teresa, the girl in our Book of Saints who was known as 'The Little Flower'. Once, while picking my way around on my own in the dimness of the Manor Wood, I suddenly came upon a Hawthorn tree in an impossible glory of scented blossom. Unusually, I picked a bouquet of flowering branches to take home to my mother as a rare romantic gift.

When she saw me walk in the door with them, she opened her mouth and eyes wide and started screaming. It's the only time I have ever seen that woman panic. Mouth distorted, arms flailing wildly at me to get back out, get out, as if she could expulse me back out the door by making enough wind with her arms from across the room. Her shouts backed me out of the house and out of our yard, across the road and got me to throw the blossoms back over the Wood Wall where they had come from.

She calmed down then and explained something I hadn't known. That the Hawthorn is the tree of the Fairy People and must never be plucked. And above all, that its blossoms must never - *ever* - be brought into a human home. I felt ashamed to have made such a mistake. But she said it was fine to play around them outside, so long as you never picked one of their flowers.

Having understood the rule, I continued to enjoy playing in and under Hawthorns. They had a much older, wilder, craggier feeling than the other types of trees, as if Hawthorns stepped directly out of the ancient Irish mythology books that were read to us at school. They are angular, dense and thorny, but for some reason it feels safe and cuddly once you are settled inside a suitable Hawthorn. Then they seem to tell you stories and lore from other times and places - stories that you both can and cannot hear.

Sycamore: thin skin. A bit remote and distant. But they countered this by sending down wonderful toys in Autumn: spindle-seeds that made their long flight down to the ground in slow pirouettes, like fancy parachutists showing off. You could stand below, dodging about to try and catch them. The seeds had a little green knob at one end and at the other end, a gossamer wing like that of a dragonfly. These little structures were covered in a fine green skin so resilient you couldn't penetrate it with your fingernail. They were very different from the burnished, triangular seeds of the Beeches. But put together with the pricelessly shiny, wood-coloured conkers of the Horse-Chestnut, those three different types of seeds made a great collection to head into the Winter with.

Camellia: Up near the Manor House, in the huge Wood that surrounded it, there was a secret, overgrown tree of Camellia that stood tall as a two-storey house. It leant against the outside of the old walled garden, covered by the canopy of the Manor's arboretum, in a corner that was always shady, wet and dripping. Very few people knew of this Camellia tree. You had to be a dedicated crawler of the undergrowth to come across it. Its big tropical flowers opened deep scarlet inside that high, wet, black-green corner. They were sensual, luxurious - almost obscene - in a way that nothing else in our world was.

By our mid-teens, we had given up those earlier intimacies with trees. Commuting to school in the city on a slow bus and coming back with much longer, harder homework kept us indoors more. But one tree did still dominate my teen years. Whenever there was free time, it called like a siren. It took a bit of effort to get there: first, because it was deep in the heart of the Manor estate and second, because it was beside the driveway, exposed in full view of the Manor House.

My companion was 18 and I was 15. We were best friends. Coming from the two Village families living closest to the Manor estate, we were lifelong, experienced trespassers who knew every growing, mucky inch of it better than its aristocratic owners ever did. From age 5 or 6, once we could climb up and over the Wood Wall, we would each separately spend our days crawling, wading and clambering through its undergrowth behind bunches of older siblings who wouldn't let us hang out with them yet.

The estate felt to us like an abandoned wonderland with its exotically planted walled garden, landscaped valleys, overgrown courtyards, floral walkways, streams, dams, mill and islanded lake. Throughout the British occupation of Ireland, it was carefully maintained and curated by teams of professional gardeners, gamekeepers and other staff, most of whom were long gone in our time. By then, the owners had retreated to spend most of their time at their other estates in England and India. They only visited occasionally for a few days' damp stay in the grand, neglected Manor.

Like resident rats or squirrels, we kids knew every inch of their estate up close. But it was my friend who showed me that particular tree when we were teenagers. Normally we wouldn't ever approach it because of the exposed line of view up to the House. It was in one of the few zones where the owners could ever spot us, so Village kids always avoided it.

But he showed me how to sprint out from under cover keeping low to the ground and - on the side of the tree facing away from the House - make the quick, easy climb up the seven or eight feet into the tree's bosom. Up there, a broad space opened out like a small room, or the palm of a giant hand. A ring of branches each a foot thick curved out and up protectively around the edges of this platform, so no-one could see you once you were in there. Not even if they stood right beside the tree.

This became the place that he and I found most relaxing at that time in our lives. It became a necessary luxury to flee there as often as possible and just lie around up there smoking, daydreaming and asking each other questions. I don't know what we talked about but in those years, conversation swilled between us in a dreamlike flow that we never had to think about.

As many of my own Crow Glen ancestors had done over a hundred years earlier, he emigrated to Australia. We've both been back to the Village since, but not at the same time. I know he always visits Norma Buckley when he's there. I know he sometimes brings his Australian husband and that they all drink tea by the fire.

But now, it's my turn to approach her. With some trepidation, I reach her door. She startles me by opening it as I'm about to knock. She says 'Ah, there you are. I saw you coming up the road.'

'I knew you'd turn up eventually', she said as she settled me by the fire with tea and plates of scones. 'I heard you were around.'

## References

*Calendar to Fiants of the Reign of Henry VIII, 1510-47, & Queen Elizabeth, 1558-1603*, London, 1601
*Wilson's Directory of Ireland, 1834*, 'Fair Towns of Ireland', available at www.from-ireland.net/category/miscellaneous/cork-miscellaneous/page/3

Chapter **2**

# The air is full of spirits

Images at the opening of this chapter:

~ A scapular
~ A monstrance
~ Rosary beads and purse
~ Sacred Heart picture and Perpetual Lamp in the home

Back in the 1990s, when my grandmother said to me *'The air is full of spirits'*, that seemed to me a good description of the religion that we practised. But it wasn't the description that I saw reflected back in the media or in books. Especially since the Church's sex abuse scandals emerged in the 1990s, the media seemed to describe parishioners as being passively led, and misled, by priests who dominated them from churches.

But what I remembered, rather than such 'parishioners', was some quite mature *practitioners*. I remembered the practitioners of the religion in Gleann an Phréacháin as doing something much more self-directed, much more complex and more intense. It wasn't just dictated to us by priests in churches. I remember the majority of it as being a whole fabric of very complicated personal practices that were wrapped around your own intimate daily life *by yourself.*

You carried a range of religious objects on your person for use throughout the day and week. You arrayed sacred objects around key points in your home, ready for use at ritual moments across each day. They were in the centre of the living room, at the external doors, by your bedside, on the infant's cot. And we paved our day and week with prayers and ritual practices, pretty much round the clock and wall to wall.

What I remembered was a whole universe of very elaborate spiritual practices that began in the home around the individual and - once the day and the life in the home were saturated with them - then spilled out into the wider landscape of spiritual sites that surrounded the Village, of which *The Chapel*, as we usually called the Village church, was just one component.

 I had never seen or heard the religion described in this way that I remembered it. So I went to Norma Buckley to ask her how accurate that memory was. And what she went on to describe in this book is exactly how I remember it being.

We were settled now by her fireside with a pot of Barry's Tea. [13] A black greyhound watched regally from the couch as Norma responded to my questions. Apparently, the creature is a regular sight on the roads around Gleann, walking Norma daily to keep her as fit and as slim as the hound is.

---

13 Barry's Tea is blended in Cork. Crow Glenners tend not to drink its rival, Lyon's Tea from Dublin, which doesn't taste as good to Cork people. Emigrants like me buy our Barry's Tea online in six-packs that Barrys post to us all over the world.

 Norma...

Well you know, I'm no theologian. But I am willing to talk to you about the religion, as you're seriously asking me to. To talk about how we do it and how we see it, and how it was in the old days compared to how it is now. I'm interested in those things too. I can only speak for myself, obviously. I can give you *my* take on the religion but remember that every single person has their own.

There are a lot of people here in the Glen of the Crow who are *so* devout, and have always been so devout, but they would never talk about it with anyone. I'm probably unusual in that I am willing, if asked, to talk *about* it, as well as to do it.

But remember we didn't - nor in my mother's time, *they* didn't - discover Catholicism! It's a living, ever-evolving thing that we have inherited, going back many, many centuries. And think how vast the whole scene of it is. Where to start? I can tell you my version of the religion but everyone has their own take on it. Each takes what they need from it themselves.

## ḣolꝡ oḃjecꞇs on ꞇhe ḃodꝡ

You're asking about all our special equipment, our personal religious objects? Oh, they were always *vitally* important - vital! You usually got your first set of personal religious things when you received your First Holy Communion at age seven. Oh, the special white Rosary beads! I still have them - my first set of beads from then. They were lovely. And of course, you had to have a special little bag to keep them in. Up until say the 1980s, everyone around here of all ages, men and women alike, would have had their own well-worn set of personal Rosary beads on them at all times, and a little bag to keep them in in their pocket, some kind of simple pouch or purse. Many still do today, but not everyone would anymore.

For your First Communion, you might be lucky enough to get a purse that came with your Communion dress, in the same fabric, on a little drawstring. You really valued those Rosary beads that you got for your Communion - the first you had of your own.

That was the age too when you were given a scapular to wear. You were each presented with one at the end of your First Communion Mass, when all the children knelt down at the altar. But to be honest, it was never explained to us what the scapulars were really about. A scapular was two little squares of brown cloth enclosed in plastic, hanging at either end of two strings, like a double-ended necklace. You put it on over your head and it was to hang down inside your vest against your skin, with one of the little brown squares hanging at the back of your torso and one in front. I think the term 'scapular' comes from the Latin word for shoulder-blades. You were meant to wear it continually and only take it off for your bath.

We knew they were important. They were protective. I suppose nowadays I'd call it a kind of talisman. I didn't carry on wearing it into adulthood, like some people did. But any boy who later went to war, for instance, there's no way his mother would let him go without being armed with his scapular under his vest, for protection.

Relics too were often a small square of cloth that had touched the original holy object, maybe the preserved body of a saint, kept in a basilica. People weren't much into relics around here but there were any number of holy medals that you could wear on a string or ribbon around your neck. They were pinned onto prams and cradles to bless babies, often with a little holy picture and prayer stitched into a plastic covering. There are many different types of medals dedicated to Our Lady, and those to the Sacred Heart, and then medals for individual saints - Saint Christopher for travelling, and so on.

Over time relatives would also give you presents of little holy pictures for your bedroom, especially in the time coming up to your Communion or Confirmation. That was the classic present to bring back if someone had been away. I received a beautiful ceramic wall-plaque of the Guardian Angel, made by Wedgewood, and that was beautiful to hang beside my bed. I've passed it on to my grandchildren now.

And then there were white mother of pearl Prayer Books, if you were lucky enough to have one, though I didn't have one of them. Anyone lucky enough to have a nun in the family, the nun would produce the white mother of pearl Prayer Book and that was *very* special. They were gorgeous, with a picture inlaid on the cover into this thick, glowing mother of pearl. They were beautiful.

You couldn't buy them in the shops. My friend had one because she had an aunt who was a Mother Superior. They got them through the clergy's supply stores, so you had to have religious connections to get them. I had one with just cardboard covers but it had two coloured pictures in it of Mass, and that was very nice - to see the coloured pictures.

For my Confirmation I got a loan of a big crucifix to wear, from my mother. It was a special object. Long ago, a young woman from Gleann was emigrating to Australia. And my mother very kindly bought her a gift of a set of underwear. The girl knew she'd be sleeping in a dormitory on the ocean liner, and she didn't have adequate underwear. It was so kind of my mother because it was very expensive and she could have done with that money herself.

Anyway, many years later that woman came back on a visit from Australia and she had never forgotten my mother's gift. She came back via a pilgrimage through Rome where she bought a solid silver crucifix that the Pope himself had blessed. She brought it back for my mother in thanksgiving, thirty or forty years after the precious gift of the underwear! That's the crucifix that I wore for my Confirmation.

In terms of clothes, the christening robe was important too, handed down through the generations in our family, and often lent out to other families. It's a long, lace-edged dress, twice as long as the baby. And for my First Communion, I had new white socks and a veil. The dress wasn't new but we got it from well-off cousins in the city, still in its box. And the tiara was of flowers, beautifully made in cloth, wired so it stood up off your head a bit. Even the Queen wouldn't have it. It was magic. Those were magical things.

Of course, women always covered their heads in the church until the Second Vatican Council in the 1960s. We wore mantillas. They were triangles of black lace that you pinned onto your hair. They were quite elegant and pretty, really. Religious guilds and confraternities also had some lovely bright-coloured satin sashes that men wore across the body for ceremonies, but they were kept together in the community hall, not at home. Jewellery was often religious. Women would wear a little crucifix or a medal on a neck-chain. And members of the Pioneers wore Pioneer Pins on their lapel wherever they went. [14]

For the boys, their First Communion meant their first proper suit. And they got their own personal Prayer Book and Rosary beads too, for their suit pockets. I remember two little fellas, one brother making his Communion and the other his Confirmation. The parents had splashed

---

14 Ireland's *Pioneer Total Abstinence Association of the Sacred Heart* is a religious association of Catholics who abstain from alcohol.

out on the local tailor to make matching suits for them. But his speciality was making horse-saddles! And didn't he make them these two big thick rigid suits of the roughest possible material! God love them, the suits were horrendous on the day.

In your pocket or bag you had your Prayer Book, or some adults would have a Missal. The Missal - a fairly thick book with a leather cover - has the full liturgical year of ceremonies that will be performed in the church. They became popular suddenly, often among people who had priests or nuns in the family. The Prayer Books were nicer I think, and more for ordinary people. With nice prayers to Our Lady, to the Sacred Heart, and to saints, and prayers you could say during Mass. That might surprise you because nowadays you're supposed to follow the Mass but in the old days it was all in Latin. There was never a translation - you didn't know what was being said. So it was fine to say prayers of your own during it.

Another thing that kept people busy praying was their set of Mortuary Cards. They are little two-sided commemorative cards that get printed up when someone dies, with their photo and dates and a little prayer for them on it. People collected them in their Prayer Books or Missals: they were a visual reminder to pray every day for the souls of those departed individuals.

People would have the Mortuary Cards of all deceased family, friends and neighbours. My father's Prayer Book used to be bulging with them. Occasionally he'd have to do a bit of a purge and put some of them aside, if there was too many building up in there so that you could hardly close the book and the day wouldn't be long enough to pray for them all. '*We can't have grief for everyone*', he used to say when he had to do a purge. But those cards were a very precious, intimate way to remind yourself to pray for the repose of the soul of loved ones, even many, many years after they had passed on.

So people spent a huge amount of time with their Prayer Books but the Bible, no - we were discouraged from reading the Bible. The idea was: '*Rome will interpret for you*'. Catholics were not to read the Bible because that's what Protestants did. My father was a strange dichotomy in that yes, he did read the Bible. I don't know how they managed to acquire a copy, but himself and the schoolteacher, they used to read it in my father's shop, hiding it under the counter. It was absolutely not allowed.

It never bothered me to be honest that we couldn't read the Bible because we had enough to be doing already, with religious observances all day long. It was a bit of a release not to have to read the Bible as well! Children's practices alone could stretch across five or six hours of the day, if you add up all the prayers before waking and sleeping and eating, and before every class at school, and the Catechism class at school every day, and the Angelus at midday and at 6pm, and the family Rosary at home at night, plus you'd often be taken to morning Mass on your way to school, or be expected to drop into the Chapel on your way home from school to say a few prayers…

We had plenty to do without the Bible bothering our brains as well. But when my first child was born, I did buy us a Family Bible. That Bible was the fattest, chubbiest book I've ever seen, with over 1,000 pages. One Winter, my husband ploughed his way through the whole Old Testament in it. They used to try to cover that up in particular - the Old Testament. Catholics were above all not supposed to touch it, was our understanding. Of course, the Gospels were read to us night and day at Mass, but not the Old Testament.

But I think that even the priests didn't bother reading the Bible in their own house. They weren't interested. Not all of them had any deep interest in finding out about it. Another schoolteacher used to stay in lodgings in the Village, and he had a copy of the Bible in his room. The woman who ran the lodgings told us about it. She didn't show it to us but she secretly read bits of it herself in his room and she used to tell us quotes out of it.

Speaking of lodgings, before he got married my father lived in lodgings here in the Village. When my parents were moving into this house here together after getting married, they were unpacking their things. And he said to her *'Where's the bell?'* He meant the little handbell that he was given in his lodgings to ring whenever he wanted to be served, at the table or whatever. My mother put him right quick enough, letting him know that there wouldn't be any *bell* in this house!

But the lifestyle of a priest in the old days was like that too. It was a very good job at the time. They were given a house and a car, and a paid servant as a housekeeper. As an unmarried man, a priest wasn't expected to ever cook or clean or lift a finger for himself in any way. The Church always supplied a housekeeper to look after them.

# Personal devotions

The thing is that people wanted and needed a lot of specific literature and holy objects in order to get on with their own devotional practices, on top of the standard ceremonies that everyone did in the Chapel. We haven't even begun to touch on all those ceremonies that people did voluntarily across the year, on top of the basics. There were the main festivals and then there were all the Feast Days on every day of the year, joining all that up.

Our current priest puts out a nice newsletter telling you which saint's Feast Day it is on each day of the year, as well as things like when the florist or the chiropodist are in the Village. He puts in all the different dedications of Mass for each day too. Not even a priest would know all that off by heart - the 365 days of the year and all their ceremonies and dedications.

Maybe 100 of the 365 feast days are for Irish saints. For instance, Saint Paul's feast day used to be a big day but now there's much more talk about Irish saints. They're being given big coverage. They might be from Donegal, or whatever. That's another recent evolution, this emphasis on the *daily* liturgy. Christmas has been slightly downgraded. It's slipping in importance. Easter is more foregrounded now, for the Transubstantiation, the Eucharist, and the Resurrection. You have all those core Catholic mysteries there really, within Easter. Christmas isn't of the same *ecclesiastical* significance. Easter is the heart of the matter now, really.

But people used to - and some still do - use those religious calendars to plan their own extra devotions across the year. That was where you could make real extra progress as a Catholic. Through penances, pilgrimages, Novenas, Missions, Indulgences and so on. Where you could be getting on with extras by yourself. That's much, much less emphasised now, of course. Now all that is boiled down more to being charitable in a practical way - being a good person and a good neighbour.

But before, they were many, many ways that you could make extra spiritual progress, and people pursued them enthusiastically of their own accord at home. They would plan these Novenas, Missions, pilgrimages and so on into their year ahead. To get more points in heaven you might say, if you wanted to be callous about it. But of course, people did them a great deal for others too, to petition for positive outcomes for others, both living and dead.

I'll remind you of the basics first, that everyone did. Up until the turn of the millennium we had Mass here in the Village every morning. You would remember going to that often yourself, on the way up to school on weekday mornings. Now we have Mass in the Village on just three days of the week, Thursday, Saturday and Sunday but the neighbouring village, Watergrasshill, has it on the other days. Since the millennium there used to be only five or six of us at Mass during the week but over the last five years that has gone up to maybe ten to twenty on some weekdays.

And on Thursdays we have the Exposition of the Blessed Sacrament after Mass. That's when the consecrated host - the Body of Christ - is displayed silently on the altar for two hours inside the most beautiful gold display stand, called a monstrance. It's shaped like a sun with rays radiating out and a circular glass compartment  at the centre that opens with a little glass door. The host is placed into that glass space at the centre. A congregation member commits to sitting in the Chapel with the Blessed Eucharist - the priest doesn't need to stay. I love that - where you just sit being present together with the Blessed Presence of our Lord before you on the altar. It's quite something, very serene and simple.

For the Sunday morning Mass, we used to fast from midnight on Saturday but that was reduced later to fasting for just one hour before Mass. And of course, everybody 'fasted' every Friday but that only meant abstaining from eating meat, and having a simple fish dinner every Friday instead. On Ash Wednesday and Good Friday, as part of the Easter ceremonies, you would have only one meal in the day, with just two other small snacks allowed. On Good Friday you had to abstain too from laughing, joking or singing as you were meant to be contemplating the death of Our Lord all that day, really.

I remember once my husband was unfortunate enough to be staying away in lodgings for work for the whole seven weeks of Lent. And he was given kippers for his dinner *every single night of the seven weeks!* It was that or nothing. He did fight in the end for a boiled egg (laughs). That was reality, honestly.

I don't know if it was quite as bad in the city, the whole fasting regime. I gave a talk recently to newcomers into the area here. I told them we didn't have electricity, running water, toilets or bathrooms when I was young, and it seemed beyond the stretch of their imagination. They all grew up in the city so maybe they had all those things there long before we did. By the 1960s we had running water in the house here but most people didn't, or didn't have indoor toilets.

Then there were the religious confraternities, sort of guilds that men could belong to, and members could gain Indulgences through them. An Indulgence earned you a reduction in the amount of time you would spend in Purgatory after you died. Men went to them maybe every Friday night, and they gained extra Indulgences through the confraternity's devotions or ceremonies.

A friend of my husband, a bachelor, used to like to go out for a drink with us on Saturday nights. But you would never see him out on a Friday night because that was the night for his religious confraternity. Here in Gleann we have The Legion of Mary and the Pioneers, both very active religious guilds to this day. [15]

I think women had confraternities too in the city, but I don't know much about that. Here in the Village we had the Catholic Girl Guides. I was very active as their leader for fifteen years. I had seen that my eldest daughter lacked confidence and I didn't want that to happen to the younger one, or to other girls in Gleann. So we set up the Girl Guides. The Guides meant a lot to me because the girls are called 'Brigíní', 'little Brigids', dedicated to Saint Brigid. And with our River Bride named after Saint Brigid and our beautiful stained-glass window to Saint Brigid on our altar in the Chapel, we have great devotion to Saint Brigid here.

It was fundamentally Catholic as an organisation but it also just gave girls a lot of outdoor activities, challenges, travel and skills. With brown uniforms and brass trimmings, we used to march in the Village Processions. We marched in the big Saint Patrick's Day Parades in Cork city too - huge secular parades. And we used to take our Girl Guides away on huge camping trips called Jamborees, where you'd meet up with Guides from many other places.

Anyway, in terms of extra practices, we always had the First Fridays, and you got extra points for that. It meant that on the First Friday of every month for nine months you would go to Confession, Mass and Communion, though by the 1970s already, they had stopped teaching children that. Jesus died on Good Friday so it was a commemoration. You did it either to honour the Sacred Heart or to gain merit for yourself, or else for a special intention. If it was exam time, for instance, you'd have a good crowd doing the First Fridays at that time of the year.

---

15  The Legion of Mary is an organisation of laypeople devoted to Our Lady. Founded in Dublin in 1921, it now has millions of members worldwide.

Equally, there used to be the First Saturdays of the month and that was a special Mass to Our Lady. You could do a Novena of the first Saturdays of every month for nine months too, but that was phased out in the 1980s. It became too much, as if devotion to Our Lady was becoming a self-sufficient religion in itself.

A Plenary Indulgence was supposed to be a full clearance of all your sins to date, wiping out all the time that you would have had to do for them in Purgatory. So that was quite something. But the most important thing - and this wasn't selfish either - was that you could get Indulgences for the dead on two days at the beginning of November. So you daren't not do that, if you had ever had someone you loved who had died.

That was for the Holy Souls. Now remember the Holy Souls means our own dead, and they weren't all necessarily that holy, some of them. But it was our job to pray for them and to make them holy *now*, so they could spend less time in Purgatory and be liberated into Heaven as soon as possible. That was a very important part of people's religious life, doing that for each other. There was a whole Novena of Masses for that on the first nine days of November as well. Loads of prayers were pertinent to that. It was totally committed, very hard work.

There were many different Novenas too that you could do for the Holy Souls, because most saints had a Novena that you could do to them, like for instance you could do a Novena to petition Saint Jude. You'd do that privately at home for the nine days leading up to his feast day. For instance, Saint Teresa, The Little Flower, my mother firmly believed in her and she is very powerful, it's true. The story goes that if you're doing the Novena to The Little Flower and someone hands you a flower for whatever reason, it's a great sign that you're being heard. Well, while my mother was doing the Novena to The Little Flower, Johnny Riordan, our next-door neighbour, gave her a flower and she was overjoyed. I'm sure he guessed that she was doing that Novena but he didn't let on he knew.

Then there's all the different *Our Ladies*. For instance, there is a very strong, powerful Novena that you can do to Our Lady of Perpetual Succour. She's for extreme cases. She's like one for 'lost causes', as Saint Jude is. In Saint Augustin's church in Cork city there is a big shrine to Our Lady of Perpetual Succour, and you'd see that whole shrine lit up with parishioners' candles on those nine days leading up to Her Feast Day. You'd see that in every church during the Novena of whatever saints they had statues or shrines to in that church.

In the city, if a church belonged to a specific order of clergy, like say The Order of the Sacred Heart, then when the Novena to the Sacred Heart came round, you'd have a *pile* of priests trotting around in there for it. But in the countryside the priests were spread much thinner, and the people did their own thing more. It all went a bit too far in the end in Cork city because the bishop built a chain of fifteen new churches all around the city. And he set it up such that you gained a Plenary Indulgence if you visited every one of them. So people were getting on and off buses non-stop to work their way around the city to the fifteen churches.

It's hard to visualise that culture now for people working a full-time week. They wouldn't have the time to do it now. But there weren't as many distractions or entertainments back then, even up into the 1990s. This for a lot of people was *it* - this *was* their cultural life and entertainment, and their method of 'personal development', as New Agers might call it nowadays. That religious form of personal development was like a passionate hobby or occupation for people back then. For instance, single young working women would say to each other socially: *'I'm doing the Novena to so and so next week - are you doing it?'* The way they might talk about watching the latest TV series now.

## Sacred Things in the home

If you were doing a Novena to a specific saint, you would have to get hold of the written texts for that saint's Novena. They were widely available as leaflets. You'd get them in churches or religious shops. The set text might be fairly short and you could add your own prayers to it. The text might only take half an hour a day that you would do for the nine days, on top of all your usual devotions.

Those were part of the religious papers that everybody had at home. They'd have their own Prayer Book, or maybe even a Missal. And that would be bulging full with the Mortuary Cards that they'd use to pray every day for their dead. And then there would be as well, loose between the pages, these texts of specific Novenas. All those papers were a personal, intimate thing to each person, a sort of a map and calendar of their own religious life and activities.

So even as children we took great interest in leaflets of saints, especially those who were new to us. A saint's picture or life story might strike a particular note with you, and they might end up in your Prayer Book as one of your Novenas and you might have a friend for life! Think what that means, if they could help in some way with the illnesses, accidents, exams and so on of your loved ones, and with their afterlife.

There were different religious objects for different parts of the home too. Here in the centre of the living room where we're talking now, we had of course the big picture of the Sacred Heart, signed in Rome to testify that this house had been consecrated to the Sacred Heart by a priest who came into the house to do that. The priest signed it, my parents signed it and we children later signed it as well. It was taken down once a year to display it in the window that faced the road, on the day that the Sacred Heart Procession would come down the Street.

And you would always have the little red Perpetual Lamp lighting before that picture in the living-room. You can only have the lamp if you have that special Sacred Heart picture. The lamp reflects that divine presence in the home, the way the red sanctuary lamp in the Chapel shows Our Lord is present in the tabernacle. So our whole family would kneel down at night to say the Rosary together here in the living room, taking their rosary beads out of their pocket. You would remember doing that yourself in the 1980s, when you were a teenager.

The heart of the home really was that perpetual lamp to the Sacred Heart. The electrified version only started after we got electricity, obviously. Before that we had a little 24-hour oil lamp burning in front of the Sacred Heart picture. You never let that oil lamp go out. The guy who came and wired the houses for electricity, he had a good little deal going on the side, with all these extras. So if you wanted, he wired in your Sacred Heart lamp from day one when you first got electricity. You had the option to have that as a little extra. We had it up until the 1990s. You could buy the special bulbs for the lamp in any electrical shop.

Now, I'm not done with the Sacred Heart obviously, but I am done with that big, old, rather dark picture. This house is still consecrated to the Sacred Heart, which is very important to me. But now instead of the picture from Rome, I have this lovely bright white alabaster bust of Jesus as the welcoming, loving, bright *risen* Jesus. I made that change as a sort of liberation. I thought it would feel less oppressive for the young people.

That's the centrepiece of the living room now, on the mantelpiece above the woodburning stove. I sit beside that all my life now. And if I have something in particular to pray for that day, I'll light a candle to Him. I've lit a lot of candles there, I can tell you! So there is certainly no less devotion to Him now in the house than before.

At ceremonial times you'd have various displays in the windows facing the road. At Christmas you'd have the Advent Candle lighting there in the evenings. And for the Processions, you'd display in the window either the Sacred Heart or Our Lady, depending on which Procession it was. For Processions we used to also fly the big yellow Papal Flag on a pole in the front garden right beside the road, to greet the Procession as it went by. [16]

Inside the front and back external doors of the house, you always had a little font of Holy Water hanging, to bless yourself with before leaving the house. You could buy them in a Catholic shop in the city. Today I still keep a little crystal bowl of Holy Water inside my door, for anyone to bless themselves with it as they're going out. Up to the 1980s we had the traditional font there, a little hanging bowl at chest-height. Everyone used it then, all visitors. Now only some women friends use the Holy Water in my house before they walk out. No-one ever used it on their way *into* your house of course - they were supposed to be safe once they were in there! It'd be a very bad sign if they thought they had to cross themselves with Holy Water on the way in!

Even now I automatically throw it over myself when I'm seeing someone out the door. Younger people around here think I'm a bit weird anyway, so they don't take any notice of what I'd be doing. But I am very friendly with them, they do seek me out. So they don't think it odd that I'd have Holy Water inside the door. Some might not have it at their own door, but many do.

Our parish priest has spoken quite a lot about recently about Holy Water, and about taking Holy Water out onto the fields to the crops. He doesn't go terribly into depth about it but he does say it often, suggesting that people bless their crops with it. He's encouraging that greatly. He spoke about it again now recently when it was time for planting this year's crops. He wouldn't have time himself to go around sprinkling everywhere, to do it himself for them. There are so few priests nowadays that they have to work very hard.

But He blesses the Holy Water in the Chapel before Mass in front of everybody - a big vat of it. And more and more people are using it for more things nowadays, so he's doing it pretty often. There's a lot of take-up. There's a big stainless-steel container of it kept at the back of the

---

16 This is the official flag of the Vatican. Yellow and white, it shows the two Keys of Saint Peter and the Pope's pointed hat or *mitre*. Jesus is believed to have given Saint Peter these two 'Keys to the Kingdom of Heaven' - one in gold to symbolise spiritual authority in Heaven, and one in silver symbolising the authority of the Church here on earth.

church and you serve yourself from that with your own bottles or whatever. That's much more popular now than it was in the past.

But in the past we did always try to ensure we had the special Easter Water. Easter Water is really special because it is blessed as part of the long, complex Easter ceremonies. You would go especially to get some of that at the back of the Chapel, to have in your house.

The only other real hierarchy in Holy Water is the water brought back from the River Jordan in Israel. Once, somebody brought back some of that from a pilgrimage abroad. And that was really, really something. Because Jesus himself was baptised in that same River Jordan. There is a tour you can do of the Holy Places in Israel - to Jerusalem and so on. Fifteen days touring the holiest places, on escorted pilgrimages run by the Church. Some neighbours went on it and brought me back a little bottle of River Jordan Holy Water. Imagine that!

They obviously brought a flagon or two to distribute around Gleann in little bottles. It was very kind of them, because water is very heavy to carry in your luggage. They say that if you could add just a tiny tip of that to a baby's Christening water, that it's a very special blessing. Even just a little tip of it, that's what people mainly want it for. They would keep it at home and bring a drop to the baptismal font in the Chapel for the Christening.

My father was devoutly religious and he had great faith in Holy Water. He came from Ballyvourney towards West Cork, where they have Saint Gobnait's Holy Well, and that's amazing stuff, the water from there. They practically *invented* Holy Water, back there. He wouldn't sleep in a house if there wasn't Holy Water in it.


## Initiation

It was quite a complex thing, our religion here in the old days, so children were initiated into it gradually. They saw all this around them in the home from the beginning, and then they were taught their first prayers at school from age four. But it was at age seven, really, at their First Communion, that they were fully inducted into the religion as responsible practitioners of it themselves.

That was 'Confirmed' further when they were 12, at their Confirmation ceremony. There was a lot of study and preparation for those two ceremonies, but especially for the First Communion. After those two they were considered fully equipped, to go on and develop their own spiritual life. They might feel drawn to become a Pioneer, or develop an interest in and devotion to a particular saint, or get into going to Knock on Marian pilgrimages, or whatever. They were up and running then!

Obviously, this was all dependent on them having been baptised a Catholic as a baby in the first place. But that was automatic for us. Until after the millennium, no-one around here would have neglected to have their newborn baptised. Unless they were of another religion, obviously, which occasionally people were who have lived here in Gleann over the years. Different religions were never a problem here, either for them or for us. They were just normal, active members of the community in every other way, and then they had their own religions that we knew very little about really.

But for local Catholics here, it was desperately important to parents historically to have their babies baptised, to ensure that if the baby died their soul was brought into the Church forever, to avoid them being condemned to Limbo. There were important secret practices around that here in Gleann an Phréacháin right up into the twentieth century - I'll tell you about that another day.

But you're asking how the First Communion and Confirmation are for children now, compared to when I received them seventy years ago? You know, I'd say there's been virtually *no* change. Just last week for her Confirmation my granddaughter wore a dress almost exactly the same as the one I wore back then. A very simple, beautiful, white dress with a lace top.

But it's all an even bigger event nowadays, if anything. They're absolutely huge now, the Communion and Confirmation. The other difference today is that children *know* more now about what they're doing. Which can only be a good thing, of course. But I think it does take some of the mystique out of it. Now the whole ceremony - and the *preparation* for it - have taken off in a huge way. Personally, I think that's totally over-emphasised now, that it takes the simplicity out of it. Now every child gets something to do during the ceremony. I think it takes the focus off the Mass itself and the lovely simplicity of just walking up to the altar and focusing yourself on receiving the Holy Communion.

Now the seven-year olds-are up on the altar doing the readings. They're like little priests! And they're reading out prayers for everyone they ever heard of. And they're bringing up *gifts*. Okay, it's when the gifts of bread and wine were traditionally brought up but now they take up gifts that are expressions about *themselves*. Footballs and all sorts. I've seen hurleys and footballs taken up on the altar. It's all gone very *theatrical* now, that's the only word for it.

They're making a different *use* of it all, I suppose. But I think they're going away too from the intrinsic depth of it. I mean, the amount of effort the teachers put into planning all this performance is amazing, quite amazing. The amount of *work,* to get even one child up to the altar and another one down, while another fifteen are waiting in line. There are a lot of *functions* happening, and that takes a lot of effort. But the simplicity is gone.

I know it's all being done for a very good reason. But I can't help wondering if it's a good way to go in terms of the true *religious* way. What the good reason actually is and the aim is, I'm not even sure - it's not very clear. I suppose the aim is to get the children to buy into it all personally and to feel it's their own. To take ownership of it. Like with the hurley and the football. That's the thing he or she is best at, so *'I'm bringing up to the altar the best of me'*. It's much more about 'me' nowadays. In our day there was absolutely nothing about 'me'! You had no ego, and no-one asked you anything about 'me'. That is *the* big difference.

Intrinsically, of course, it's still the same. But with a big *show* built up around it now. Now it starts months before the Communion Day. And one Sunday Mass on every one of those months is given over to some aspect of the preparations. All the children are there and their parents, and maybe their grandparents. You can't get a *leg* inside the church! For instance, a good friend of mine who goes to every Mass that's held all year, she has mobility issues and has just one place where she's comfortable in the church. And on those Sundays, she can't get to it. She's asked to leave it and go back to the back, with failing eyesight! But she's there every day of the year that Mass is said, whereas we won't see those parents again until their child's Confirmation in five years' time!

*'Do this in memory of me…'* Well, it's a memory alright because they'll hardly ever be there again! They'll dive in for the months of preparations and the hurley and football on the altar and the big ceremony. But then they won't come back to Mass on Sundays once the big ceremony is done: they'll be off playing football and hurling!

So they feel free to serve themselves from the ritual in absolute *fullest* technicolour. And then they'll quite comfortably leave it again until the

Confirmation five years later. *Comfortably.* That's so the opposite from how it was even fifteen years ago. I find all that fascinating, to be honest.

There's an obvious win in it for the Church in that they get great mileage out of it during the months of preparations - but then they'll never see them again! But the priests go through it all in the hope that - if they have 37 children each year for First Communion and Confirmation, like they had this year - they might keep those seven afterwards. My gosh, imagine if they got seven out of it, who kept attending Sunday Mass from then on. Because that'd be seven whole families. But I haven't seen it happen yet, and this has all been going on now for several years.

Although to give credit where it's due, I have seen maybe four families stay on every Sunday in recent years. You'd think surely that if all those parents are getting their children put through the Holy Sacraments, that some small proportion of the families would find they have a *natural* feeling for it, and would want to keep doing it? There must be some *ingrained* desire or reason for it, in at least some proportion of people.

But I suppose many parents now just see it as a rite of passage for the maturing young person, like they have in different cultures around the world at that age when we have Confirmation. Big moments that you go through in life just one, two or three times. Whereas of course the Church considers that they're giving you something that you will do at least weekly for the rest of your life. But today, the parents feel able to use it just for those special occasions. It seems odd: why would you put such huge input into it, if it's just for one day? But it's for the *show.* You *have to* be a part of it! It's *pantomime!*

But isn't it a bit like a couple having a huge, big wedding day, and then never having anything more to do with each other afterwards? Of course, couples do that now too: they're all dying to have a big wedding day in the Chapel, and then they never come back there again! It's the same thought process, whatever it is.

But my own First Communion and Confirmation, they were great for us as children and we looked forward to them hugely. We didn't know as many prayers and hymns and all the rest of it as the children do now. But what we did know, I think we learned properly. And we *wanted* to learn them, and we could see the importance of them. It meant a huge amount, it meant I became a proper Catholic. (Of course, in those days there was no question of describing yourself as 'a Christian' - it was just *Catholic*, and to hell with everyone else, almost literally!) But it was *so* important. It was a step - it was an initiation, I suppose.

There was a real mystique to it. It gave you a little flutter in your heart, going up to the altar to receive Holy Communion in your little white dress. You knew you were actually receiving God and the Holy Spirit into yourself, and you were well prepared for it. So, however it was transferred to them, the child really believed and felt 100% that they were experiencing a spiritual mystery. They really did get that, whatever about anything else. It was a very special moment in a child's life.

It was a bit of an anti-climax I suppose once the day itself was over. But I don't know where in God's name that must leave today's children, after all their massive preparations. How do they *come down* from that afterwards?

I don't like to admit it but for my age group, believe it or not, our First Communion was the first time that we ever saw soft fruits in the Village - pears, oranges, bananas. None had ever come into the Village since the rationing after World War Two. Our parents had known those fruits but our age-group had never seen them. So that's part of the First Communion memory for me too.

Learning to go to Confession was a huge part of it too. It is a very big concept to learn, as a child. That you could do something wrong, and be *forgiven* for it. Previous to that I had thought that if you did something wrong, it was there in a great ledger forever more!

And then in Communion there was the mystery of Transubstantiation, as it's called - the bread and wine being actually transformed on the altar into the Body and Blood of Christ. They didn't go into that very much with us. But I mean, give 'em a break! Transubstantiation is a bit challenging even for adults, not to mind a child. Maybe it's one of those things you don't want to go into too deeply (laughs).

They just told you that was happening and they didn't say any more about it. 'The Body of Christ', we were told, but they played down the 'Blood of Christ' part, so that it wasn't too graphic. And in those days the wine was only for the priest anyway. But I wouldn't want to have a class of 37 seven-year-olds in front of me and have to explain Transubstantiation to them! I know from being a Girl Guide leader that you'd get a lot of awkward questions! I'd say steer clear of Transubstantiation, tactically!

Whereas of course Confession, especially for a child, is a much more understandable, natural thing. Even the smallest child is already used to being taught that there are rules and they shouldn't break them. It's such a human thing, to say you're sorry, and you can go into it as deeply as you like, or not.

Except for *the box!* Everybody in my class at school was terrified of going into *the box.* The Confession box was black and dark and oh - *'we have to go into that?!'* And once we did start going to Confession, I'm afraid we used to make up sins to tell the priest because we didn't have enough real ones to tell him! Imagine that! I think most children did it. *'I told lies, I hit my sister...'* But you know it was such a religious society and you were policed from the moment you woke up to the moment you went to sleep, so you had very little margin left for sinning!

And for children there was corporal punishment as well, both at school and at home. So where in God's name would you get the time or the chance to be sinning?! I hardly ever saw a child commit a sin in the course of my childhood. So you had to make them up for Confession, didn't you, if you didn't have any real ones to tell? Which wasn't a great plan either of course because then you were telling lies to the priest inside the Confession box, by claiming that you had told lies when you actually hadn't! But you didn't have any other sins to show for yourself.

Everybody used to say in Confession that they told lies. *'I told lies, I was disobedient, and I didn't say my prayers as often as I should have.'* I suppose it was okay to say that about prayers because you could never say enough prayers, no matter how many you said. But to say 'I told lies' was of course a blatant lie in itself. But if you think about it, it was no longer a lie by then because you had indeed just walked into the Confession box and told the priest a blatant lie! So there you have it. I often thought that: they *made* me a sinner! What a nation of little liars we must have seemed to the priest! But there wasn't 5% of them were actual real lies. You wouldn't dare tell real lies!

And telling him *'I was disobedient'* - when I certainly *wasn't!* I hardly ever saw a child be disobedient in those days because you'd get thoroughly slapped for it. But you had to find something to say in Confession. Everybody in their childhood did that.

Confirmation, on the other hand, for girls that involved *style* starting to come into it. You were more innocent for your First Communion and not as obsessed with your dress. But by the time of my Confirmation, nylon had just come in, and that cloth would fluff right out.

Confirmation was a bit confusing because you were told you were becoming an adult - but an adult at twelve?! The bishop came and tapped you across the face. I think I confused that a bit with knighthood, where the Queen tapped people on the shoulder with a sword. But the most important thing was that you received the Holy Spirit, or the Holy Ghost as we used to say then. Like the Apostles did after Jesus' death when the Holy Spirit came down on their heads, looking like tongues of fire. I think it was probably my father who drummed into me the importance of that for your whole lifetime ahead. To this day, it's very important to me. When the Holy Spirit comes to you like that at Confirmation, He brings you seven spiritual graces, or gifts or protections. He brings wisdom, understanding, fear of the Lord, and so on. That was the kernel of Confirmation, strengthening you for adult life ahead, and it was very important.

It's still always the first thing I do whenever I walk into our Chapel, to this day. I say *Hello* first to Our Lord in the tabernacle and then I look up at the Holy Spirit, represented as a dove above our altar. He has seven rays coming out of Him, representing those seven spiritual gifts, for you to take ownership of and develop throughout your life. I think that is so fundamental and I've never lost touch with that in almost seventy years since my Confirmation Day. You said earlier that your grandmother said 'The air is full of spirits'. Well for me, the air around me is full of the Holy Spirit in that way, once I remember to tune into it.

*

Norma's elegant greyhound was getting restless, stepping around in little circles on her couch. It was time to leave them to get on with their day. I went back to my own childhood bedroom in the Village, and sat on the bed to listen to the recording of Norma's interview. I felt I was on track. Without any prompting from me, Norma was spontaneously using terms from anthropology to express her own thinking about the religion. She had talked about the '*uses*' and '*functions*' that ritual practices had and have for people in Crow Glen. She talked about '*initiation*' ceremonies for the youth. About material objects being external symbols and triggers for experiences that happen *in the mind*. And how all these practices are a tradition that gets '*inherited*', changed and '*evolved*' over time. You have there a summary of some of the **core ideas of anthropology** (they are highlighted in bold script below and in all my commentaries on Norma's interviews). [17]

When she talked about the '**use**' that parishioners make of the various religious practices available to them, she described people as - both in the old days and today - selecting for themselves specific practices that had certain '**functions**' for them, as she put it.

She described some religious rituals as initiating young people to become full 'members' of the community, both socially and spiritually. It's striking that what she calls the '**initiation**' of Confirmation that she received 67 years ago is still actively benefiting her, she believes, in ways that she can palpably feel in the course of her day.

She described too how today's parents often use Communion and Confirmation as initiations for their children, while declining the rest of the Church's offer. It reminded me of one Irish anthropologist's remark that this 'twenty-first century religion (in the tradition of the many centuries that preceded it) is anything but easy to pin down'. Like Norma, he describes generations of younger Irish people 'who choose to remain outside while fondly retaining some of the practices of the organized religion that they shy away from'. [18]

I was surprised how comfortable she is with what she describes as the constant flow of changes and **evolutions** in her religion. Describing it as '*inherited*', she actively expects it to constantly change with the times, for better or for worse. Limbo, Holy Water, First Holy Communion - she recounts watching with 'fascination' as they surge in and out of fashion according to what people want from them at any given moment.

She has made her own deliberate changes and adjustments too, for instance around the Sacred Heart picture at the centre of her family home. In one way, it's just a change from a rather dark picture to a statue with a brighter aesthetic. But it also reflects what she sees as a core shift in the religion, towards this 'lightening' of the spiritual atmosphere around her.

I hadn't chosen Norma as an unusual practitioner of the religion in the Glen of the Crow, but as a typical one. I was surprised now to see how just much maturity and insight there seemed to be in her spiritual practice.

17 Lavenda, R. & Schultz, E., *Core Concepts in Cultural Anthropology*, Oxford University Press, 2019
18 Salvador Ryan, National University of Ireland, Maynooth, 'The Quest for Tangible Religion', *The Furrow*, Vol 55, 2004

For instance, she is clear-sighted about the distinction between temporal, worldly aspects of the religion that she feels can and should be changeable - and what she sees as 'intrinsically' spiritual levels that, in a positive way, never change. Around this sense of pure spirit as unchanging, she is happy to let external aspects of religion come and go or, as she puts it, '*evolve*'.

She is clear-eyed too about the relationship between ᴄʜᴇ ᴍᴀᴛᴇʀɪᴀʟ ᴀɴᴅ ᴛʜᴇ ꜱᴘɪʀɪᴛᴜᴀʟ. Whether a beautiful landscape, a bright stained-glass window or a lovely mother-of-pearl Prayer Book, she sees material beauty not as contradictory but as complementary to spirituality. For her, the beauty of the material world is like a trampoline to spiritual states, a tool that will help you get there. As that Irish anthropologist of religion put it, 'God speaks through the very ordinary bits and pieces of the material world that he created'. [19]

I noted with interest what Norma said about ɢᴇɴᴅᴇʀ - that in the traditional religion, men were in no way afraid of seeming 'feminised' by their practice of it. This was a memory that was still vivid for me. The rugged, rough-dressed countrymen of my youth would kneel against an armchair in the living room and draw from their pocket a soft leather pouch holding their well-worn Rosary beads. With head bowed they would finger the beads tenderly, murmuring *Hail Mary*s. The humility, the submissiveness, the gentleness, the intimacy of it… even as a small child I had my own (gender-prejudiced) ideas that this all seemed somehow feminine, and at odds with the men's roughness at other times. But the countrymen of those days saw no contradiction there.

I made a note too about Norma's comments on Holy Water being used in the fields, and brought back from pilgrimages abroad. I saw an opening there for what I wanted to ask her about next time: religious practices out in the landscape.

## Reꜰᴇʀᴇɴᴄᴇs

Lavenda, R. & Schultz, E., *Core Concepts in Cultural Anthropology*, Oxford University Press, 2019
Salvador Ryan, National University of Ireland, Maynooth, 'The Quest for Tangible Religion', *The Furrow*, Vol 55, 2004

---

19  Salvador Ryan, as in Note 18

# Chapter 3

# A black ship and a silver bus

Images at the opening of this chapter:

~ Photo from article on 'Glenville's Bonfire Night: Community-Run and Family Focused', John Ahern, *The Avondhu*, 27-6-2018
~ Handbell that called tenants to the cart for the coffin ship
~ Nineteenth-century etching of Famine victims
~ Coffin ship *The Avon* that took the Carneys to America in 1847

# Leaving

Someone is leaving Crow Glen. In fact, ten are leaving. A mother, a father and their eight children. They are leaving in the back of an open farm-cart pulled by a horse, with a driver sitting up front. These ten won't ever be back. They are leaving forever, going to a different universe. Like dying, but still in this life.

After three hours of banging along roads of dirt and stone, they will smell that they are drawing near to the water at Cork. Tall as a castle, a dark wooden ship looms up against the quayside there. With hundreds of others, they will be herded into its closed underbelly. It has been prearranged. When their small group stumbles up the plank into the ship's loud-creaking hull, the children will get their first ever glimpse of the city, and of seawater.

This kind of ship has come to be called a coffin ship. This one is named *The Avon*. It is bound for a land of ice called Grosse Île. Their bodies already broken by famine, up to a third of the wretches in the bottom of these ships die during the two-month Atlantic crossing. [20]

They don't know it yet but in a few weeks' time, the father of this group will be one of those statistics, losing his life in the crowded hull of the coffin ship. The mother and the eight children will face America alone.

Her name is Johanna Carney. She is from the beautiful, intensely green hillside of Doon, in Gleann an Phréacháin. She dreamt that God was calling them to America, giving them a way out. She saw a watery, heaving route on which they could travel away from the deaths of the neighbours. She decided that they must go now - they couldn't wait any longer. Another week would see the children dying off, one by one. They must try the very tiny margin of luck that is left to them, on that ship.

There was nothing left around them at home but the four cold, wet walls. Everything had been sold, or burnt for a spark of warmth. Anything that could conceivably be boiled, they had tried to eat it. Leather, cloth, tree-branches. Stew it, shred it, break it down somehow to swallow it. A knife-twist in her gut told her to stop thinking about that now. In her stomach

---

20 The Avon seems to have been even worse than most coffin ships. On one of its voyages, 'it had 552 passengers, and there were 236 deaths in the voyage'. Seamas MacManus, *The Story of the Irish Race*, Devin-Adair, 1983

she had pains the like of which she hadn't felt since the birth of the youngest twenty months earlier.

So they had decided. They would tell the steward from the Manor House when he came to carry out the dead from the houses along their laneway. They would tell him that yes, they accepted the Manor's offer of one-way passage for them all on the coffin ship, in exchange for leaving the land and the house back to the Manor landlord forever. They would go with the children into the ship, where they would each receive a bowl of liquid swill every day during the crossing. And maybe, please God, they would find some way to stay alive on the other side.

The day the cart pulled up into the yard for the journey, the landlord's man rang a loud handbell, over and over. Like a smaller version of the funeral bell on the church in the Village, it was the well-known signal for the cart for the coffin ship. It often rang out across the fields. But today it was ringing for them.

At first, jolting along the road in the rain, she could feel only pain. Pains in her bones and muscles, pains in her stomach, pain in her head. But the beat of the horses' hooves and the swaying eventually brought a kind of numbness, a blessing she hadn't experienced for a while. It was pierced by the flash-memory agony of leaving the house a few hours earlier. Touching the walls, close-up and in slow-motion, as her feet moved her towards the door, while the bell clanged demandingly outside. Never - however long she might remain alive - would she forget the clangs of that bell, like blows raining down on her.

It was 1847, when Pat and Johanna Carney left Doon for the coffin ship. Historians describe that year, often called 'Black '47', as the worst year of the Famine, when 'the dead, the dying, and the starving could be found all over Ireland'. [21] The National Folklore Collection describes how the Hudson dynasty at Gleann's colonial estate methodically profited from the famine through evictions, buying up the land of the starving very cheaply, thus expanding their estate as far as the foothills of the Nagle Mountains, north of the Village. Crow Glen schoolteacher Ó Suilleabháin recorded that in the area known as Chimneyfield and The Commons, north of the Bride River Valley, the local people 'were almost completely wiped out during the famine years. This commonage was purchased by Hudsons and such occupants as were there were ruthlessly evicted and replaced by

---

21  Adrian McGrath, 'Coffin Ships and the Great Hunger - An Gorta Mór', *Irish American Journal*, 30-8-2017, available at www.irishamericanjournal.com/2017/08/coffin-ships.html

others, servants and such.' [22] By the time the Famine was over, Hudsons' colonial estate was so massive that to the north of the Village alone it extended for eight miles, beyond Bín na Sceithe towards Killavullen.

If you stood today on the green slopes of Johanna's homestead in Doon and looked around you, you would wonder how the horrors of famine could ever have unfolded in a farming landscape with such fertile land and a benign climate. The answer lies back in 1650 when Cromwell led the English army all over the arable parts of Ireland to 're-conquer the country on behalf of the English Parliament'. [23] Ireland had been colonised by the English since the twelfth century, but not thoroughly enough for Cromwell's liking.

In the twelfth century, the English King Henry II had already granted 'half the kingdom of Cork' to one family of aristocrat settlers called De Barri. In 1180, England's Parliament 'granted' to Robert de Barri 'the eastern portion of the kingdom of Cork', which included Crow Glen. [24] Meanwhile, the Irish clans maintained as best they could their own Gaelic-speaking culture, and they continued to rebel. By Cromwell's time in the seventeenth century, the English wanted an end to those rebellions and that persistent Gaelic culture. They wanted a tighter, more methodical and more profitable occupation of Ireland's fertile arable land by English settlers.

So Cromwell invaded and waged an immense war on the natives, clearing them off their lands. They were either slaughtered, exiled abroad, or displaced onto the barren wilderness of Connaught on the western seaboard, which was of no interest to the English. In 1652, the English passed legislation that they called an 'Act for the Settlement of Ireland', which brazenly doled out ownership of all the arable land of Ireland to English aristocrats, many of whom would never even see the vast tracts of farms that they now owned there. The massive rents and taxes that they now drew from the natives would be sent on to them in England.

The Irish were allowed back onto the land as serf labourers or to work the land as tenants, so that they could send rent to their absent aristocrat landlords in England, in exchange for the right to subsistence-farm small sections of what had formerly been their own lands. In the early

---

22  D. Ó Súilleabháin, National Folklore Collection, Gleann an Phréacháin, Roll No. 450, p. 148, available at https://www.duchas.ie/en/cbes/4921858/4896707
23  David Wallace, *Twenty-Two Turbulent Years, 1639 -1661*, Southgate, 2013
24  Ann Galbally, *Redmond Barry: An Anglo-Irish Australian*, Melbourne University Press, Melbourne, 2013

eighteenth century, Gleann's Manor estate was established in this way, and its small tenant farmers were able to survive on it for the next hundred and fifty years.

But during the 1840s, the potato plant - the only food-crop allowed to the locals as tenants - was hit by blight. Meanwhile the weather, other crops, normal farming practices and the export of harvests out through Cork harbour to the British Empire - all that continued as usual. But because the potatoes of the tenant Irish failed in the following years, they starved to death. Historians describe how at the same time, 'there was an abundance of fruit, vegetables, dairy products, seafood, and even meat, and indeed beef, in Ireland. So, why did the Irish starve? (...) Nightmarish scenes appeared at Irish sea ports as British ships packed with livestock and food stuffs, guarded by British police and soldiers, set sail for Britain or for sale overseas, while Irish peasants starved to death all around these ports and along the city roads leading out to the countryside.' [25]

In 1997, on the 150th anniversary of the Famine, British Prime Minister Tony Blair visited Cork and formally apologised on behalf of Britain, declaring: 'That one million people should have died in what was then part of the richest and most powerful nation in the world is something that still causes pain... Those who governed in London at the time failed their people through standing by while a crop failure turned into a massive human tragedy. We must not forget such a dreadful event.' [26]

## Midsummer Learnings

In the year 2000, Norma Buckley created her own exhibition about the Famine in Crow Glen, and it was the first time I had ever heard anything about Famine in the Village. She displayed it in *The Old School* in the middle of the Village, now used as a community room since a modern school had been built further up the Street. She put the display on during the ancient midsummer festival, which draws hundreds of revellers. Even people who have migrated to the city or beyond come back for this long day of ritual and celebration that culminates in a night-time street party around *The Bonfire*.

That night, I was back from abroad for Bonfire Night and I threaded my way through the crowds to get into the Old School to see this home-made

---

25 Adrian McGrath, as in Note 21
26 Kathy Marks, *The Independent* (UK), 'Blair Issues Apology for Irish Potato Famine', 2-6-1997

exhibition. In there, I could scarcely believe what I was seeing. Norma had gotten glued together on paper a close-up map of the Village, showing each house and the familiar names of the families who had lived there for more than two centuries.

As a child I had been inside every house in the Village. With my sister, when we couldn't sleep, we would play a game of mentally going into every house, from the Crossroads Below to the Crossroads Above, remembering what each house was like inside and describing it to each other.

Norma's close-up map drew each house as a box lined up beside the next house. And inside each box was written the number of people who had died of starvation in that house during the Famine, using official records of the bodies that had been carried out of each house by the authorities. The name and age of each corpse was transcribed onto the map from the records.

I ran my finger down the hand-drawn map of these houses whose interiors I knew so well. Inside most, a range of people had died of starvation, across a spread of age-groups. Mary O' Sullivan, 61. Her granddaughter Minnie O'Driscoll, aged 4. Jackie O' Driscoll, Mary's son-in-law, the child's father, aged 31.

Mike Murphy, a present-day cartographer at Cork University, had been in my class at school in the Village, and he still lives there. In 2018, Mike helped mount an exhibition at his University, rebuilding a typical Famine shack (a '*bothán*' in Irish) where people starved to death during the Famine. In an article, he explained: 'People died in harrowing ways. For example, the mother was often the last of the family to die, and she was sometimes found dead just inside the door of the *bothán*, with the bodies of her family around her. As a mother, she would have struggled to preserve privacy by closing the door and allowing her family some dignity in their final moments.' [27]

I had never been told about any of this in the Village, neither by my family nor at school. There had been no mention of it ever, anywhere. We were taught a few remote, summary facts about the Famine. Like everyone else, I had seen the creepy nineteenth-century drawings of writhing skeletons dying by the roadside, foaming at the mouth from trying to swallow handfuls of grass. But the houses in the Village were not *bothán* shacks:

---

27  Mike Murphy, '*An bothán*, a symbol of Famine misery', *News and Views*, University College Cork, 2018

they were solid, well-built, respectable stone-and-plaster homes with heavy slate roofs. How could anything like that ever happen in there?

I had somehow assumed that the Famine had nothing to do with the Glen of the Crow. That it had all happened in farther, wilder reaches of Ireland. In the West, in Connemara, where the land had always been rocky and barren. The land around the Village was like a different universe. It was as lush as a hallucination. Grass grew impossibly thick and green there. Trees, shrubs, flowers, weeds - everything planted there became an uncontrollable riot of dripping greenery. Crow Glen farms placidly gave good yields in dairy herds, beef, potatoes, other vegetables and animal feed. I had always assumed the Famine had happened *elsewhere*.

And now, I saw in Norma's exhibition that in just the two years from 1850 to 1852, the Famine had already killed 47 people in the tiny Village of Gleann an Phréacháin. [28] And that was only an early dribble in a decade of starvation to come. Fully five years earlier, on the 17th of March 1847 (a St. Patrick's Day, ironically), Gleann's parish priest, Father McCarthy, wrote to the *Cork Examiner* newspaper as if the worst were only then beginning. He wrote:

'On Tuesday a man brought to my door a corpse of a girl about ten years old on his back, craving for food... In this locality... absolute famine stalks abroad with fearful pace... And if some steps not be immediately taken to meet the dreadful wants of the famishing population, the districts must 'ere long be tenanted alone by the dead.' [29] Dead tenants would no longer bring profit to their colonial landlords, the priest was publicly pointing out.

Father McCarthy lived then in the house where the cartographer, Mike Murphy, grew up in the 1970s. 'Going in and out the same door...', Mike points out in his article, with a map-maker's sharp awareness of physical space. [30]

It was *Black '47* when Father McCarthy wrote to the newspaper, the year that Pat and Johanna Carney were put on the coffin ship. Nell, the cosy granny that I grew up beside in our house in the Village, was born in 1909,

---

28 The Irish National Famine Museum at Strokestown Park, County Roscommon in Ireland tells that 'between 1845 and 1850 alone, two million of the then eight million people who lived in Ireland disappeared. One million died of hunger and related diseases and the other million left Ireland for permanent exile.' Adrian McGrath, as in Note 21
29 Mike Murphy, as in Note 27
30 Mike Murphy, as in Note 27

just 62 years later. Yet neither she nor my grandfather had ever mentioned a word about it to us.

So Norma Buckley's display that night in the Old School was like having a bucket of cold water thrown in my face. And yet there was also something faintly thrilling about this one-night exhibition on that millennial midsummer. The Old School had always smelled of nineteenth-century mortar being eaten by damp and mould. All the old walls in the Village gave off that smell when broken into or crumbling. The walls of our own house had yielded it when my father opened them up to build an extension.

When we were children, that smell was oddly exciting. It was like a breach in the wall of normal domestic life. It meant a building was being transformed, whether by being worked on, or by slowly falling down. And that often meant we could go and play in those altered spaces, whether for a few hours, or for years if the building had been abandoned.

The Old School had that weirdly enticing smell. Only community officials had its keys, and we children got in there only occasionally, by dodging past their legs. It was the storage place for the ritual objects used by Gleann's guilds and associations for their meetings, parades and festivals. It was quietly amazing to walk around inside the moulding-mortar smell of the Old School and see the sacred objects that created our festivals lying in wait, as if asleep naked. Banners, statues, sceptres, sashes, badges and flags lay there inert like theatre costumes backstage, waiting to be put on.

Outside in the Village, we only ever saw these untouchable objects *in action*. Held up proudly during religious Processions, carried aloft, waving in the breeze, worn across the body - they sprang exotically to life, bringing our festival days with them. Those days hovered outside time in a cloud of awe and excitement.

It was almost indecent to see these transformative objects lying about in the empty rooms of the Old School. It was like a famous king - only ever seen parading in full pageantry - now glimpsed curled up, sleeping like a baby.

That Bonfire Night, as I ran my finger down Norma's hand-drawn exhibition about our Famine dead, I saw that the official records, with typical English precision, stated where each of the dead had been found in their house. 'Agnes O' Reilly, 27, curled up in corner of back room'. 'John O' Reilly, 61, in the bed in the side room'.

This deadly information under my finger coincided with the primitive excitement of the street-festival outside. Through the open windows, you could smell the hot take-away foods at a stall. Music throbbed in from the street. There was dancing, and the first crackle of the Bonfire as it roared up into the night like a dragon, lighting up the faces around it.

There was some kind of deep, carnival thrill in the contrast. Somehow we had survived what was in that exhibition, or at least some of our people had survived it. Enough of them for the rest of us to be there, that night, at the Bonfire.

I didn't give the exhibition much thought over the following years as I was whipped away, busy with my own life and work abroad. I hadn't ever gotten the chance to ask Norma Buckley the questions that later occurred to me about it. Where did she get that archival information? [31] Why did she create that exhibition for that one night? And why had we never been told any of it before, either in the Village or at school? Why was it not part of the official Gleann an Phréacháin history that we all took such pride and interest in?

In her exhibition, I had glimpsed those facts - that reality - for a moment, as if a thick curtain on a stage had been lifted away to reveal a scene, before being dropped back down again. I had stepped out of my *unknowing* about the Famine for a moment, and then I dropped back into it again for many years more. On that midsummer night in the year 2000, I knew nothing as yet about Johanna Carney. I did not know that 17 years later, her Famine reality would erupt vividly into my own life, as if she were rising back to life in front of me out of the rich black earth and thick green grass of Doon.

And there were so many things that Johanna herself did not know, that day in 1847 when she hustled her cold, wailing infants up the gang-plank into the dark ship by the quayside in Cork. She had no way of knowing whether they would each live or die as a consequence of her decision to go. She only knew that if she had not taken this action, they would all definitely have died.

The other thing that Johanna did not know, and could not know, was that 170 years later, in the year 2017, twelve of her descendants would return from America to Crow Glen. That they would arrive in Cork city and be

---

31 I later learned that Norma had accessed a heritage grant to employ a local youngster to research the topic as a summer job. That was Sinéad O' Keeffe, at the time a history student at University College Cork.

driven in a luxurious silver minibus that they hired for the occasion, to find the homestead that Johanna and Pat had had to leave behind. That they would come there to honour herself and Pat as their fore-mother and fore-father.

When I got a phone-call abroad from Norma Buckley inviting me to join her in welcoming those Americans on that visit, I did not know why she was inviting me. I did not know then that the arrival of that silver bus would profoundly alter what I thought I knew about the Village and my own people's role in it.

On the day when it finally pulled up outside Norma's house where she and I stood waiting for it, the Americans' silver bus looked sophisticated enough to have flown them all the way from Washington, where they were coming from. Parked in the middle of the Village, it looked every bit as strange and beguiling as the *Wanderly Wagon* that used to come flying in on our TV screens when I was five years old.

## References

Crowley, J., Murphy, M. & Smyth, WJ, *Atlas of the Great Irish Famine*, Cork University Press, 2012
Galbally, Ann, *Redmond Barry: An Anglo-Irish Australian*, Melbourne University Press, Melbourne, 2013
MacManus, Seamas, *The Story of the Irish Race*, Devin-Adair, 1983
Marks, Kathy, *The Independent*, (UK), 'Blair Issues Apology for Irish Potato Famine', 2-6-1997
McGrath, Adrian, 'Coffin Ships and the Great Hunger - An Gorta Mór', *Irish American Journal*, 30-8-2017, available at www.irishamericanjournal.com/2017/08/coffin-ships.html
Ó Súilleabháin, D., National Folklore Collection, Gleann an Phréacháin, Roll No. 450, p. 148, available at https://www.duchas.ie/en/cbes/4921858/4896707
Wallace, David, *Twenty-Two Turbulent Years, 1639 -1661*, Fastprint, Southgate, 2013

# Chapter 4

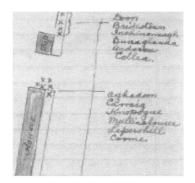

# When places are blessed

Images at the opening of this chapter:

~ Part of a hand-drawn map from the 1920s, showing where men from each townland used to gather in the Village to socialise after Sunday Mass
~ The Gleann Procession
~ Carraig an Aifrinn, the Mass Rock at Gleann
~ The pilgrimage island of Lough Derg

In the days before the Americans arrived, I had time to sit down with Norma again to ask her my next questions about the religious practices in Crow Glen. My memory was that there was a whole elaborate map of outdoor practices too, across a kind of spiritual geography that spread out well beyond the Village. As well as happening in the Chapel, rituals overflowed out from the home into Processions through the Village, pilgrimages to the two ancient sacred sites further out in the landscape, and ceremonies called Stations out on the farms beyond them.

On this visit, I was formally introduced to the greyhound, apparently called Miriam. She watched suspiciously from the couch while I took up so much of her minder's time. Every so often the hound would stand up to rearrange the silk, satin and velvet cushions that formed her daybed, before turning in a circle and sinking back down onto them with a weary sigh.

 Norma...

## The Chapel

Oh, religion is definitely not confined to the indoors around here, and it never was. But before we talk about ceremonies outdoors, I just want to say too that I personally find *great* relaxation of mind and body in the Village Chapel. Maybe now more than ever, now that I'm older and I enjoy a simpler practice of just *being* in the presence of the divine, without having to do lots of prayers and ceremonies. Spending time in the Chapel is a total haven for me in that way - a peace and a refuge built up over the years.

That's when I'm there alone or with just a few others. But of course in the old days and right up into the 1990s, Sunday morning Mass in the Chapel was a huge event for everyone in the parish, socially. Everyone came in from all the isolated homesteads all over the mountains. Until the 1960s, they would all come in open horse-drawn carts, even when it was pouring with rain. It was the big outing of the week for them. There were several different shops in the Village then, and they would all be open after Mass for the country people to get their weekly provisions. In the 1970s there was a butcher's and a fish-counter too, that only came to the Village for that

Sunday morning slot. And people would stand around in groups the length of the Village talking for a long time before, and especially after, Mass.

Remember that fabulous hand-drawn map that you showed me, done in the 1920s, of exactly where the men from each townland used to stand in the Village to socialise after Mass? [32] Well, you'll remember yourself that right up at least into your time in the 1980s, your cousin Denis O' Mahoney from the townland of Bunaglanna above the Bride River Valley did indeed used to stand exactly where the 1920s map says that Bunaglanna men stood in the Street after Mass!

For me, what I just said about the Chapel as a haven, it applies to any church to an extent, even churches of other religions or in foreign countries. What I really feel in them is the devotion of the good people, in their thousands over the centuries, who brought their pure spirits in there. That's what I feel buoyed up by. It's like the imprint of the spirituality of all those people who have been there over the centuries, and what went on there. The feeling of good people having been there.

But what isn't in other religions' churches of course is the same presence of God in the tabernacle on the altar. The tabernacle is the solid gold box holding the consecrated bread and wine that have been turned into the Body and Blood of Christ. In Catholic churches they are kept in there at all times, at the centre of the altar. So you feel and you know that the real *Presence* is actually there. You're going in to meet somebody, albeit a spiritual being rather than someone in a human body. And the red light on the altar, called the sanctuary lamp, will always be on if the consecrated bread and wine are there in the tabernacle.

Once when I was a child and our church in the Village was being renovated, the sanctuary lamp went missing! It was probably taken away for safe keeping but it never came back. We had a new priest at the time and I said to him that we *must* get a sanctuary lamp. He happened to be invited to the Manor House for dinner that week and he mentioned to them in passing about the missing lamp. He thought they looked a bit

---

32  Shown at the start of this chapter, the map can be viewed online at https://twitter.com/duchas_ie/status/1019164182573453312 It's from the 234-page folklore collection gathered from farms and townlands around Crow Glen in the 1920s by the local schoolteacher Seán Ó Duinnshléibhe, who will appear again many times across this book. His original manuscript is part of the National Folklore Collection in Dublin (Roll No. 12542, p. 221-467). *The School Collection, Volume 0382: Áth Dúna, Gleann an Phréacháin, Mainistir Fhearmuighe – Béaloideas.* It can be read online at www.duchas.ie/en/cbes/4921859/4896737/5190225?ChapterID=4921859

uneasy around the table. After the dinner Colonel Hudson, the owner of the Manor House at the time, called him aside and said 'I think it's in one of our out-houses'. And of course, it was. Anyway, it was handed back and we were so glad to have it! And you remember that the perpetual Sacred Heart lamp in the centre of the home is a tie-in to that sanctuary lamp on the altar in the church.

My husband worked in the heating, plumbing and ventilating of churches, convents, monasteries and schools, so I've seen a lot of church buildings around the country! We recently had our own church here in the Village renovated again. The priest wanted to add roundels of stained glass to all the windows down the two sides of the church. But I said to him 'You know, you'd want to be very careful. It could end up looking like a themed pub in America.' He was a bit taken aback by that but he did change the plan and we have a really beautiful decor now, chosen mainly by the local women.

But in terms of moving outwards from the home to the Village and the landscape... Well, first, the 'Churching' of women, do you know what that meant? It's all part of the fabric and the intricacies. You see, after having a baby, a woman had to be 'Churched' by the priest before she could be allowed back into the Chapel. You had to go to there to have a special cleansing blessing before you could be allowed to go to Mass and receive Holy Communion again after having a child! Modern women didn't like being told they were unclean, but it was just part of it. You were just after producing this lovely baby, thanks to be God. And now you had to be cleansed?! What was that all about?! Personally, I dreaded the whole thing. I wasn't feeling it was any kind of 'blessing'. I was thinking: what has the devil got to do with me? Why on earth does he need to be ousted from *me*?!

And look, I have to touch on this as well. For the Church in the old days there was only one sin in Ireland and that was sex! You could shoot your neighbour if you wanted but sex was the absolute sin, whatever way you looked at it. And women did bear the brunt of that view more heavily, I think. I have read and studied a lot about the thinking of the Church down through the years. Now of course that was their *private* teaching in the seminaries. The congregation knew nothing about what priests were told about women in the seminaries and in the old theology. You know that priests abusing children very rarely abused girls - always only boys.

And yet when I think of the actual innocence of the people back then! Recently the Pope made an apology for all the clergy's sex abuses. There has to be forgiveness, but there has to be more too here in Ireland because the wrongs done were so vast.

But in my case, I was very lucky because I didn't get 'Churched' when I should have been after my first child was born. Instead, the priest invited me up to his house for it and gave me the ceremony in private. He said, 'I've something to offer you'. I thought it must be Rosary beads or a medal or something and I said, 'Oh father, that'd be lovely'. 'Well', he said 'it's a blessing.' He had the Holy Water ready and all, and he did the whole blessing there and then. Of course, it was in Latin. And he said, 'You can go to Mass now whenever you feel up to it.' I said, 'But Father, I'll have to get Churched first.' And he said 'No, you don't need that now, it's done.' I was so grateful. He didn't tell me not to say it to anyone else, but he knew well I wouldn't, because other women were still being Churched. But by the time my second child was born four years later, they weren't doing it anymore - it was gone, thank God.

## Processions and Stations

In the Village we always had two Processions in the year - the Marian Procession in May and the Procession of the Blessed Eucharist on the feast of Corpus Christi, the Body of Christ, in June. But it had died out and up until recently, we hadn't had one for 18 years. I said to the priest 'Look, did you ever consider that what we need to do is to bring Jesus out onto the Street again? It's time to bring back the Processions. Bring back taking Jesus out and walking the Street with us - out of the tabernacle and back in amongst us.' The priest was very busy at that time and he said 'Norma, if you insist on doing it, you organise it!' But of course, the association of local people called 'The Legion of Mary' came onboard and they were keen to do it.

But we had none of the ritual gear left from the old Processions. We had no canopy to carry above Our Lord. The men carrying the statue had no sashes to wear across the body, and so on. You see Processions were a thing of the past by then. You were meant to go to big PR mega-events organised by the Church in Dublin, rather than doing your own little thing in your own little village where no one would see you and it wouldn't be in the media!

But we went over to the next village and borrowed their paraphernalia and the men's sashes and so on. For the Procession, a local man drove the car and led the decades of the Rosary and the hymns through a loud speaker, all at the same time. And the altar boys were spreading incense, and the First Communion girls were there in their white dresses. We had masses of incense. We paraded up and down the street, reciting the decades of the Rosary and singing hymns. We got a priest in from the next village to officiate because our own was away. But it's well established now again, and we do it every year, which is lovely. The Legion of Mary run it, and it's in safe hands. And I'm sure the Church, when they sees it's going well, will buy all the equipment for it again.

The Stations, then, are another way of basically taking the Eucharist and the Sacraments farther out into the wider landscape and onto people's farms. It's still important today. There's a calendar or rota set up for the year whereby on a given day of the year the priest comes and offers Confession and says Mass in a given farmhouse. People are cleaning and decorating for weeks beforehand. It's a really big moment for the household when they have the Stations. And it's a huge hospitality thing because all friends and neighbours around are invited into the home for it. So there's a lot catering to do for them as well, to give them a good sit-down meal afterwards. It's just another way of taking the religion way out there to the people and onto the land itself. It's almost like a way of giving the farmers more ownership of the Sacraments and the Mass, to have them in their own home. [33]

## The holy Well

Then, every midsummer, the community here in Crow Glen make our annual pilgrimage to a sacred site about two and a half miles from the Village - our Holy Well. This has been done since time immemorial. A local pilgrimage like the one to our Holy Well here, it's called a Pattern Day, because there is this pattern to what you do. Not every area has it by

---

[33] A historian of these Stations in Ireland explains that 'Stations of Confession', as they were originally called, 'first appear in the documentary record in the 1780s in association with dioceses located in East Munster'. He explains that 'at one level, a Station was a community event. Everyone in the neighbourhood was welcome to attend. It was not uncommon for more than a hundred people to attend a given Station.' Interestingly, he comments that 'the practice flourished in Ireland well into the 1860s (and in some places into the twentieth century)'. However, in Crow Glen it is still a popular practice to this day. Most scholars consider that Stations must have begun in response to the seventeenth-century Penal Laws that outlawed Catholicism, causing Catholic practices to be done in secret in unofficial places. (Michael Carroll, *Irish Pilgrimage: Holy Wells and Popular Catholic Devotion*, Johns Hopkins University Press, 1999)

any means. The nearest one that I know of that's as significant as ours is in the next county of Waterford, in Ardmore, where like us they do rounds and drink water from a holy well. [34]

We all do this annual pilgrimage to our Holy Well every midsummer, before gathering in the Village later for our annual Bonfire Night street party. [35] Families go along to the Well individually during that day. All day you'll meet people coming and going along the lane to the Well, either having done their visit or on their way to do it. The foot-traffic is heaviest just after suppertime when people have finished work.

As you know, the Well is on the land that used to belong to your own people, near the homestead where your grandmother Nell grew up in Doon. The Well is inside an ancient ringfort there, with a lovely grove of trees growing around it inside the ring, like a protection. Our annual ceremony is that each person says the Rosary in front of ancient stones that are embedded in the ground there around the Well. After each decade, you use a smaller stone to trace a cross three times onto the old, cross-marked stone in front of you, and then you move on to the next stone for your next decade. The stones are grooved three inches deep from generations of people marking them with crosses like that. Those grooves are centuries old. And when you consider that people mostly only marked them on one day per year, you can see how old the practice is!

Of course, in pre-Christian times, these were already agricultural festivals that were offered up to the nature spirits for fine weather, good crops or whatever. And the early Christians just put Christian saints' names onto them. Ours was dedicated to Saint John the Baptist at that point. I have great faith in the Doon pilgrimage, even if only through thinking of the centuries of people who have expressed sincere devotion there.

But in recent years I felt it was important to bring to public attention in Gleann an Phréacháin the fact that, up until the Vatican stopped refusing unbaptised babies in their consecrated graveyards, locals used to bury their unbaptised dead babies in the tiny graveyard at the Holy Well. Your ancestors, the Sweeneys, used to assist locals with their unbaptised dead

---

34  For a book-length study of the Ardmore Holy Well tradition, see *The Holy Well Tradition: The Pattern of St Declan, Ardmore, County Waterford, 1800-2000*, Maynooth Studies in Local History, 2002, by Stiofán Ó Cadhla, Professor of Folkore and Ethnology at University College Cork.

35  You can join in with the Villagers' pilgrimage online by watching one of the heritage videos created by Crow Glenner Tony Kennedy. Called *Doonpeter Well, Glenville, Co Cork, 23-6-2017*, it's on his Youtube channel, *Real Cork*, at www.youtube.com/watch?v=-z0MIRwd69g

babies. Bereaved parents could use the private path from Sweeneys' house to carry their infant to the Holy Well unseen. Your grandmother used to say that living there as a young girl, she would every so often see men passing through the top of their yard in the evening with a shovel and a small box under their arm.

It brought people some comfort because Crow Glenners still remembered that way back in the year 1199 the Holy Well had actually had a consecrated burial ground, which the Vatican had never gotten around to deconsecrating. So when people were smuggling their infants into the arms of Our Lady at the Well, they felt their babies were actually getting a consecrated resting-place. Unlike most ringforts, our Holy Well does include a tiny Catholic-consecrated graveyard left over from that first little Catholic church that stood inside the ringfort in the year 1199. The footprint of that very early chapel is still there. But people had to bury those babies in secret because ironically, if it was known, the Church would have stopped it, deeming unbaptised babies unworthy of consecrated ground.

I have a newspaper cutting of an article written by a priest who went around surveying holy wells in the 1930s or so. He said the Gleann Well was 'widely renowned for its curative effects'. I remember that the older people would always put their finger in the water and bathe their eyes with it because it's supposed to be good for eyesight.

When the father of Nell, your grandmother, was old, he became blind. I used to go to Doon visiting and I'd sit with him on the side of his bed, as he didn't move around much then. Every time I saw him he'd talk to me all about the Well, as it was on his land of course. He told me about the 13-year-old girl who came there once looking for a cure. She had come all the way from Carrigtwohill, a village about 15 miles away, because the Well was so well known for its cures in those days. People with great faith in it would come from several parishes away.

It was well known for cures but this was the most spectacular one. She was on crutches and because of the rough ground crossing the fields to get to the Well, she had to be carried in there by two men. She was lowered down beside the Well and I believe her feet and hands were bathed with the water. And when they were helping her to get up, she moved them away. And when they gave her her crutches she said *'No, I can do it'*. And she stood up and walked back out of there by herself. Her crutches stayed there for many years, hanging on the hawthorn tree beside the Well.

Believe it or not somebody stole them eventually. Can you imagine doing that? Trying to steal a cure? It doesn't bear thinking about.

When your grandmother Nell was a child back there, her first cousin was brought out from the city for a stay at the farm because she had tuberculosis. She had been in a sanatorium for it and wasn't cured. So she came to stay and she was taken to the Holy Well for a Novena of nine days in a row. And at the end of the nine days she was cured. She went off back to town, and she died just a few years ago, a fine elegant city woman at the age of 86. You would have seen her visiting here in this house many times.

There were lots of holy wells around the country but the difference is that they didn't all have a cure - only certain rare ones. And there weren't that many of those. There were a few around County Cork, as West Cork was very traditional and religious. Of course, there's Saint Gobnait's Well in Ballyvourney - I'll tell you more about that another time. But to be honest, I can't think of another one other than ours until you get back west as far as Banteer, and that's already a long way towards the Kerry border.

How people saw the Holy Well was that they approached the whole site with the same reverence as a church. In the old days people used to go there a lot on their own unsupervised, maybe to pray for a Special Intention. They'd walk all the way over there from the Village.

I feel that if any place is to be special, it has to have rising water - a spring or a well like there is at Doon. You feel this so much when you go there. But at the holy wells, I believe there is more - much more. I feel Doon has a spiritual power of its own as a place. A church building takes you inside, indoors, into the human world of all the past worshippers. But the Holy Well is bringing you out into the universe.

You're talking here about the spiritual coming through the material - the water coming up from the depths of the earth through its own energy. The Holy Well is coming up from the depths of the earth and I do believe there can be cures in those wells. Of course you must first believe that God initiated the material universe as much as He did the spiritual one, and it seems nobody can disprove or contradict that very well to this day. The cure is partly in your own mind and body of course, if you have enough spirituality to believe in it - to raise your own spiritual energy to that level where a cure can happen in you.

Remember, in the Penal Times in Ireland when all Catholicism was outlawed, it was an indescribable loss to the people here. There were no churches anymore but people could still go to their Holy Wells in secret. And they were still able to connect there with the spirit of God, without any break in the connection. I think those people who went to the Wells and the Mass Rocks under such duress and such danger, way out in the countryside in holes in the rocks - they helped to make them into places of profound spirituality. They are as near as you can come to touching spirit in this world.

Once a woman came here to be a schoolteacher in the Village, and she became a great friend of my mother's. My mother took her back to the Holy Well once, on the midsummer pilgrimage. Well, my mother was crossing the stones there and doing the whole ritual seriously, of course. But the teacher was teasing her, saying 'Are you really going to do all that nonsense?' You know, as the well-educated sort of person that the teacher was.

Well, when my mother had finished, they were starting to walk out towards the perimeter ring. The teacher was walking ahead of my mother and next thing, she turned round and said 'What did you do that for?' My mother said, 'Do what?' And the teacher said, 'You hit me on the back of my head!' And my mother always swore that she was nowhere near her, and hadn't touched her. My mother was as shaken by it as the teacher was. The teacher never again said a word against the Holy Well after that.

## The Mass Rock

Well, you have Mass Rocks and Mass Rocks, and ours happens to be a place of mind-blowing beauty. A place of rock and water and green ferns and the leaf-canopy overhead. It is *so, so* spiritual. We went there with my mother sometimes when I was a child, for a long Sunday walk. You'd go with a few women friends or you'd meet friends there. But you'd be going to say prayers - there wouldn't be any picnicking or anything secular like that. Prayers were part of our entertainment, to be honest!

One time recently I took a bus of Scandinavian men to visit our Mass Rock. They were coming as anthropologists to look at it, and they were sent to me to guide them there. They had the courtesy to clarify to me beforehand that they were all agnostics. Our dog preceded me onto their bus and that broke the ice nicely.

We spent the day outdoors at the sacred sites around the Village. At the end of the day we went to the Village pub. They were like northern giants in there under the low ceilings, because they were all huge. They were on a tour of these sites around Ireland but nearly every one of them came up to me and said there was something different about our Mass Rock. They hesitated to say 'spiritual' but they did. 'It's not the first time we've felt that at an Irish site', they said, 'it's the second time'. They said the other time was at Saint Kevin's Bed in Glendalough in County Wicklow, a famous ancient pilgrimage site.

At our Carraig an Aifrinn, you go into a tiny valley and you have no distractions. All you have around you is natural beauty, under the safety of the tree canopy.  It's like a natural amphitheatre. Even agnostics can meet a strong natural spirituality there. Then the place was made special by Mass being said there, and centuries of devotion.

There is a deeper connection too between the Holy Well and Carraig an Aifrinn. In the middle of the seventeenth century, Catholicism was completely outlawed by the British in Ireland. Priests caught saying Mass were in danger of being executed, or at the very least deported for life. And parishioners attending Mass at a Mass Rock would be jailed too, at least. So it was a very, very dangerous and difficult undertaking to try to attend one of these banned Masses in Penal Times. And the site of the Holy Well in Doon was used for that purpose for years, just as the Mass Rock was later on.

Doon was quite suited to the purpose in the sense that it was isolated. There was very little access to it and you could have look-outs well positioned to watch over it. So the site of the Holy Well was used regularly for Mass in the early Penal Times, before the Mass Rock ever was. The back field there is still called *Párc na Sagairt*, Irish for 'The Priests' Field'. And then *Cumar na Sagairt*, an outcrop and a little ravine further on, means 'The little ravine of the Priests'. In Penal Times, believe it or not, the priest used to live in there, under that outcrop of rocks.

But it must have all been discovered by the British because the word went out one Sunday 'Don't go to Doon this Sunday'. People didn't go, and it was indeed raided by the British Army. During the raid on the Holy Well site, the priest managed to stay hidden there in Cumar na Sagairt and they didn't find him. But that was the end of Doon for his secret Masses.

Then, surveying the countryside, the people landed on the Mass Rock as the next hiding place. They moved the secret Masses on from Doon, just half a mile across the Bride River Valley to the site of Carraig an Aifrinn. They say that a very wise old man was one of the party who scoped out the spot and he declared: 'This is the right place. No-one but Crow flying overhead could see us here. There's no other way of spotting it.'

So the secret Mass moved over to the Mass Rock, which stayed active from the seventeenth century until the Penal Laws were fully brought to an end around the start of the nineteenth century. So between them the Holy Well and Carraig an Aifrinn hosted almost two hundred years of completely secret practice of the religion. That's why I feel that that whole area - that triangle across the Bride River Valley - is so, so sacred. Because it's been traversed *thousands* of times by people doing their secret devotions and risking their lives for it.

And remember, before the Village was built by the Manor House, the centre of population was way off to the south of the present Village. It was in Graigue, which was like a little village of its own. The Village as we know it today was only built around 1799. So during the Penal Times, the people used to travel all the way from Graigue and the surrounding townlands, to get to Doon and the Mass Rock for their religious practices. That would be four or five miles each way. They were travelling quite a way just to go into that sacred landscape, at the greatest risk. So that area has been thoroughly traversed in the pursuit of religion!

Of course when I was a child we were taught Catholicism round the clock every day of the year but at that time the official Church taught us nothing about Doon or Carraig an Aifrinn - not a word. They were only interested in the present-moment Vatican Church, and that was it. I think that for a long time after the Penal Laws stopped, people still felt it was too soon, it was too dangerous. Until 1920 they were still colonised and occupied by the British Army, and they felt lucky to have what they had and to be able to worship legally again at least. They thought they had better get on with it and not look back, but just close that chapter. Up until their victory in the War of Independence, I suppose people felt anything could happen - things could revert back to the worst of what they had been. And it was great in the meantime to at least be able to practice their religion openly again, compared to how it was during Penal Times. The awful, terrifying memory of it all was too recent.

But in recent times there's been a really great revival of faith and interest in the Holy Well and the Mass Rock. Because of course, places like that can restore a certain kind of ancient, authentic faith for people. That was literally the faith of our fathers and mothers - outdoors in nature risking their lives for their spirituality when it was outlawed. I've also seen foreign descendants of people who emigrated from here coming back and gaining a burning renewal of faith through visiting the Holy Well and Carraig an Aifrinn. It can be a huge spiritual awakening and strengthening of faith, through connecting with all that history.

You know, in 1921, when the Irish finally won their independence, a huge Mass was said at our Mass Rock with a congregation of thousands who came from all over the county. My mother was there at that historic occasion, wearing her Confirmation dress because it was such a special day. I have an old photo of the event. It was finally, on the day of independence, that they could safely start to turn and look back gratefully at the Mass Rock, now they knew they would be free to run their own country from then on.

That was a very close intertwining of religion and politics, wasn't it? Imagine, that thousands came, including all the way from Cork city, in 1921 when travel wasn't easy. So it was a famous site countywide. And that was the first ever *official* moment at the Mass Rock, when it could be publicly celebrated. We had a huge Mass there again in the 1970s, for the centenary commemoration of the Famine. My family were all there. It's harder to imagine that happening now, that the Church would hold a Mass to commemorate a *political* event in Irish history.

## Farther pilgrimages

Well again, in terms of taking religion out into the landscape, in the 1980s there was a whole phenomenon of new apparitions of the Virgin Mary around the south of Ireland. There was one in Ballinspittle in County Cork, and another up in Tipperary. Our family went along to the Ballinspittle one to have a look. Literally thousands of people started to gather there once the word got around. You'd have to park your car and walk a long way, there were such long lines of traffic queueing. But I think it was mass hysteria, to be honest. I think they collectively all imagined together that they saw it.

It was at a time when the society was suddenly modernising, ironically. It was the first time that people weren't completely under the authority of the Church anymore. People were meant to be getting less religious, not more so! But maybe it was to refocus. As to why it happened, I wouldn't be surprised if there was some little bit of divine intervention that got it started, but then people ran with it themselves as a mass hysteria out at those sites in the countryside.

For me, the site of the Marian apparition in Knock in County Galway still retains some sense of the Marian mysteries. Lots of local people here go on pilgrimage to Knock many, many times in their lifetime. Some would go almost every year. There was a lovely, homely atmosphere there - something a bit magical. I still like the simplicity of Knock. I couldn't tell you how many times I've been there.

You start by reciting the decades of the Rosary as a whole crowd of you circumambulate the old Knock parish church together. And there's a statue of Our Lady that you pass on the gable of the church. I was there once with my eldest son when he was a small child. When we got to that point he stood back and shouted out 'Look, mammy, that must be where she landed!' As if she was a helicopter. Everyone tittered but no-one minded really. Knock still does invoke that reverent feeling even in adults.

Some friends here in the Village gave me a gift of a trip to Lourdes after my husband died. I was deeply touched at this lavish gift. To get a real sense of direct connection with Our Lady in Lourdes, I found that the nicest place wasn't the grotto, which is busy, but to go away on a little walk across the fields to a place where there's a statue of Saint Bernadette kneeling with her sheep around her. There was no depiction of Our Lady there but I somehow felt even more connection with Her there. Saint Bernadette was what I took away from Lourdes - that simple young country girl wearing a headscarf out in the field. If I would wish to go to any other foreign pilgrimage now, it would be to Fatima in Portugal. There were three children in Fatima and so far as I know to this day none of them have been 'knighted' as it were - I mean canonised, obviously.

Another foreign pilgrimage that I enjoyed very much was going to Glastonbury in Somerset in England. It's reputed that Saint Joseph of Arimethea arrived there by boat with Mary after Jesus died. There's a beautiful Holy Well there too, called Chalice Well. It's a remarkably atmospheric place. There's a long tradition of Catholic pilgrimage and retreats there, at the Abbey in the centre of the town. But people of all religions and none flock there too nowadays, just for the amazing atmosphere in the land there. While I was there with my daughter, as well as going to the old Christian sites, we visited a Hare Krishna Ashram or monastery, and a Pagan Goddess Temple!

But the pilgrimage that always really stands out for me is what's called Saint Patrick's Purgatory, on an island in a lake called Lough Derg, up near the north of Ireland. I think it's three times I've done that one. And that's no holiday, I can tell you. You have to leave your shoes behind you on the mainland. You get on the boat barefoot and they take you over to this tiny rocky island with a huge basilica on it.

Thousands of people flock there. And throughout your 48-hour stay, you get given *black tea only*! For a keen tea-drinker like me, that is painful. And of course, it's not even tea at all. It's basically boiled water that comes out of the bog that black colour. And you get hard, dry bread. No butter, milk or sugar. It's a hard, wholemeal bread that they make there. It's awful but you chew through it in the hope it'll sustain you, because you know that's all you're getting. And then you stay up one whole night. You don't see bed at all that night, and on the second night you get about six hours sleep.

The platform there for circumambulating the basilica is cantilevered out over the lake. It has wooden slats on the floor and if you have small feet like me, you're slipping down through the slats because you're in your bare feet, no matter how cold it is. But you can pray there, that's for sure, because there is absolutely nothing else to do.

I used to come away from the place feeling great - thoroughly renewed and refreshed. There certainly is nothing at all remotely commercial about Lough Derg! There's not even a religious shop - no medals, nothing in your face to buy.

More recently, I also go now on an annual three-day retreat to a small retreat centre run by the Order of the Sacred Heart in West Cork. It's very basic but you do get cooked food there and you can make yourself a cup of tea. And they'd even have a plain biscuit, like a 'Lincoln Cream' (though of course there's no cream in a Lincoln Cream!). And there's a nice simple dormitory with an en-suite bathroom. That too is a place where you do genuinely pray. All the priests running those retreats, they've all been to the Missions out in the Third World. And that changes them, there's no doubt about it. All those priests are very open-minded, I find.

At those retreats these days, the priests know they're not talking to children. And they all have different takes on life, so it's stimulating as well. They give talks if you want to attend them. And there's Mass both morning and evening, with beautiful grounds to wander in by the seacoast. One of them is an amazing gardener - it's his life, looking after their landscaped gardens.

Cork Diocese had a Mission in Peru so here in Gleann we often had parish priests who were back from there, or from other Missions around the world. It didn't always change them for the better, but I saw that it often did. But I've read too that a lot of them experienced a lot of freedom out there, and they really struggled to get used to the restrictions once they come back to their parish roles here.

The first open-minded priest I ever knew, he was one of our parish priests, Fr. Colm Moriarty. He changed my life completely, as he changed many other people's lives. He was an amazing person, on a *scale eile* altogether. [36] He had a brilliant mind but the Church misused him, in my opinion, and he eventually ended up leaving the priesthood.

You know, talking of foreign places, people often can't believe how many connections I have with people from all over the world, just through reaching out from my little 'office' here in my side room, without ever having left it. People seek me out when they return to the Village to look for their ancestors. So I have good friends now in Australia, South Africa, Canada, Switzerland - everywhere, really. Writers, businesspeople, lawyers, all sorts.

One was a writer from America, for instance. The pub sent him down here to me and he spent the whole day here. He brought me his novel that was set in Ireland in post-Famine times. And he wants to base his next novel here in Crow Glen. He knew nothing about the place before coming here, but his father had lived near here. And the writer felt it is a magical setting.

\*

After leaving Norma that day, I reviewed my recordings of her interviews again. I noticed that in talking about **spiritual places**, Norma always associated them strongly with **presences**. The sense of a presence there seemed to be what made a place spiritual for her (as perhaps it does for anyone around the world who experiences a given place as 'spiritual'?). She described her strong sense of the 'good people' who had done spiritual practices at these places before her. Or the feeling of 'pure spirit' coming through nature in the water of the Holy Well. She felt the Holy Spirit itself was present above the altar in the Chapel, like a good friend that you can drop in on any time. And that Jesus is always 'present', as she put it, in the tabernacle, as promised by the red sanctuary lamp.

---

36 *Eile* means other in Irish, so 'scale eile' means 'on a completely different scale'.

This sense of homely familiarity and friendship with spiritual beings reminded me of the Irish anthropologist I mentioned in an earlier chapter, who describes parishioners 'giving each statue in the church an affectionate rub before leaving the building after Mass. A lingering rub was often reserved for one's favourite saint or, perhaps, for the Virgin Mary.' [37]

In a very human sense, the idea of dropping in easily on friends is absolutely central to the way of life in Gleann. Even if you book in advance as I do, it's still almost impossible to get a whole afternoon alone with Norma Buckley. Village neighbours and friends from farther out around the farms drop in continually on impromptu errands, to bring a piece of news or a package or an invitation, or just to say hello and have a leisurely cup of tea. I've lived in many different places abroad but I've never seen a place that has such a wide *geographical* circle of ɪnꞇɪmacꞅ - I mean literally the range of distance at which you would casually drop in on a household. That range might be four miles in each direction for Norma Buckley in Gleann. In Cambridge, where I worked in England, it would not usually stretch to four doorsteps along a small row of terraced homes. [38] This sense of there being many known, friendly *human* presences spread out across a relatively big landscape is just second nature to locals in the Glen of the Crow, and I presume in other traditional Irish villages too. I could see how in Gleann - as opposed to say, in Cambridge - that could more easily translate into experiencing friendly *spiritual* presences across the landscape as well.

As in our previous recording, here again too were all those changes in the religion, with practices falling in and out of 'fashion' according to people's needs and preferences. I was starting to get a feel for the gentle tug of war or polite battle of wills that my interviewee was describing between the people and the Church over the decades, each pressing to advance their own preferences but neither side wanting to push farther than the other would accept.

She described clear moments of leadership and oᴡneᴙꙅhɪp coming from the people's side, like when they arranged to bring back the annual religious Processions through the Village. And on the other hand she

---

37 Salvador Ryan, 'The Quest for Tangible Religion', as in Note 18

38 I've written about the notorious privacy of English homes in my book *Asylum under Dreaming Spires: Refugees' Lives in Cambridge Today*, with the Living Refugee Archive, University of East London, 2017

described practices by the Church that eventually just pressed too hard against what the people felt was reasonable to accept: those things had to be 'quietly phased out', as she put it. They included 'Churching' women after childbirth (which she particularly hated); condemning unbaptised babies to eternal Limbo; and not recognising those unbaptised babies secretly buried at the Holy Well in Doon.

Yet all this 'evolution', as she calls it, isn't quite predictable or linear either: it can revert in circles. She points out how the **apparitions** of Our Lady at Ballinspittle in the 1980s happened just when society was supposedly 'modernising' and people's lives were supposed to be becoming more secular. Interestingly, those apparitions came entirely from the people, and were neither initiated nor particularly welcomed by the Church.

Similarly, the ancient country folk-practices of the Holy Well and the Mass Rock were *out* of fashion with the Church back when she was a child. But they are very much back at the heart of the faith in Gleann now: the outdoors, nature and **sacred sites** on the land are things that people are hungry for now as part of the local religious offer.

Over these first two recordings, Norma had answered my many questions about the material aspects of the religion - holy objects on the body and in the home, and rituals spread out across physical sites on the land. But my own memory was that those things were still only the outer layer, like the wrapping on a gift. They weren't the core of the matter. Surely, what all those ritual objects, places and activities pointed towards was the spirit world *itself* - the **spiritual dimensions** and the divine beings who dwelled there? We hadn't really touched on that at all yet, and I was keen to get her to talk to me about it. But would she?

## References

Carroll, Michael, *Irish Pilgrimage: Holy Wells and Popular Catholic Devotion*, Johns Hopkins University Press, 1999

Hoffman, Marella, *Asylum under Dreaming Spires: Refugees' Lives in Cambridge Today*, with the Living Refugee Archive, University of East London, 2017

Ó Cadhla, Stiofán, *The Holy Well Tradition: The Pattern of St Declan, Ardmore, County Waterford, 1800-2000*, Maynooth Studies in Local History, Four Courts Press, Dublin, 2002

Ó Duinnshléibhe, Seán, National Folklore Collection, Roll No. 12542, p. 221-467. *The School Collection, Volume 0382: Áth Dúna, Gleann an Phréacháin, Mainistir Fhearmuighe - Béaloideas,* viewable at www.duchas.ie/en/cbes/4921859/4896737/5190225?ChapterID=4921859

Ryan, Salvador, 'The Quest for Tangible Religion', *The Furrow*, Vol 55, 2004

# Chapter 5

# Drink again from the holy Well

Images at the opening of this chapter:

~ The silver bus of the Irish American Carneys
~ The Holy Well at Doon, Gleann an Phréacháin
~ Essie Cuffe's pub at the heart of the Village, run by her descendant
Barry Kennedy who provides an *Afterword* for this book
~ Some of the Irish American lunch party at Norma Buckley's house
(from left: Norma, Mary Carney, brother-in-law Bob, sister Chris Carney,
and the author; Mary and Chris Carney both speak in Chapter 6)

# News

On an unusually warm, sunny morning in August 2017, Norma and I stood outside her house in the Village, waiting for the twelve American Carneys to arrive in their bus. I had come especially from abroad to help her welcome them. And an hour earlier, surrounded by the yellowing archives in her side room, she had revealed to me why she had invited me.

On the day before one Christmas Eve, a stranger had come knocking at her door. He told her he was an American named Carney. Like so many others before him, he was looking for the homestead of his people who had left Gleann an Phréacháin in the nineteenth century. As she did for all the others, she brought him in, gave him tea and went to look up her records in the side room. And she did indeed find his homestead - in Doon, a couple of miles from the Village. But the other thing she saw as she ran her finger down the names on the crinkly old papers would change forever my own view of life in the Glen of the Crow.

I had always believed that my people had always lived in Crow Glen, for countless generations. On my mother's side we were archetypal, *could-not-be-more-more-rooted* Crow Glenners from a homestead in Doon, the same hillside that Johanna and Pat Carney had lived on. But on that day in the old papers Norma saw that in fact, my people had only moved to Crow Glen from another part of Ireland around 1848, to take up their homestead in Doon. And the homestead that they moved into was the one that Patrick and Johanna Carney and all their children had been thrown out of, the day they were put on the coffin ship to America in 1847.

This news hit me hard. I had a lot of trouble digesting it in the hour before the Carneys arrived. Apparently, the new reality was that these unknown Americans arriving in the bus any minute were actually more *Crow Glen* than I was. And my people were suddenly some sort of collaborators with the Manor landlord. I was mortified to hear that our family had moved in on that poor woman's home like cuckoos, kicking out the young who had a right to live there. It was with those slightly sickening feelings that I stood waiting with Norma for these unknown Americans.

The plan for the day was that their bus would pick us up, and she would direct its hired driver up through the Village, straight through the Crossroads Above and on for half a mile to where we would turn left to take the long private lane to what had been the Carney homestead in

Doon. Later, we would visit the Holy Well, which happens to be on the land of that homestead, and then we would go on to Carraig an Aifrinn.

I had no idea what these Americans would think of it all. There is no denying that the land in Doon is particularly beautiful - a gentle slope looking down into the Bride River Valley below. The Valley now has special protected status as a 'Special Area of Conservation'. Its rare 'flora and fauna, environment and heritage' are now protected for futurity by Cork County Council's Local Area Plan. [39]

To me this shallow Valley had always seemed a kind of heartland. When I was growing up, my grandmother was always sitting by the fire in our house in the Village, the house she had married into. But it was clear to us that she wasn't a Village person. We knew that she came from Doon, and that her spirit was somehow derived from there.

The Bride River Valley that her homestead looked out over contains the main sacred sites of the parish - the ancient Holy Well on its south slope and the Mass Rock on the north, tucked into the landscape like a secret. Miles apart by road, there's just half a mile between them as Crow flies across the Bride river. And the nineteenth-century school in Chimneyfield, perched at the foot of the mountains above the Mass Rock, had long been a place of traditional Gaelic learning, before schooling was moved into the Village in modern times. I saw my grandmother as a more authentic Crow Glenner because she came from that landscape.

As I was mulling over this, the Americans' bus pulled up in front of Norma's house. It was sleek and elegant as a silver bullet. It looked like a luxury sports car. Its black windows must surely hide celebrities. It was a top of the range Mercedes-Benz, and the hired driver was very proud of it.

Keith, the man Norma had told me about, got out of the bus and came up into her front garden to greet us. She casually introduced me, and I remember that I walked up to him, put my arms around him and hugged him. This embarrassed us both. We were strangers but I felt an irrational urge to take this man in my arms like a long-lost brother. Many months of

---

39 The Plan states: 'The Bride / Bunaglanna Valley, to the north of the village forms a proposed Natural Heritage Area... (This) 'tributary of the Blackwater... has been designated a... Special Area of Conservation and a... Natural Heritage Area (because its) biological communities are notable and include some very rare species... The aim of this plan will be to preserve this unique landscape setting, particularly the scenic and amenity values of the Bride River Valley.' Cork County Council, *Local Area Plan, Cobh Municipal District,* Vol 1, Section 4, 'Main Policy Material', available at http://corklocalareaplans.com/cobh-municipal-district

discoveries would follow before I would start to understand all the reasons why.

The Carney group had breakfasted well at their hotel in the nearby tourist spot of Blarney, and were ready for the day's explorations. Norma and I got on the bus and sat in seats left spare for us at the front. The dark interior of the bus stretched away, full of faces that we just glimpsed before sitting down. She directed the driver until we turned off into the long lane that leads to the homestead in Doon.

The lane is neatly tarmacked now but as you move along it farther west into the land, away from roads and houses, it still feels like inching into another dimension. The Bride River Valley opens out to the north on your right, and stretches out into the west in front of you. Norma remarked that the farmers on the slope opposite would be amazed if they looked out their windows now and saw this exotic silver bus gliding through the pastureland towards the hidden heart of Doon.

## The homestead

Finally, we reached the end of the lane, where the Carneys' home had stood. On its footprint now is an attractive modern house built by the people who bought the land in recent times. Norma had contacted the woman of the house. She came out to visit with the Carneys and welcome them onto the land.

For some reason, on that exceptionally warm, balmy day, the land there was swathed - *swimming* - in a sort of hallucinatory beauty that I had never seen before. Something about the way the heavy yellow light lay across the Valley made it seem to glow internally. A shimmering mist of green-gold beauty seemed to breathe up out of it.

One by one, twelve Americans stepped down from the silver bus and I saw them all face to face for the first time. There were Keith's wife and two teenaged children, his elderly mother and various cousins, aunts and uncles. Wordlessly they poured out of the bus and walked slowly forward onto the land in front of it. I stayed by the bus with the driver, watching them. They stepped forward a yard at a time, as if advancing into some unknown substance. Their hands, hanging by their sides, seemed to feel the air tentatively.

Some had tears pouring down their faces. Even the driver, well used to taking Americans around Ireland in luxury buses, took off his hat and lowered his eyes as if at a funeral. Not much was said. What could anyone say in the face of such beauty - with right beside it Johanna, coming out the door of her cold, empty house...

As she passed us, carrying her sobbing children, there was no chance for the Carneys to speak to her. To say 'It will be okay. You have no idea now but this will work out, this thing you're doing. We twelve here are the descendants of your boys Patrick and William, sitting over there in the back of the cart with their heads down. Those two will stand tall in the future, Johanna. They're ashamed now that they can't do anything to help their mam and dad. They know they just have to go. But Johanna, with your help those boys will survive and grow and make new lives on the other side of this big, round world. We twelve here are their descendants who have come back to prove this to you, as you leave today. We are so sorry that you can't stop to hear us now.'

The cart-man's bell clanged loudly over all our heads and Johanna had to go on. She couldn't pause to hear anyone say 'It will be ok'. They wanted to tell her 'We have done well, mother. We have thrived thanks to the action you are taking today. We're healthy and educated. We're teachers and nurses and lawyers, Johanna. Thank you for everything, beloved mother.'

But Johanna couldn't pause to hear any of that. She couldn't see or hear them standing beside her, helpless to help her. All her attention was on this gruelling moment, as the cart-man helped her step up onto the cart.

Her husband, Pat, paused to look back for a moment. Johanna didn't look back. She kept her face steeled forward towards the lane and the unimaginable odyssey that lay ahead of their starved, near-broken bones.

But Pat, for a moment, did seem to see us. He squinted across the air to where we were standing. Just weeks now from his own death on the coffin ship, he had less time to look forward into. Maybe more of his awareness was available here, for his last moments in Doon. His eyes seemed to flicker on us as if he sensed us standing there, looking at him.

Keith stepped forward, square-shouldered in his expensive suit, and looked straight into the space where Pat was standing. He looked into the man's pale, starved eyes and said wordlessly: 'Father, we are here. We've come back to help you through this worst moment of your existence. Let it help you, father, to hear what we can tell. All your children will survive the journey. Johanna will live well cared-for to a ripe old age. We are the future children of your boys there, Patrick and William, and we've come back to try to soften this moment for you, and to help you carry it.'

Keith said 'I am strong, father', and he took Patrick's arm and helped him climb up, shaking and gasping, into the horse-cart behind the children. Keith said: 'I promise you that we will see them on the other side. You don't need to worry about anything. We'll be there waiting, and they'll all be looked after. And I promise you that in 170 years' time, we will come back here to Doon on your behalf. And we will look out over your beautiful land here in prosperity, not in hunger and poverty. We will come back here to celebrate you and Johanna. And we will have a party, father. So you can go in confidence now. There is nothing to worry about.'

Pat slumped back against the side of the cart, his eyes rolling back in his head as if in a fainting relief. He could let go soon. For some reason that he didn't understand, he knew now that he just needed to get them all onto that ship in Cork harbour that evening, and his job in this lifetime would be done. At some level he knew now inside himself that others would take care of the rest.

And that in 170 years' time this inexplicable son Keith - whose strong hand he had felt on his aching, bony elbow - would be looking after the family. And that he would somehow bring them back for - of all the most unlikely things - *a party*. A proper party like they used to have in Doon in the good times before the spuds started to fail on them.

The cart-man cracked his whip and the horses pulled away, cantering eastward out along the lane. Like a puff of smoke that moment in time was whipped away, and the ancestors who were living it were whipped away within it.

Visibly shaken, the Americans turned back towards the west and stepped on further out into the land. The lush peace of the vista that I saw enveloping them at that moment seems impossible to describe. This beauty was theirs to reclaim now, as Keith had promised Pat that they would come back and do. Their mouths hung open as they gaped at the plenitude being given back to them - this 360-degree ring of natural beauty that they were standing in. There was some kind of magical arena around the Valley that day. It was just there and given. I don't know why it was there but we all saw it, and I've never seen it before or since.

As they headed back onto the bus, one of the Carney women, Mary, paused near me. She looked back out over the land to the west and muttered, mainly to herself it seemed: 'This is *spirit to spirit*'.

We all got back on the bus, it crept back out the lane and we drove a couple of miles along the road to the gateway that leads in to the Holy Well. There is still an old private footpath from the Carney homestead to the Holy Well, but we drove round by the road so our bus could park nearer to the Well.

## The cure

As we approached, I felt the surge of homely excitement that we Crow Glenners always feel when we go there, like visiting Santa's grotto as a child. I had always gone on the annual midsummer pilgrimage to the Well, and had hardly ever been there at any other time of year. Like Santa's grotto, you kept it as the special occasion it was meant for. But this visit with the Americans was an exception.

As you get near the site, you first see the circular stone perimeter that surrounds it, about six feet high, two feet thick, covered with earth and grass. Inside, a lush grove of trees and flowering bushes surrounds the Well itself. A small homely gate painted silver guards the opening in the perimeter. Inside that, on a standing stone, a glass-covered niche contains a statue of Our Lady, with small offerings that people have left at her feet. A few coins, a ribbon, a twist of dried flowers, a set of Rosary beads.

Here you pause and with head bent, prepare yourself for stepping into the spirit-world that you will be walking through simultaneously, while also walking the physical ground around the Holy Well. You don't move on down the sloping path until you feel you've made some kind of shift from your normal awareness to something more heightened. Today we all paused at the statue and Norma told the group the history and significance of the Well, as she had told it to many other groups that she had guided there on heritage visits.

In fact, this mysterious place has had several different uses reaching back not just over centuries, but over millennia. Its name, *Doon*, is the anglicised form of the Irish word 'Dún', meaning ringfort. Ringforts were circular, fortified settlements mostly built during the first millennium AD:

archaeologists carbon-date them to between 500 and 1000 AD. [40] They describe ringforts as 'the home and farm of a free man' (as opposed to an indentured labourer, serf or slave, which were all common at the time). [41] A ringfort was a desirable residence in that era of early cattle-herding, when cattle-raids by marauding clans were the norm.

These ringforts - whose perimeter originally defended a household and their livestock - still pepper the Irish countryside. In the Irish language, the smaller ones were also called 'Rath' or 'Lios', which is why Ireland has so many placenames beginning with Rath- or Lis-, as well as Dun-. But as historians put it, 'Dún was the term for any stronghold of importance'. [42]

You can see why the one in Gleann an Phréacháin merits the term. It's well positioned at the top of a fertile slope of grassland with 180-degree panoramic views over the Valley below. It has its own spring water inside its perimeter wall. And a small, fish-laden river, easily accessible for the cattle to drink at, runs along the bottom of the slope.

It must have taken long weeks of many-handed work to raise and finish that perimeter wall of earth-covered stones, as well as a wood and wattle building inside it for the household. One can imagine that eighth-century cattle-herder being well satisfied with his creation when he stood back to admire it, finished.

Around the 1900s, the local schoolteacher and folklorist Seán Ó Duinnshléibhe described having himself found what he considered 'an underground passage and chamber' inside the ringfort. [43] I am not aware of any other documentary evidence for that but archaeologists confirm that underground chambers, which they call 'souterrains', are very common in these well-built ringforts. They functioned 'as an intriguing combination of defensive measure and subtle housekeeping device - as a secure larder or cellar... They were the granaries... of the ancient inhabitants, in which they deposited their corn and provisions, and into

40 Matthew Stout, The Irish Ringfort, Four Courts Press, 2001. Ireland's Heritage Council confirms these dates, with 'most dating to between 550-900AD'. Heritage Council, 'Significant Unpublished Irish Archaeological Excavations, 1930-1997: Ringforts', available at https://www.heritagecouncil.ie/unpublished_excavations/section13.html
41 Hilary Bishop, Sacred Space. A Study of the Mass Rocks of the Diocese of Cork and Ross, County Cork, PhD thesis, University of Liverpool, 2013
42 Bishop, as in Note 41
43 Seán Ó Duinnshléibhe, Gleann an Phréacháin - Béaloideas, as in Note 32

which they also retreated in time of danger… Current estimates suggest there are between 3,000 and 3,500' such souterrains in Ireland. [44]

Today, 1,300 years later, you can still admire the handiwork of that eighth-century cattle-herder in Doon, in the aerial photograph on the cover of this book. (It was taken with a drone organised for Gleann's Community Council by Norma Buckley in 2019.) In the photo you can see that the raised perimeter is still a ring of haunting beauty and symmetry.

At some stage in the early Celtic era, after this family had erected their ringfort there, the spring inside their circle would have started to be noted and honoured for more spiritual, as well as practical purposes (unless the herder who built the ringfort had already noted the spring's spiritual qualities from the beginning and deliberately fenced them into his own home).

In either case, experts consider the Gleann an Phréacháin well to be typical of those used to honour the nature spirits of the old Celtic religion, long before its spiritual power later became attributed to the Catholic church. [45] Before Christianity arrived in Ireland, the natives had prayed to the spirits of nature at specific rocks, trees and waters that became renowned as sacred sites in their landscapes. [46] Between about 400 and 800 AD, Christianity spread around Ireland. It was gradually amalgamated by the natives into their own nature-based religion.

Once the Catholic Church got organised, it excelled at taking over these ancient sites and adapting them for Catholic use, rather than trying to suppress or abolish them. Researchers view Gleann's Holy Well as a typical 'site for pagan rituals that was taken over by the Catholic Church'. [47] The ringfort would have been about five hundred years old already when, in the twelfth century, 'it was mentioned in a decree from Rome in 1199' because 'a church of approximately 24 by 20 feet stood there within a medieval enclosure'. The church was destroyed by Red Hugh O'Neill in 1599, when the local chieftain refused to join his army to help him fight the Battle of Kinsale. [48]

---

44  Eileen Battersby, 'Going Underground', *Irish Times*, 2-2-2002

45  Hilary Bishop, 'Classifications of Sacred Space: A New Understanding of Mass Rock Sites in Ire land', *International Journal of History and Archaeology*, 2016

46  Hilary Bishop, as in Note 41

47  Hilary Bishop, as in Note 41

48  Seán Ó Duinnshléibhe, *Gleann an Phréacháin - Béaloideas,* as in Note 32

One historian describes how, during her own recent survey of the Gleann Holy Well, 'offerings were found' there because it remains to this day 'associated with numerous cures' in folk memory. Authors believe this modern practice that locals have of leaving small offerings at the Well 'reflects a continuation of the ancient ritual of votive offerings during the pre-historic period'. [49]

Just as Norma Buckley had told me, this expert confirms that 'Catholic communities up to the nineteenth century chose to bury their unbaptised infants at sites such as ringforts' when the Catholic Church wouldn't allow unbaptised babies to be buried in their graveyards. [50]

And before our group moved on that day from Our Lady's statue at the entrance, Norma explained that that is exactly what Johanna and Pat Carney had to do for their last son, shortly before they had to leave Doon. He had died at birth before they could get him baptised, so they had to bury him there in secret, inside the ringfort.

We could see that this meant a lot to the visiting Americans - that the bones of one of their ancestors still lie there. That newborn child had a fate that was different from the rest of their family. By dying as soon as he was born, he was the only one of the now extensive Carney clan who had stayed in Doon uninterruptedly to this day, lying enfolded beside the Holy Well. One historian goes so far as to describe this few square yards of official burial space inside the Gleann an Phréacháin ringfort as 'the second oldest Catholic graveyard in Ireland, as recorded in Rome'. [51]

Since that early Christian chapel that was recorded there in 1199, priests didn't visit the Holy Well again for centuries until people like Norma Buckley started asking them in the 1980s to start going there again to do public ceremonies and commemorations. In 2012, Norma helped to get a formal plaque erected there to tell the story of the unnamed infants who were secretly confided to the Well's burial ground. She convinced the parish priest to hold a major public ceremony of forgiveness and commemoration there. You can see a solemn video of the event online. [52]

Meanwhile, academic surveyors of Gleann's Holy Well describe it as also having the '*bullaun* stones' that are characteristic of the most ancient sacred

---

49 Hilary Bishop, as in Note 41
50 Hilary Bishop, as in Note 45
51 Seán Ó Duinnshléibhe, as in Note 32
52 *Burials at Doonpeter, Glenville, Co Cork, Ireland*, 30-9-2018 available on the Youtube channel of local video-maker Tony Kennedy, *Real Cork* at www.youtube.com/watch?v=mNuNv67Z_T8

sites. [53] They explain that these standing stones that jut out of the ground are 'often found at holy well pilgrimage sites'. Archaeologists describe how they contain one or more man-made depressions gouged out over centuries where 'pilgrims inscribe crosses on these stones'. [54]

I confess that until I read those words recently in the archives, I thought it was unique to us at Gleann an Phréacháin, this practice of making these stone markings during our annual pilgrimage to the Well at midsummer. I thought no-one else in the world did that - each pilgrim using appointed smaller stones to trace crosses onto the bigger standing stones after they completed each decade of the Rosary. I had never heard that they existed anywhere else or that there is a name for them - 'bullaun stones'.

We marked our Rosary decades at each stone because our ancestors had always done so, in a ritual that drew special, powerful blessings from this special, powerful place. Why would you not do it? It felt important. And when you came back out through the small, silver-painted gate in the perimeter ring, you felt cleansed by having completed your annual rounds of marking the stones. You felt rejuvenated - ready for anything the year ahead might throw at you. And ready to party like hell at the Bonfire in the Village that night.

Today, Norma led the Americans on down the little path to the Well and took them through the ritual that Crow Glenners always did there. The culmination of it is when you have completed your Rosary, marked all the rounds of stones, and you've earned the right to step forward and drink from the Well, using one of the little glasses that are always there for the purpose.

No-one spoke while one after the other, each of the Carneys solemnly knelt down beside the Well and scooped up a little glassful to swallow. Watching them, I knew they were thinking that Johanna and Patrick would often have drunk from these same waters, both for the midsummer pilgrimage and on many private occasions, as the Well was on their land.

Before we left the ringfort, I paused to admire the well-tended grave of my granny's father, Michael Sweeney. But lying in that grave, there were further realities that I didn't yet know about. And I didn't know that as we left Doon that day, they would get up out of that grave and follow me home. That I would spend the ensuing months coming to terms with

53 Walter & Mary Brenneman, *Crossing the Circle at the Holy Wells of Ireland*, University of Virginia Press, 1995
54 Hilary Bishop, as in Note 41

them. That I would eventually be glad that they had risen again into the land of the living, and would write this book about them.

We all repaired back to Norma's house in the bus, and the fifteen of us (including the bus driver) fell upon the hearty lunch that she had prepared for us before she went out that morning. It was the kind of food that calms, bonds and satiates people the world over. Local meats, cheeses, smoked fish and sandwiches. Home-made cake, scones with jam and cream and pots of tea. Simple foods like in a fairy-tale, on a table laid with love. [55]

Those Americans could afford to buy their dinner in the world's finest restaurants. But it was clear that the gift of being welcomed back to eat their fill in the place that their forefathers had been starved out of, was nourishing to them in a way that could not be bought. Some fundamental underlying tension seemed to be released in them by those plates of sandwiches and Norma's china teacups, balanced on their knees. As if they were eating and drinking on Pat and Johanna's behalf, resolving once and for all an unforgivable, 170-year-old hunger that still gnawed at their guts.

Looking at the scene I wondered: why does Norma, already 76 years old at that time, do these things for people? It occurred to me that she has a deep, natural understanding of the power of ritual. She knows that an action taken by a single individual, if it's charged with the correct intent, can ripple out a healing effect onto situations much bigger than themselves. So when she sees an opportunity, she steps in in person to organise her own reparation for collective wrongs done in the past, even though it wasn't she who did them. Norma has organised many big events but that day in her kitchen, I saw how her simple ritual of providing a special lunch for the returning Carneys dropped a little healing stone into the pool of a centuries-old injustice.

## Rocks and stones

Our final visit of the day would be to Crow Glen's other sacred site, the Mass Rock, on the opposite slope of the Bride River Valley from the Holy Well. We took to the road refreshed and on the way there, Norma explained the Mass Rock to the visitors.

---

55  One table of that lunch party is pictured at the start of this chapter.

We saw in an earlier chapter that over 150 years of Penal Laws had outlawed all practice of Catholicism in Ireland, under pain of death or banishment. So the Irish moved to practicing their religion in secret, often using the pre-Christian sites of their older religion which had for hundreds of years already been amalgamated into their Catholicism. These were places where they could worship outdoors 'on the run'. Buildings were too easy for the English police to raid, and too small for many to gather there safely. Instead, rebellious communities chose strategic spots that were hidden from the wider landscape, could be protected by lookouts, could hold large numbers of people for the duration of Mass, and could be escaped from in many directions if English forces were approaching.

These places came to be known as Mass Rocks. And if you ever have the good fortune to visit the Mass Rock in Crow Glen, you will see how well it meets all those criteria. [56] It's a hollow and hidden but spacious place. It has a lookout hill jutting out over it like a roof. And it has wild, open mountain country to the north to escape into. [57]

The Penal Laws, as they lasted for almost a century and a half, kept whole generations of priests hidden, outlawed and offering Mass in secret illegal places like this. Historical records show that many such priests around the country were indeed executed by the English forces or deported to far-off English colonies. The oral tradition in Gleann an Phréacháin records that unfortunately, at least one priest was executed in this way in Gleann during Penal Times, somewhere around the Bride River Valley near the Holy Well and Mass Rock. There are several references to the incident in the Gleann manuscripts at the National Folklore Collection. [58]

The physical suitability of the Gleann site as a Mass Rock is obvious. But historians add that such 'sites also appear to have been chosen because they already had been made sacred by repeated ritual use in the past'. One archaeologist who formally surveyed the Gleann Mass Rock noted that 'numerous crosses had been etched across the rock face', just as she had found at the Holy Well across the Valley. [59] She read this as confirmation that the Gleann Mass Rock had also been a place of worship for the earlier

---

56  You can visit online by viewing the video *The Mass Rock in the Glen, Glenville, Co. Cork, 9-11-2014,* on the *Real Cork* Youtube channel at www.youtube.com/watch?v=o0nsKdcWpnw
57  This book's associates, the Avondhu Blackwater Partnership, give a guided walking itinerary for a loop that joins the Holy Well to the Mass Rock at www.avondhublackwater.com/glenville-holy-well-loop
58  D. Ó Súilleabháin, National Folklore Collection, as in Note 22
59  Hilary Bishop, as in Note 41

nature religion, long before the Penal Laws made it necessary to pray there again.

Arriving there by road, you see nothing but a picturesque stone bridge. But beside the bridge you can open a small, silver-painted gate just like the one that admits you to the Holy Well. You walk down a sloping grassy path with trees arching overhead. It's like a vivid green tube fully enclosing you. And at the bottom, you come out into an open clearing. On your right, on the opposite side of a gurgling river, a cliff rises about 40 yards high. It arches out like a ledge over the hollow cliff-face that it cradles beneath it. At the foot of this cliff is a platform of rock about 40 yards long parallel to the river, and jutting about 20 yards wide from the foot of the cliff to the water's edge. This is the Mass Rock, Carraig an Aifrinn in Irish.

From where you arrive on the near side of the river, the Rock across the river looks like a stage-set. You could imagine an atmospheric rock concert there with the band playing on the rock platform under the cliff, and the audience spread out in the grassy clearing around you, on this near side of the river.

And that is indeed how Mass was said there. Large crowds could assemble on the grassy side to look on. A small footbridge allows passage across the river to the sacred rock for the priest and his attendants. You only cross that bridge reverentially, as the rock 'stage' over there is basically the altar. In Catholic churches, ordinary people don't walk on the altar. And I personally have never walked across the river onto that sacred rock where Mass is said. But if you do step over there via the footbridge, you must first pause and contemplate the miracle seared into the rock on the riverbank beside it, on the audience's side of the river.

Here four round depressions in the shape of horse's hooves are sunk about four inches deep into the rock. This is where a brave horse miraculously marked the rock in Penal Times while leaping across the river to carry his priest rider away to safety when the English approached. Children have always loved these hoof-prints and it's still the first thing locals gravitate to when we visit the Mass Rock, as if to verify in wonder that they really are still there each time.

The whole site is a deeply atmospheric place of white rushing water, blue-black slate rock and dripping ferns, with a cathedral of tree-canopies arched over the lot to hide it from view. On the day when we visited, a local Irish speaker, Brian O' Donoghue, had been invited along by the

Carneys. Now he stood by the Rock and sang for us the emigrant's lament '*Áird Uí Chaoin*'. It rang out in Irish in his hauntingly clear, beautiful voice, at once expert and natural, in the *sean-nós* or 'old style' tradition. [60]

Later, the Americans were unanimous in feeling that of the three places we visited that day, the Mass Rock was the one that vibrated with them the most, reaching into their very core. Keith told us that as he stood on the Rock, he suddenly understood the rock-like spiritual faith that their family had retained across nearly two centuries in America. 'I get it now', he said. '*This* is where it all comes from - our faith as a family. It's from this specific rock: this is just *how our faith feels* to me.'

We walked back up the sloping green path that brings you out of the Mass Rock site and crossed the road to study another plaque that Norma had gotten installed there. Hand-painted in Gaelic calligraphy, it includes a colourful painting of Crow, hovering knowingly over a map of this, his local landscape. A dotted line traces out the 'Famine Walk' that stretches across the fields and fords the Bride River, joining the Holy Well to the Mass Rock. We could see the Well's circular grove of trees in Doon, just half a mile away across the river as Crow flies.

Abhorrent in my eyes, this Famine Walk was one of two 'charitable works' run by the occupying British in the Glen of the Crow during the Famine. Instead of returning to the starving locals even a pittance of the riches that they were exporting from the land through Cork harbour, the British instead gave the starving an artificial, temporary 'job'. This was to ensure that the people dying of starvation *earned* the daily soup given out to them at the end of the day, rather than being *given* it. The invented job was to labour all day carrying a pile of rocks from one pointless place to another, to lay down a 'Famine road' in the middle of nowhere that was never intended to be used by anyone.

The notion that it's purifying to do pointless physical labour comes from jails, where being sentenced to 'hard labour' means lifting rocks backwards and forwards, supervised by wardens. This punishment was still in place in twentieth-century apartheid South Africa where the barrister Nelson Mandela was jailed for 27 years for demanding equal rights for his people. In the film of his life, *Long Walk To Freedom*, you see his dignity while carrying those rocks back and forth inside the prison walls all day, never

---

60 You can hear this beautiful song performed by a *sean-nós* singer at www.youtube.com/watch?v=CSnhzI3DWVQ

wavering in his certainty that the fairness of their cause would become clear one day in the eyes of the future world.

I nearly threw up the day that I found out recently from Norma that the old Wood Wall that surrounds the colonial Manor estate and runs up through the Village - the one I scaled daily as a child on my escapades into the estate - is a 'Famine Wall', built in the same way as the 'Famine Walk'. To think that my footholds in that stone wall - which I could still find this minute blindfolded - were lifted up there by local people whose elbows were breaking from starvation, like those of Pat Carney when Keith helped him up onto the cart for the coffin ship. I felt as if I had hurtfully climbed my full weight up onto their sore, skinned hands.

As our group stood looking at the Famine Walk plaque near the Mass Rock that day, an odd thing happened. We heard the swift clopping of a horse's hooves on the road, and around the corner came a sight I had not seen since childhood - a local using a horse and cart as his mode of transport. He trotted up to us as if arriving directly out of history, and pulled up his horse when he reached us. Apparently as real as we were, he gave us a frank looking over. But the cart was no retro-chic hobby. He explained that he was one of the Traveller family who have always lived in a caravan on that part of the mountain. Unlike everyone else in Crow Glen, he was still poor. Without sentimentality, he said the horse and cart were by far the cheapest way for him to get around.

I had never spoken to this man, but I knew that we had lain in the same cradle as babies. My mother had owned a beautiful cradle made of solid wicker-work, with a solid wicker hood that curved up over the baby's head. When her babies had finished with it, she gave it to that man's Traveller mother to use for her newborns. Years later, the woman came back to our house one day to ask if she could borrow a good coat overnight, so that she could look presentable at a family funeral next day in West Cork, where she had come from before she married a poor Travelling man to live on the side of the road. One can imagine the emotions she must have felt that day, approaching someone's door with such a request. My grandmother gave the woman her second-best Sunday coat, and said she could keep it. The woman always wore it to Mass afterwards, with a quiet dignity. Apparently some local women, recognising Nell Sweeney's coat, whispered behind their hands that Nell should not make so familiar with Travellers.

By the time we got back on the Americans' bus to head back to the Village, we all felt drunk with the emotional intensity of the day. Keith suggested we stop for a real drink in the Village pub - a welcome call back to reality. Built in 1799, this stone pub has for centuries been a social haven at the centre of the Crow Glen landscape. Lonely men from all over the surrounding mountains have always found a simple, nodded welcome there. Pat Carney would have sat on its wooden benches in better times, with no idea that a Famine would soon hit them like a tidal wave, washing him away into an early Atlantic grave.

In Pat's day it was run by the same family who run it now, called Cuffes then and Kennedys now, the name having changed through marriage. But Keith had done his research. When he said to Norma 'Will we stop in at *Essie Cuffes'* for a drink?', we understood that he was still accompanying Pat Carney, this time to sit and lean his back against the wall where Pat had leant his, chatting to other farmers over a pint.

The pub was opened by Mike and Essie Cuffe. Essie was a well-regarded teacher at the Village school across the road. But as one historian explains, 'it was forbidden for teachers to live in public houses, forcing her to live next door to the pub'. He adds: 'and as if that were not enough, she had to forfeit a year's salary for living in the pub in the first place'! [61]

You bend your head to go in the narrow stone door and you pass through into dim, cosy, stone-lined rooms. You can slouch at the bar or disappear into snug corners. The place smells comfortingly of a thousand nights - quiet, wordless nights and raving party nights. My father came in here most nights of his working life to sit over a pint of Murphy's stout with other Gleann men, discussing whatever it is they discussed for thousands of nights on end. Then he'd walk the 300 yards home to join my mother in their bed. [62]

At the end of that day with the Americans, it was soothing to lean back against those cool stone walls, as if discharging some of the day's emotion back into them. We made plans to meet again a few days later. Meanwhile, the Carneys would tour around Ireland on their bus. And for later in the week, Keith had somehow arranged that the Manor House in Gleann an Phréacháin would receive our group for dinner. By paying an undisclosed sum, he had - unbelievably, to me - purchased an evening whereby the lady of the Manor would open up the House to us, give our group a tour of the House and gardens, and a formal dinner would be served to us in

---

61 *Fleming / Mulcahy Family Tree*, 'Glenville at the Turn of the Century', available at https://flemmultree.wordpress.com
62 A rival to Dublin's Guinness, Murphy's stout, brewed in Cork, looks identical but to Cork people it tastes milder, more sophisticated and better.

the Manor's wood-panelled dining hall. The bus would collect Norma and myself outside Norma's house. We felt like disbelieving Cinderellas invited to a ball.

To me, this was a far more surreal and heady prospect than anything from our first day with the Americans. I was well used to the intense ambiance of the Holy Well and the Mass Rock but the Manor - I had only ever approached it on my belly through the undergrowth, pulling myself along on my elbows. A thousand times I had loitered under its perimeter Wood Wall until no-one was passing so I could climb over it, proceeding through the bushes to whatever part of the estate I was interested in that day.

I had never entered the estate through its gates and had never thought I would. I had seen them open on occasions when foreign dignitaries were visiting there - for instance, obscure European royalty accompanied by their uniformed bodyguards. But I had certainly never been in a vehicle moving up the driveway. The idea made me feel physically sick. As children we fancied our 'survival' in that jungle depended on *never, ever, being seen on the driveway.* You had to move unseen through the dense bushes that border it.

For me, the driveway was like the infamous strip along the old Berlin Wall that could never be approached by East Germans. I fancied it electrified, fatal. Then suddenly, on a given day, the East Germans were told they could now walk up to the wall without electric shocks or being shot.

I assume the Manor aristocrats wouldn't have shot us, if they had ever found us on their estate. But with a child's relish, we enjoyed thinking they would - believing that those were life-and-death safari raids that we were on, and priding ourselves on never once getting caught.

I had spent my adult life abroad, working in fine positions in fancy places and jetting around in airplanes. But the prospect of going up the Manor's driveway inside a bus felt genuinely disturbing to me. I lay awake on the nights leading up to it, tossing and turning on my childhood pillow in the Village. I couldn't imagine what it would be like, nor how it could possibly work out.

References

Battersby, Eileen, 'Going Underground', *Irish Times*, 2-2-2002
Bishop, Hilary, 'Classifications of Sacred Space: A New Understanding of Mass Rock Sites in Ireland', *International Journal of History and Archaeology*, 2016

Bishop, Hilary, *Sacred Space. A Study of the Mass Rocks of the Diocese of Cork and Ross, County Cork*, PhD Thesis, University of Liverpool, 2013

Brenneman, Walter and Mary, *Crossing the Circle at the Holy Wells of Ireland*, University of Virginia Press, 1995

Cork County Council, *Local Area Plan, Cobh Municipal District,* Vol 1, Section 4, 'Main Policy Material', available at http://corklocalareaplans.com/cobh-municipal-district

Fleming / Mulcahy Family Tree, 'Glenville at the Turn of the Century', available at https://flemmultree.wordpress.com

Heritage Council, 'Significant Unpublished Irish Archaeological Excavations, 1930-1997: Ringforts', available at
https://www.heritagecouncil.ie/unpublished_excavations/section13.html

Ó Duinnshléibhe, Seán, National Folklore Collection, Roll No. 12542, p. 221-467. *The School Collection, Volume 0382: Áth Dúna, Gleann an Phréacháin, Mainistir Fhearmuighe - Béaloideas,* viewable at
www.duchas.ie/en/cbes/4921859/4896737/5190225?ChapterID=4921859

O' Leary, Brendan, Glenville National School Website at www.glenvillens.wordpress.com

Ó Súilleabháin, D., National Folklore Collection, Gleann an Phréacháin, Roll No. 450, p. 148, available at https://www.duchas.ie/en/cbes/4921858/4896707

*Real Cork* Youtube channel, *Burials at Doonpeter, Glenville, Co Cork, Ireland*, 30-9-2018, available at www.youtube.com/watch?v=mNuNv67Z_T8

*Real Cork* Youtube channel, *Doonpeter Well, Glenville, Co Cork,* 23-6-2017, available at www.youtube.com/watch?v=-z0MIRwd69g

*Real Cork* Youtube channel, *The Mass Rock in the Glen, Glenville, Co. Cork,* 9-11-2014, available at www.youtube.com/watch?v=o0nsKdcWpnw

Stout, Mathew, *The Irish Ringfort*, Four Courts Press, 2001

# Chapter 6

# Johanna's children speak

Images at the opening of this chapter:

~ The Nagle Mountains above Gleann an Phréacháin
~ Ringfort around the Holy Well at Doon
~ Entrance to the Holy Well ringfort
~ Site of the Gleann Mass Rock

At the end of that first day with the Americans, before they left for their tour around Ireland, there was a pause back at Norma's house where I got to sit with three of the Carneys, listening to and recording what they felt about the day. For them it was a little window of reflection, a pause in this intense pilgrimage that they were making from America.

It seemed hard to believe that the two Irish American women sitting in front of me could have such a physical, immediate link to the Famine-era Johanna - but their father was one of Johanna's grandsons! He was the son of one of Johanna's boys, who had sat in that farm-cart leaving Doon and survived the coffin ship crossing, while his dad died in front of him on the ship along the way.

Mary, now living in Rhode Island, USA, had been a senior nun of the Sisters of Mercy Order, and a former head-teacher. Chris, living in upstate New York, was a retired nurse. The sisters grew up in Connecticut with six other siblings. Keith Carney, who lives and works in Washington DC, is their much-loved nephew.

Keith seems like a central, organising hub for this wide but tight-knit clan. They are now spread all over the United States but seem to retain an extraordinarily close sense of *family*. I notice that when they say '*our family*', they mean not their own household but the great pyramid of their extended family, sweeping down through the generations, which seems to be a core part of their identity.

In the background of the recording, Norma's china teacups clink comfortingly in our saucers. She has put a plate of jam and cream scones between us by the fireside, and left us to talk. Later, Keith will give me his own account of what the Glen of the Crow means to him. But first, I ask Mary and Chris how they are feeling about the places we've been to that day. And how the Catholicism that they've seen here in Gleann compares with the one they know in Irish America. Chris speaks first. Slowly, with a warm, soft American accent that lovingly *drawls* over her first words.

 Chris and Mary Carney...

# Sacred Ground

Chris: *Walking* onto the land earlier with you and Norma, and *seeing* this *vast* plot of land, and *knowing* that our relatives had to *leave* this *beautiful* spot…

The biggest emotion for me was wondering how it actually felt for them to leave. I have goosebumps just thinking about us coming back to their land today and walking where they walked. And then when we walked on to the far end of the property. That vista, just to see it… It was *unbelievably* beautiful, that piece of land. And how do you find the words for all that they must have felt, and that we felt today, standing where they stood?

Mary: For me too, the overwhelming feeling was the sheer *beauty* of that piece of land. As long as I live, I don't think I'll ever forget it. It must have been so hard for them to have to leave that *beauty*. To have worked that land, to have touched it and lived off it, and then to have to leave it forever.

In walking and doing this journey, it just all seems like sacred ground to me. Walking it and seeing it all today, and seeing the Holy Well and the Mass Rock… There's just something very sacred about it.

For me, spirituality *is* connected with the land. Basically, I think spirit is spirit. And my spirit, standing there, could feel… I could *feel* our relatives!

Chris: For me, spirit is an energy. And today it came from the land. Almost like a bolt of lightning, spirit to spirit. I get that more from the land than I do in a church. I mean, Irish-Americans' Catholic ceremonies seem to be about the same as those here in Ireland. But I think our family are more about feeling the energy of spirit directly. Some of us are very sensitive to that. On a sacred place in the land, we can feel it directly through our whole body.

Mary: I was an ordained Sister of Mercy but I feel that my whole experience in life is more about spirit than about formal ceremonies. As far as I'm concerned, I feel that I walk with God. I just experience that directly. At times ritual, because it's familiar, can be wonderful. But I don't have to have ritual. I don't know whether it's the same for the people here in Ireland or whether the ritual is 'it' here. I don't know them well enough to know that.

But going to those different places today and experiencing, first of all, the homeplace in Doon, and then the Holy Well further back on their land…

And to know that one of our ancestors is buried there as a newborn baby. And that our ancestors would have been drinking ceremonially from the Holy Well, as we did today.

And then - probably the most emotional of all for us - going on to the Mass Rock. I guess it's because all the feelings about all those relatives that we have heard about - well, that is the spot where they were, and where they worshipped. I'm getting goosebumps again, just thinking about it.

After the homestead in Doon, to go on and see this other *incredibly* beautiful place that was their Mass Rock. And to realise it was actually a hiding place. In my mind, I hadn't really realised this thing that at one point in history they had to hide their faith. Because we don't have to hide our faith. In America, they wouldn't have had to hide their faith. And to see with our own eyes this place where they had to hide their faith, that's quite something.

The thing about the Mass Rock is, we as a family group have very strong faith. It was passed on to us. And I feel it was passed on from here, at that Mass Rock. For all of us here together as a group experiencing it today, it was the most emotional thing. We all felt blessed. Blessed.

## Questions

Chris: Would we have had Johanna's courage, or would we have said '*Okay, I give up*' ? The fear of facing onto that ship, not knowing what she was taking all those small children to. What did they take with them - nothing? They would have had no body fat on them either, they were starving to death. But we're from a line of strong women. I've always known that.

And then we have so many questions going forward with Johanna. To know where she went, how she went...? We have so many fragments of stories. We did genealogy searches, and Keith found the names of Johanna and Patrick at Grosse Île in Canada. That was where their ship arrived. We had assumed she would have come in to Ellis Island in New York, but we didn't find their names there. But there in Grosse Île, Keith found them. And he took us there. There was a big glass wall with so, so many names of those who arrived on the coffin ships from Ireland. And there were so many other Carney names there too.

So here Johanna comes, arriving into this vast unknown country with all these kids, after her husband died on board ship. And did she get some help on arriving at Grosse Île, that she was able to travel further on? Amazingly, we have an article that was put in *The Boston Pilot* newspaper, searching for Johanna. It was put in there by a man called Michael Riordan from the Glen of the Crow who had also, like so many others, taken the Famine ship to America. In it he asks whether anyone has seen, or has any news of, Mrs Johanna Carney and her children, from Doon, Crow Glen, in Cork. See, this is the newspaper ad he placed, asking for any news:

**Of MRS. JOHANNA KEARNEY and her children, Mary, Ellen, Thomas, Maurice, Patrick, William, Richard and Peter, natives of Doone, parish of Arduaguna, co. Cork, who sailed from Cork on the 1st of May, 1847, and landed in Quebec; afterwards proceeded to the State of Vermont. Any information respecting them will be thankfully received by Michael Riordan, care of John Foley, 21 Hamilton street, Boston, Ms.**

63

We think he must have heard about her husband dying on the voyage and was looking to locate her, to connect her up with the assistance that new arrivals could get from their own local Irish community of fellow-emigrants in the States. If he did find her, that could help explain how she managed, after arriving alone with all those children.

And Norma was able to tell us who that man was. There was one family of Riordans here in the Village and Michael was one of them. Right up to the end of the twentieth century, that family still lived in the Village, right next door to Norma's house here, on the right as you're coming up from the Crossroads Below. They were close friends of Norma's, the niece and nephews of that man Riordan, as they all grew up together here.

The *Boston Pilot* article said that Johanna had moved on from Quebec to Vermont. That's quite a journey. But how, and why…? And another story was that she went to California. And did she go with all the children? Or did she drop some of them off somewhere along the way? Yet somehow they eventually settled back in the East in Salem, Massachusetts, because that's where her grave is, where she was buried as an old lady. And all the names of the children are on there, though that doesn't necessarily mean they're all buried there.

Our father didn't talk a lot about it until the end of his life. He was retired then and he had a *shellalegh* and he'd take the grandchildren for walks in

---

63 Arduaguna is a misspelling of Ardnageeha (Árd na Gaoithe in the original Irish, meaning Windy Height).

the woods. [64] He'd walk with Keith when Keith was young and he'd tell him stories about the family having come over from Ireland. But up until then, he just didn't talk about it. He didn't talk about the Famine, the hardship of how they got there.

Mary: There was great love there and a really strong sense of family. But there was no talk of how it had all happened. *At all.* Even when he talked about it with us, he'd talk only about his mother Julia, who had come from Clonakilty in West Cork. We always heard about Clonakilty, and that she had stayed in touch with her people back in Clonakilty. But very little detail was passed down. And we heard nothing about his dad's side coming from here in Gleann an Phréacháin.

But now that I understand more, I realise that part of that silence may have been shame. The shame of not having been able to look after themselves. And shame is part of survivors' guilt too.

But I'm searching for another word too other than shame. I guess it's pride. The pride of having survived, of belonging. And also loss: all that was lost, all those who were lost... You've told us that people in the Village here often stay silent about the Famine too. That even when you ask them, individuals tend to go quiet and not really want to pursue the conversation. So in my mind that makes me ask about them: *And you, who did your people lose...?*

## Remembering

Chris: Our dad's uncle, Dan, was a priest. And I remember that he had, in gold, that exact same kind of cross that was over there today up on the Mass Rock. And our dad too studied and trained in a Jesuit seminary for over twelve years, right up to coming up for ordination as a Jesuit. I think he got into a deep depression at that point and he asked if he could delay, for a year out. They said no, it's now or never. So he had to leave the Jesuits. He was 33. At 36, he got married and went on to have eight children. But he *carried* that *strong*, strong faith that was so meaningful for him. And I'm sure that it came from this... this *lineage* here.

---

64 The *shellalegh* is a traditional Irish walking stick made from blackthorn wood cured for a long time, traditionally in a chimney. Associated with folklore and storytelling, they were in history also used as fighting cudgels.

Mary: The other sense I had today was of survival. That the only reason they left was in order to live. Because otherwise they would have died. And for me, what gives me goosebumps is that because of their courage, their survival, we have life. It's because of their courage that we are here.

Chris: And yet, I'm very aware too that when they came over to America, the education of all of them just seemed to... *blossom*. We definitely have very highly educated ancestors, after they made it to America. For instance, imagine that our dad's father - one of Johanna's very *sons*, straight off the coffin ship - became Secretary of State for Massachusetts!

But oh, how sad it was when we visited the Famine Heritage Centre yesterday. To see it all displayed in front of you. They had interviews with a priest, a labourer, family members of victims who had starved to death... They spoke about it. They explained that potatoes were all they ever had to eat anyway, as serf tenants of the colonial landlords. The people had been cleared off their lands by the colonisation. And they were allowed back as tenant labourers, because the colonial farms needed local labour. And they explained exactly how many potatoes it took to feed a family. And how other foods were still being exported out of Cork harbour by the colonial system while the people starved.

We also went on the Famine Ship tour in Dublin. We were shown how they survived in cubby holes down in the hold of the ship for the two months of the crossing. And there were often storms where they'd be delayed at sea for weeks longer, without enough rations.

Chris: To me, walking onto that ship was very visceral. It was harrowing. I'll never forget it. Feeling these were *my* people. It was like walking into a time capsule. Seeing what they endured, it made me want to throw up over the side.

Mary: I was probably more prepared for that because I've visited a lot of sites about Black slavery in America. I was in education for 47 years and I took a lot of students on tours to study slavery. For me it's very similar. The Famine ship gave me just the same feeling.

But you have to go inside the wrapping of all that trauma, to find the other emotions and to eventually find it empowering for yourself as an individual. I don't know if you could ever find it empowering by just hearing about it. But we have been through this actual experience - we have made in reverse the journey that Johanna made, and we have emerged feeling blessed by this return.

I've always known that we in our family are very strong women. We come from very strong roots, on both sides. And I'm just looking at Johanna now in total admiration: the courage, the *strength* that she had, to make that journey to America, and then across it…

On social media we're sharing this journey that we're making here. Sharing it with our next generation of nieces, nephews, children, as well as having some of them here with us on the trip. And I see them seeing the faith in completely new ways through this visit. Learning so much and getting so interested, getting hooked… So it's kind of coming full circle. And we're trying to pass on all this heritage and lineage in a healthy way. It's up to us to pass on in a healthy way what has been passed down to us. Because if it stops, it stops. That's why it's been so delightful to hear that the whole community here in Gleann still do all those rituals, out there in their landscape.

Chris: We don't want any of this to be lost to the future generations of our family. It's going to be wonderful to take back to them this clear sense we have now of where our people came from. To bring that back and share it with them - the sheer emotion and beauty of it. And I hope they'll want to grasp that for themselves. Because it's brought us back to a much deeper, richer level of ourselves.

Many of them don't even know the simple facts yet - the history of where our people came from and how and why, and what they brought with them spiritually and emotionally. Some of the young people in our family are sensitive souls and I think they will really want to grasp this.


# Nature

I think in the States, some aspects of Catholicism have become quite commercial. It doesn't seem to be the sheer *faith* that I see here. It's often more about 'What can we build? How much can you give us?' That type of thing. And partly because of that, I see an awful lot of people there having walked away from Catholicism.

Mary: Compared to what we've seen here in Gleann, Catholicism in the US has a lot less connection with nature, the seasonal cycles of the year, the outdoors and the land. But for me privately, nature has always been the way to God. Even as a child, my spirituality has always come from the earth. I feel that nature and the earth somehow act as a channel that helps us to experience spirit - our own spirit meeting the spirit of God. I know that some in the Church have sometimes seen nature-based spirituality as a threat but I think they're just trying to protect their own view and they're missing out on the genuine spiritual beauty that comes through - that can reach us and touch us through nature.

Catholicism is in fact a lot about energies, and direct experiences of spiritual energies through the sacraments. But somehow parts of the Church and some priests seem to have the idea that if people feel spiritual energy coming through to them from nature, that that isn't the same thing - that's not the Catholic God coming through. I don't see it that way. But you know, we are a bit rebel, our family! I would say all of us are, in our own ways.

Chris: We grew up being taught a very traditional, institutional Catholicism. We knelt together as a family to say the Rosary and so on. But ultimately it wasn't enough for us.

Mary: For me, that was all fine but I needed more too. I started to go off for walks in the woods and I found my real spirituality there. Even as a small child, I made my own shrine to Mary outdoors in our back garden. And to me, she was 'Mary of the Woods'.

And when I came to Ireland for the first time in 1978, it was the sheep grazing on the land that I fell in love with! The sheep really did it for me. Keith used to tease me about it, and ask me why. But in fact, as a young teenager my favorite psalm was 'The Lord is my Shepherd'. That all just came from me as a child by myself - that ancient tradition of the spirituality of the land emerging through me.

Later, I became a Sister of Mercy. That was a progression for me. I felt drawn at that stage to the deep silence of the contemplative life. We had one hour a day when we spoke. That was for the five years of my training. My novitiate was at Long Island Sound on the East Coast, on the waterfront facing the Atlantic. And I loved it, I absolutely loved it. It was a deep grounding before then going on to train as a teacher within the Order.

Chris: I on the other hand migrated away from the formal Church. But I felt that within my profession in nursing, I was in church every single day! As a nurse, that's what I did: I helped people. I wanted to serve, and I was serving *something*...

Mary: You connected spirit to spirit with your patients, I could see that straight away.

Chris: The ceremonies of the Church were no good for me at that point so I poured my heart and soul into my nursing as a way to serve and care for others. And church ceremonies remained of no use to me until - well, actually - up until this past week here in Ireland, to be honest, when I feel I've had the chance to see things differently.

 Keith Carney...

## In the footsteps of our ancestors

Let me say first that, to be honest, I can hardly understand myself the depth of feeling that is constantly drawing me back to the Glen of the Crow. Some force that keeps me searching for more, something that is making me want to return again and again like a young lover yearning for his mate. I find the place magical - this simple village and quaint acreage, and rolling hills filled with thousands of years of history. A microcosm of Ireland's mystery and magic, her conflict and gentleness... Each time I arrive at the Glen of the Crow, I prepare myself for what I may discover. I make the Sign of the Cross on my forehead to open my thoughts, on my lips to speak with true voice and on my chest to open my heart. And each time I arrive in the Village, I know I will learn something new.

And it is *intense*! The analogy I often use is that it's like 'drinking from a fire hose'. For instance, Mary, whom you've just heard from, had been to Cork before and Chris to Dublin. But neither had been this close before to what we have searched for, for generations. For them - and for my other family members - being in Crow Glen today was quite overwhelming. The Mass Rock in its little glen, the Famine Road, the Traveller man that we met there, Doon and the Carney homestead and farmland, the Holy Well, its graveyard and ring fort, walking in the footsteps of our ancestors - I could go on and on...! It is a massive amount of events and emotions that could not all be processed in one day. They have both told me that the trip has been life changing for them.

You know, America is a land of immigrants. And Americans have a burning desire to find their heritage - the history and origins of their families from their motherlands. Many who emigrated to America did so because of war, famine, oppression or for sheer survival. When they departed, they left the old world behind and too often, they never discussed or wrote down their family history. Not much was known in my family of our Irish heritage in Ireland. Where in Ireland did our family come from? When did they depart? Under what circumstances did they leave? Did any of the family stay in Ireland? Where they kings, or horse thieves? All these questions remained unanswered over the generations of the Carney family in America.

I find the Irish race particularly reluctant to talk about tragic events. Perhaps this is human nature, but I know in Irish-America, there was always reluctance to discuss the Famine, or what it took to come to America. It may be an inherent coping mechanism that blanks out tragedies and terrible memories. But I feel the Irish bring this to a brilliant level of skill!

For instance, when I was young, my grandfather would try to tell me stories about Ireland - mostly rebellious ones. And his Irish American wife, my grandmother Eileen McKenna Carney, would let him know very quickly that there would be *No Irish stories* in her house! That's when he and I would head outside to walk a local path in the woods, taking his blackthorn *shillelagh* stick along to keep *the caint and the craic* going. [65]

Over the course of my lifetime, I began to discover further small clues to my Irish heritage. Piece by piece, the puzzle began to come together into a picture of my family. When I was a child, I got titbits from my grandfather on those long walks. Family folklore was discussed during holidays gatherings, but little detail was available. When I found out the names of my great-great grandparents - Patrick and Johanna Carney - I gained significant insight, and information started flowing faster. There was a serendipitous encounter over the internet with distant cousins Terri Carney Reisert and Bill Fawcett. They too were descendants of Patrick and Johanna. They were the first to come to Crow Glen and blaze the trail for my family, and all descendants of the Carneys, to follow. Terri and Bill introduced me to Norma Buckley, the *seanchaí* of Crow Glen. [66]

I have been blessed to know Norma, who is for me like an angelic keeper of Crow Glen's history and lore. In this remote Irish village, I have discovered what is like a spiritual *Trinity* for our Carney family. For us, this Trinity is made up of the Carney homestead in Doon, the Holy Well

---

65 An Irish-language expression for chat (*'caint'*) and fun (*'craic'*).
66 A *seanchaí* is a traditional Irish storyteller or folk historian.

(which was once part of the Carney land), and Carraig an Aifrinn, the Mass Rock.

Today, the Carney homestead is just the site where Patrick and Johanna's home once stood. Their home had been destroyed on the day they were escorted out of Ireland. Ruined by the landlord and the authorities to send a message to others in the area not to occupy the property, and to ensure that the Carneys would not ever try to return. Today on the footprint of the Carney home stands a modern Irish house.

But the location still holds the spiritual energy of that large Irish family that once lived there. As my aunts mentioned, they felt *the Spirit* there. As a descendent of Patrick and Johanna, it is a very emotional place to visit today. Not much has changed in the Bride River Valley where the land is located. I try to prepare my relatives for their first visit, but I find it better to let them come with no expectations and discover the spiritual emotion for themselves when they arrive.

Visitors to Doon today see the same views as the Carney family saw when living there in the early nineteenth century. You see the same sun and cloud shadows cross the slopes of the valley. You breathe the same air, smell the same smells as you walk over the paths and fields of your forefathers. I have returned several times in recent years with waves of my direct family, with Norma Buckley leading the way. I see the looks on my family's faces, their tears welling with emotion, their body language that of an amazing, near-physical surrender. I felt and acted the same way the first time I visited. I watched with great joy as one of my female cousins recently made her first visit. She had never been to Ireland before. Always boisterous, never shy, she has never been a person at a loss for words.

But when she stood on the ground of our family's home she was speechless, tears filling her eyes, biting her lower lip to try to mitigate the emotion she felt. She stood silent, gazing over the landscape of the valley, trying to absorb the reality of generations of our family who had occupied this land some 170 years before.

The Holy Well is located on the land of the original Carney farm, deep into the fields of the property. Due west on the south side of the Bride River Valley, the site of the Well can be seen in the distance from the Carney homestead. No roads lead there, only ancient paths travelled by so many to this well that was in use for at least a thousand years before the Carneys arrived. The well's origin: pre-Christian. Its structure and form: round, built defensively on a hillside, to protect its original inhabitants. Its more recent history: a Catholic Church site destroyed by feuding Irish clans. And its medicinal powers: healing episodes, well documented.

## Sanctuaries

Johanna Carney's *Obituary* in America states that she lost an infant child just before departing from Ireland. Eight other children were born into the Carney family in Doon - this one was the first to pass over. The Great Hunger must have compounded significant weight on top of this grief of losing their child. And in Ireland in 1847, unbaptized children of Catholic families were not permitted to be buried in Church graveyards: consecrated ground was off limits to these unfortunate souls. The Irish felt that Holy Wells were the only hope for their unbaptized, deceased family members to rest in a spiritual peace and get to heaven. That Carney child would be buried there - on their property, safe and secure under a non-descript stone.

Today at the Holy Well, within those safe, circular walls that have protected it for centuries, there are so many such non-descript stones covering the ground. Stones not placed in clear patterned rows like a neatly kept cemetery, but randomly laid over the ground by grieving families long ago, who guiltily placed their loved ones in any open space they could find. Each time I visit, I say a prayer as I look at the earth covered in stones, wondering which one was a member of my family.

During the Holy Well visits, Norma guides all in attendance to drink the water. This hole in the earth that has flowed healing powers since before Christ is now protected by a Cross and a statue of the Blessed Mother, keeping a vigilant eye over it. Into a dark well of water just below the earth's surface a pitcher is gently dipped, and its contents poured into small glasses. Amazingly, the water poured into the glasses is crystal clear and the vessels pass from one family member to the next with reverence.

The water from this Holy Spring not only refreshes the body of those partaking, but also their souls. All in attendance are invited to offer prayers or words that allow us to reflect on the gravity of the moment. Norma showed us the cross-marked stones on the ground, suggesting that we take up a rock and trace the Sign of the Cross onto the stone to show that we have visited. The years of this practice had carved deep, cross-shaped crevasses into those stones.

For me, the Carraig an Aifrinn Mass Rock was the most spiritual experience of my life. I had learned of Mass Rocks during my own research on the Catholic faith in Ireland. These were most typically a large single boulder in the countryside, often hidden by hedges or trees - makeshift altars for priests to conduct Mass during Penal Times, when our faith was outlawed by the colonisers. I knew they were secret places, hidden and out of sight of the authorities who scoured the countryside to punish Catholics for practicing an outlawed faith. Catholic priests were hunted and killed by the British occupiers if caught saying Mass. There was always a lingering term in my research, saying that generations of Irish were forced to *practice their faith beyond the hedgerow*: this was a concept hard to comprehend as an American. America as a country was founded on freedom of religion and the clear separation of Church and State.

Within my own personal Catholic faith, I have always been drawn to churches where I could feel the presence of the Holy Spirit. A comforting presence that fills my soul, surrounding my physical body and mind with a release of day to day troubles, to open up and welcome God into my heart. Throughout my life, I found this presence in only a few churches in the US, but I found it in nearly every church I visited in Italy: in Rome, at the Sistine Chapel, in St Peter's and in numerous great basilicas there, both major and minor. Those massive buildings were built by blessed artisans, craftsmen who dedicated their talents to building monuments to God. As soon as you walk into those cavernous sanctuaries, your eyes gravitate skyward and to the altar.

When I visit the Mass Rock in Crow Glen, it is the same experience for me as entering one of those sacred cathedrals. You go in through a small hill entrance by the roadside, over a slight climb and then descending into the most beautiful glen. The sanctuary is a small grassy area surrounded by large trees, supporting a canopy of leafed branches. Your eyes are immediately drawn to the sky above, as if to the ceiling of a church. Then to the altar, trimmed low by the bubbling stream of the River Bride, gently rolling down into the Bride Valley below. It curves its flow in front of a natural rock wall where the outlawed priests would celebrate secret Masses for Crow Glenners. This natural wall formation served as the altar, in that time when priests celebrated Mass facing the altar and away from the parishioners.

On my first visit to the Mass Rock, I was brought there by Norma Buckley. I was accompanied by my wife and our two children. My wife and Norma stood in the little glen as my kids and I went across a small, thin footbridge to stand in front of the natural altar. I could feel the presence of the Holy Spirit, my heart opening as if I were in a church for Mass.

But the emotion then and there ran deep. I felt as if I were weightless. Flanked by my children on each side of me, I held them close to me and looked intensely at the altar of stone. I could not control my emotions, and began to sob uncontrollably. At that moment I felt the weight on my shoulders of 800 years of oppression that my forefathers had endured. Their religious persecutions, their enslavements, their evictions and injustices all rushed onto me at that moment, 170 years after our family was forced to leave the Glen of the Crow.

It was the greatest spiritual moment of my life and I was so blessed to be able to have my children - the next generation - be there by my side at that moment. Before retreating back across the bridge, we each picked up a small rock and traced crosses on the stone wall. Our tracings were done on top of previously etched crosses, lovingly traced over those done by thousands of visitors before us, as a sign of their respect.

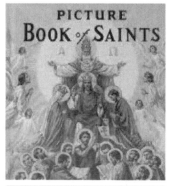

# Chapter 7

# The zones of the spirit world

Images at the opening of this chapter:

~ Our Lady Queen of Heaven
~ The Communion of Saints in Heaven and on earth
~ Hierarchy of divine beings in Heaven
~ The Holy Spirit with the Risen Jesus

The Americans had left on their silver bus to spend several days touring around Ireland. They would return to the Glen of the Crow for our evening together at the Manor House. I had time now to go back to Norma Buckley and try to get her to talk to me about the *spirit world* as Crow Glenners saw it - the dimensions beyond this physical universe.

My memory was that when I was a child there, we believed that a whole wider universe of spiritual realms lay wrapped around this brief human life. In those realms were all the spiritual beings and presences that we prayed to every day. We couldn't actually see into their realms during this current part of our journey that was this human life. But soon enough, when our consciousness left our body at death, those spiritual realms would become *our* environment too, and our bare consciousness would have to navigate its way through those realms, for better or for worse.

But as well as waiting for us in the spirit world, our culture also believed that loving beings from the spirit world could and did 'step down' and move though our human world as well. They could befriend us, interact with us and assist us in daily life, if we were open to them doing that. So as we saw it, the more familiar you could be with them, the better, because they could help you and your loved ones greatly both in your human life and throughout your afterlife in the spirit world.

My memory is that that was the worldview of the Crow Glen culture I lived in until I emigrated. But I wanted to ask Norma Buckley now how accurate that memory was, and what people in the Glen of the Crow think about the spirit world today.

Miriam, the greyhound, watched as usual from the couch. Her long, elegant feet and toes were laid out in front of her on cushions. To my consternation, I noticed that on all four feet, the dog was sporting a full manicure of bright, metallic-blue nail polish. The work of an overexcited grandchild, Norma assured me.

 Norma...

The zones

So Marella, you'd like to talk about the spirit world, would you? Well, let me ask *you* now: who can describe the spirit world? Because for instance, in this moment- are we *there* right now, or are we *not* there?!

Seriously though, from talking to you over the past few days, I can see *huge* gaps in your religious education. Things have evolved so much since you left in the 1990s. I can see that you're stuck in the old ways, as if it's all preserved in aspic in your head. But it's not like that. If you're actually here living the religion, it moves and it changes, because it's a living thing.

For instance, you're asking me about the different zones in the spirit world but sure, the zones and dimensions are gone entirely now. You'd rarely even hear of Purgatory now. And Limbo is no longer with us! It's no longer discussed under *any* circumstances.

I suppose you thought we'd have a great flaming landscape of spiritual countries to talk about - Hell, Purgatory, Limbo, the Communion of Saints, the Highest Heaven and the Transmigration of Souls making their way through it all. But I might disappoint you. Because I'm after giving up thinking about all that, trying to figure out or imagine what it's all like. Because nobody knows really, do they? So aren't you wasting your time? There's a *veil* over it, from the point of view where we're standing now, and that's that. And won't we find out soon enough?

But one thing I do feel sure of is that there are many shades of Purgatory, *as a state of mind* as much as anything else. States that are for cleansing, purifying and learning in the spiritual dimensions after you die. For instance, I don't feel that I'd be ready to just walk into Heaven direct. Jim Barry, a wit here in the Village in the old days, used to say: 'Sure, there'd be no use my going to Heaven 'cos I'd know no-one there!'

I would quite readily believe that the spiritual dimensions are states of mind rather than physical places - that the soul or the consciousness in those dimensions is having a lot of *experiences* mentally rather than them being in a physical location. But having this whole map or framework of 'zones' makes it more concrete, to help people imagine and understand what we can't actually see right now.

Apparently modern physics claims that there are many universes and many different dimensions, overlapping our own. I've discussed this with someone trained in comparative religion, who also has a long education in Buddhism. Most people don't realise this about Buddhism but it actually includes a very detailed map of all the spiritual zones, and they are almost identical to those of Catholicism. They have, in their own way, the

Transmigration of Souls, they have levels of Purgatory, they have a Limbo and many of what they call 'Hell-Realms', and so on.

Speaking of Limbo, you remember again that up until the end of the twentieth century, the Church wouldn't allow unbaptised babies or people who committed suicide to be buried in consecrated ground? Those unbaptised babies had to go straight to Limbo, supposedly. It must have been such a trial for bereaved parents, as if they weren't suffering enough already. And remember Limbo was supposed to be for *all* unbaptised people, not just babies. For everyone who wasn't a Catholic, basically. So that must be a crowded spot, mustn't it?! But they say no more about it now, though there has never been an apology for it or anything like that. These things just get quietly phased out.

Purgatory isn't as sharply defined as it used to be, either. And as for Hell - well, it hasn't exactly frozen over but again it's *much* less defined and discussed now. I wouldn't say you could do away with Hell entirely because otherwise, where would you send Hitler? But I think Purgatory has many, many shades and degrees and dimensions - more than enough to hold the vast majority of people when they pass over.

Hell is still mentioned occasionally but it's the absolute bottom rank. You wouldn't meet many of your friends there! I'd say about seven-eighths of the focus that used to be on Hell has now been moved over to Purgatory. And Limbo, as we know, has been softened and downplayed. Of course, it may not be that people are more virtuous nowadays and that there's no need for Hell anymore. If anything, people were more innocent in the old days and had less opportunity for sinning, yet we had Hell stuffed down our throat every day of the week.

Purgatory in the old days was really important. It was the holding area. It was assumed that we were all going there, because there's no way we can assume we're ready to go straight into Heaven. So praying for people in Purgatory was a massive part of the traditional practices in the old days.

Listen, this is funny. Can you hear that there happens to be thunder and lightning in the sky outside at this minute, while we're here talking about hellfire and brimstone below?!

Those who are no longer living - where do I think they are? We have no idea where they are. But what we do know, I firmly believe, is that as it says in the Gospel, there are *many* mansions in the house of God the Father. And I think you go to whatever level you've reached, the level you've earned or attained spiritually.

I think your future in the spirit world is all down to how you live your life, though whether we're doing that right or not, I'm not at all sure. But I believe that when people die and their consciousness leaves their body, then their level of spiritual attainment or progress - well, they start to experience that more directly as the main experience of their consciousness.

As children we were told an immense amount about the spirit world. This life was only a brief stopping-off point, like a springboard into what came next, which would last for all eternity. But my own personal angle now is I believe that there is a God, and that Christ and the Holy Spirit are both part of that godhead, that they're both really there. With regard to saints, the older I'm getting, the more I'm inclined to go directly to God instead. Well, to Jesus because he became man so that makes him very approachable.

You remember that in the Holy Trinity, they are actually three equal entities within one god - the Father, Son and Holy Spirit. They are equal in all things. God the Father isn't greater or more powerful than the others. Obviously, the Son I love, of course, and he's very approachable. I don't pray the Rosary so much anymore because I find it too long and I get bogged down in it. There's a much simpler devotion now that you can do on the Rosary beads to the *Divine Mercy* aspect of Jesus and I love that, it's very nice. He's very approachable in that form. I often have a little siesta in the afternoon and I do that then, when I'm lying down.

And the Holy Spirit I feel as sort of encompassing. I've always felt that great connection with the Holy Spirit since my Confirmation. When He descends on your head at Confirmation, you make that connection for life, hopefully. Then He's always around you above the top of your head. In your energy field or in your aura, as they'd say nowadays.

So that's about the entire length and breadth of my definite beliefs nowadays really. That's all I feel I need to know. I've a fairly 'stripped-down' approach you might say, compared to all the complexity of spiritual beings and practices that we used to have. But yes, I do believe the spiritual realms exist, though I have no idea where they are physically at. Maybe they're not a physical dimension at all. But I hope to attain the right side of it all myself. The 'many mansions': I assume that they are states of being - mental states, basically. So maybe they don't have to take up any physical space anywhere. For instance, I probably do believe that Purgatory is a mental state. And that you go to whatever part of that you need to be in, to have your consciousness refined until you're pure enough to move on.

But I often joke with religious women friends, saying 'There's no hope for us at all compared to how devoted the previous generation were - the *amount* of their lives that they spent in prayer!' There were people among them who genuinely saw this human lifetime as just a spiritual journey, and they'd be constantly meditating on the passage of their soul into the spirit world after death and preparing for it. And they felt nothing else was as important as that. A bit like full-time monastics would do nowadays still - just that is what you are choosing to do with your life. But these people I'm talking about were ordinary people living in their own homes, farming people with families.

## The Communion of Saints

For me it does all start with the Communion of Saints - that's the cornerstone of everything and within that, the forgiveness of sins. The Communion of Saints means all the souls who have ever been in the Catholic Church, both deceased and present-day people. Because we all have the potential ability to become saints, eventually. The Communion of Saints is this connection between all those who were ever in the Church because you never leave it, whether living or dead.

That holds and contains us all at the highest and deepest levels of our being and our soul. So, we're not alone, ever, even when faced with our own sins and shortcomings.

The spirit world encompasses our whole universe, and I might be wrong but I think local Catholic people here would say that too, still today. Because it's everything really, from when we're born into this human life, to being baptised, to when we die and join the Communion of Saints, hopefully. And hopefully, our whole lives are sort of bounded by that and guided in that direction. Generally that's our overall ethos, even though you have some days when you think of it less.

We're now well into the twenty-first century with all its science and technology. And we know that the Catholic Church has misbehaved badly, with all the sex abuse cases. But I think many people here still retain that general overarching sense that there is some sort of spiritual universe. That this world that we see is set within that wider spiritual universe, with all its levels and domains.

It's difficult to give a full answer because different people - even very learned people - at different times look at things and situations differently. For instance, think of the soul coming into the body of an infant, and then the soul leaving the body at death and travelling on through the dimensions. The soul coming in and going out again - we just can't get any kind of grip on that within this physical, temporal human life that we're in right now. All that is *atemporal*, in the other dimensions.

So I think it's more about focusing on what we do perceive, feel or experience as spiritual while we are here in our own human bodies. And for me, that's the natural material universe as I believe God made it. Because God created it, I see no contradiction in finding spirituality in the natural world. Apparently, some parts of the Church do have a problem with that, but I don't see why.

I know it's weird and wonderful if you like but for instance, you've seen me hugging big old oak trees. The great oak does draw me and my attention. But what do you think I'm thinking at that moment? I hug the oak and I look up and I'm saying to the spirit of the tree: 'You are so old and have been here so long. Please bless this place and all who are in it'.

Parts of the Vatican may have considered that irreligious, or even dangerous. But sometimes they're not especially openminded. Think back to Galileo - one of the greatest thinkers and natural scientists there ever was. By observing the natural world, he figured out that the earth orbits around the sun, not the sun around the earth as everyone had thought before him. And look what they did to him for it! [67]

I think the Church were maybe afraid of the natural universe in the old days. Instead of venerating it, thinking it was made by God, you were encouraged to keep away from it. In the old days you weren't encouraged by the Church to go out and dream about the stars, I can tell you!

It's true that the Catholic Church has behaved terribly around the clergy's abuses of children here in Ireland. But people have the common sense and the insight to know that you have to separate human wrongdoings from the reality of the spirit. Just because humans misbehave - and equally so if they're priests or bishops - that doesn't stop the whole spiritual universe existing as if it was put out with a bang. People are mature enough to

---

67 The Catholic Inquisition imprisoned Galileo for life in 1633 for making the scientific discovery that the earth revolves around the sun. *The New Scientist*, 'Vatican Admits Galileo was Right', 7-11-1992

make that distinction, even when they have been horrified by cases of clerical abuse.

You get good and not so good people in every avenue of life. The Catholic Church has taken a battering and deservedly so, and there's probably more to come yet and it'll never again be the same. But to my mind the spiritual level will of course always be the same. You have to see the distinction between the spiritual world and the temporal world of living people, which includes the Church and clergy. There's a wider spiritual dimension wrapped around this immediate human life that's playing out in front of us here. There's the Communion of Saints, there's the forgiveness of sins, there's the life everlasting of the soul and the spirit. Human lives good and bad come and go within that much bigger dimension.

I believe fundamentally in the forgiveness of sins, though not always in all the ways it's carried out. For instance, I don't go to Confession as much anymore. Because to be honest, I don't feel I commit a lot of sins to confess. You don't want to be like the innocent little children inventing sins to tell the priest every Saturday because they had no real sins to offer! That's one of the biggest changes in recent years. Even 25 years ago my parents wouldn't be able to go to bed at night if they didn't feel they had had Confession recently enough. The big emphasis on an individual was on your individual sinning: that was your big thing to focus on personally, and tackle.

But I believe that when people die and pass over into the spirit world, they just, in a way, join that world. Like my father did, I pray every day to Saint Joseph as to me he's the patron saint of a happy death because he died with Jesus and Mary at his side. I pray for a happy death, which to me means that these spiritual beings that we pray to will be with us and support us. I pray for their strength to be there and to come and take me to the right place. Of course, I pray equally at the same time for people who have already died.

I still pray individually every single day for all those in our family who have died. I go right back to neighbours who died in the 1950s, or in the 70s. I can't know how much effect I'm having. But I'm certain that a loving, positive thought for them can't do any harm! We do it, trying to make contact with their situation in Purgatory and trying to help or influence that. But can we really help? I don't know. Anyway, every morning I get up and go to the window and look out and I say this prayer, which is actually a very old one. I say: 'Oh Jesus, through the pure heart of Mary, I offer you all the efforts and fruits of the day, for all the intentions of your Sacred Heart and for the dear departed souls'.

I firmly believe that the couple of hours straight after death are very important. It's an active time, a time for your spirit to actively pray and turn to your spiritual beings. That's what I pray to them for every day, that's what a spiritual person is preparing for - that transition - that you can make the most of it.

There's an old saying that I saw written on a little notice once in a rural church way back in West Cork. 'Whenever you pass this way, come in and pay a visit, so when at last they bring you in, the Lord won't say: *Who is it?*' I always think of that. These saints and divinities have to be like your very best friends, so familiar, to be with you at that moment. So that there's no gap between you and them really, so that when your consciousness leaves your body, you will just automatically dissolve into their arms, as it were, for them to take you on into the next dimensions in the way that's best for you.

## Glimpses of the zones

Whichever way you look at it, I'm firmly convinced that there's more to life, to heaven and earth, than we see or are aware of. Maybe it's all around us staring us in the face and we're just not aware of it. I believe there's 'more' but often we just can't see it. For instance, I've sometimes known people who have insights into those realms, who can maybe partly see into them sometimes. They might be artists, or a bit psychic or whatever. Yet that's outside the Church too, isn't it? Or for instance, horoscopes - the Church were really afraid of them.

In the old days there was a very official, precise map of the spiritual world, and people who were not priests were not authorised to be travelling around in those dimensions. It was absolutely forbidden. Whether through dreams, or making art, or foretelling the future, or mediums talking with the spirits of people who had died, or whatever. Or telling the future through cards or tea leaves - it was all forbidden. The walls and doors between the dimensions were very firmly held by the Church only, and no-one else should get involved with those dimensions in any other ways. Priests could help you move between the dimensions in their own defined way, but I've also known rare people who experience the other dimensions by themselves sometimes.

For instance, we have a person around here who can recognise energies, for the good of all. He's a water diviner as well. He can detect the presence of water deep under the ground just by holding out two small rods, and they direct him to the hidden water deep underground. I was very keen to have a diviner go over the Holy Well site at Doon, to see whether they would pick up any strong spiritual energies in the land there, as well as the spring-water. He went there recently and dowsed it for us and he was really shaken by it, in a good way. The rods reacted in his hands very strongly, because of the Well of course. But he also found the earth energies were extremely powerful there - stronger than anything he had ever felt anywhere, he said. He went there to check the energies in the earth basically, not for the water.

Once a man here moved into a house and he felt very uncomfortable in it. At his request, this dowser who understands energies went to the house and walked all around in it. In one bedroom he said 'Well, this bedroom has to be locked up and not slept in again. The rest of the house is fine, no problem.' They had confidence in him so that room was vacated and abandoned, and they never had any problems again. Now he didn't actually do anything about the room, but maybe he just didn't want to make a big drama about it.

Another neighbour of ours used to read your fortune in the tea leaves left in the bottom of your cup, and she was very accurate. You probably remember her doing it here in this house, don't you, when she'd come visiting? She read my mother's tea leaves once and she said: 'There's a woman coming to your door with a very awkward package.' And sure enough a few days later someone arrived with the gift of a live chicken, wrestling with it at the door! But once that woman who used to read tea leaves went away on a Marian pilgrimage that was led by the priest, and he knocked it out of her somehow. She never read the tea leaves again after she came back.

I think that in the old days some people may have been able to travel in the other dimensions, to some extent. For instance, I had this old uncle, Tom O' Mahoney, who used to sit in the corner of the fireplace in our cousins' house over in Bunaglanna above the Bride River Valley. He was a very strong-minded individual. He could cope with stuff. Well, one night at home when I was child, we were thinking of going to bed. And I just calmly said to my mother: 'You'd better put curlers in your hair tonight because you won't have time in the morning'. She said, 'What are you talking about?' And I said, 'Tom is just after dying'. And he hadn't been sick or anything. She said, 'How do you know that?' I said, 'I just saw a ball of light passing outside the window, and I knew it was him'. My mother said to my father, 'Should I do my hair, so?' and he said drily: 'Well hardly, based on that medical report!' But in the morning, our cousins came banging on the door asking my mother to go over quickly and help to lay Tom out, because he had indeed died unexpectedly the night before.

But my father downed that immediately - the fact that I had seen Tom's soul passing. He just wouldn't entertain it, and they never mentioned it again. How else could they handle it? They wouldn't *want* to believe that anyone could see a soul passing, because that was outside the Church rules. They knew that if someone had died, their soul would be departing - but you shouldn't be able to see it! And still today if people experienced anything like that now, they wouldn't talk about it now either because they'd be afraid they'd be laughed at.

## Faıry Core

And then there was all the old lore about fairies, and their fairy forts. I don't believe the fairies exist now, anyway. Any definite instances have been lost in time, if anything like that ever did exist in reality. But the landscape definitely has some very special spots in it, and they're often called fairy forts and there's probably good reason for that. To this day no farmer would interfere with a fairy fort on his land. That's believed to bring bad luck. Our Holy Well in Doon, for instance, is in a ringfort and that is definitely a very special place. But we see that as positive spiritual energy, blessed by God.

But my mother did once hear the Banshee, and it shook her to the core. Basically, people believed that the Banshee was an entity - a sort of fairy spirit or whatever - who took lives. And she cried out to let people know she had taken someone. But if you heard her cry, it was too late, it was the moment of death or death had already happened.

That time my mother heard her, the Gleann football team were all at another village playing a match. They had all travelled away in the back of one big lorry, hanging on - the whole team and the supporters. My father was with them because he was an organiser for the team. Anyway, dusk came that evening and they should have been back. My mother stood out to look up the Street to see if there was any sign of them up the Village.

And she heard a terrible *crying* in the air. Soon, someone ran in and said young Tadhg Callaghan, one of the Gleann footballers and a fine active young man, was after dropping dead on the sports field. They had to bring his body back that evening in the lorry.

Another time when I was a child, there was another young man in the Village, a fine, big, tall, splendid man. And he got quite sick all of a sudden - seriously ill - but he couldn't be cured. And yet he wasn't sent to hospital. So there must have been more to it than met the eye. Because the doctors were there in the house with him, in and out. And I think there was even a doctor brought from Cork city too, and they could do nothing for him. The next thing the priest went and spent two or three hours on his knees in that family's house, praying for the sick man. Well, didn't the patient suddenly pass him walking down the stairs, looking grand and not a bother on him. He was fully cured.

But at that moment the priest became ill himself. That priest was a fine big man too with a blond head of hair. He was like a teddy bear, a big bonny fellow. But his hair turned white and he was never fully well again. It was all very hush-hush, the talk about it in the Village. I was just a child but we knew there was something going on. But it wasn't explained to us any further than that. He was bonny no more, the priest. Maybe he had volunteered to take on that illness, we don't know.

Of course, we are a nation of born storytellers and there were always, *always*, ghost stories for entertainment, although priests wouldn't have encouraged that kind of talk either. But with all those stories, it was hard to know in the end what was made up for entertainment and what had really happened. For instance, Village man Jim Barry had a set of ghost stories that he used to tell for fun. But then another neighbour had first-hand experiences of ghosts. He used to be cycling the mountain roads at night, way far back in Coome, courting his future wife there. There's a bendy bridge back there and on several nights, the bike just stopped dead - stuck in the road in front of the bridge, and he couldn't move it. He got an awful fright from that. Those things nearly always happened at night when people would be outdoors in scary places. [68]

---

[68] Prof. Dennis Gaffin, *Running with the Fairies: Towards a Transpersonal Anthropology of Religion*, Cambridge Scholars, 2013 explores such experiences in modern times.

In the old days talk did go on too about changelings and so on - people who could change their form, for instance to appear as an animal. [69] But I think that when I was a child, even by then people already thought that the faeries themselves were just mythology. The stories were there still, the fairy folklore, but they were told more for fun really. The old belief had been that certain people could change their form. Oh, we were terrified of that idea. It was not a good sign because it was a cover for bad deeds. If you were up to no good, turning into a hare and running off was a good way to escape, wasn't it? Changing form is attached to our oldest mythology too, in a harmless way. For instance, in the old mythology the Children of Lir were changed into four swans, to protect them. But locally in front of you, someone changing form would not be a good thing.

My elder daughter doesn't understand these things. She has a more modern outlook and she said to me: 'You lack faith! Don't you believe that God can handle and overcome all these little things? A single drop of Holy Water would do it. Any of these great divine beings like the Blessed Virgin Mary or the Sacred Heart, or a strong saint. For them it would be like wiping a fleck off a windowpane. All those things and any bad intentions dissolve away to nothing in front of even the mention of divine beings like them.'

But she doesn't understand that those are separate worlds, and you don't mix them. When I told her that, she gave me a right lecture. She said: 'After spending your life on your knees, wouldn't you expect that much in return? It's like paying out all your life for an insurance policy, and then refusing to use it when you need it! Do you not think that the Sacred Heart of Jesus is more powerful than some superstitious idiot who might be wishing bad luck on someone? But you think you mustn't involve the two together with each other? Jesus would be happy to help. If you just say *'Sacred Heart of Jesus, preserve us from all ills and from this present evil'*, it'd be sorted in a moment. Sure, that's what spirituality is for, to protect you against such things.'

But I said to her: 'No. That would be sacrilege. Holy Water is the protection we've been given against ill fortune, and that's that. That's the belief and you can't dabble against it.' Traditionally, Holy Water was used

---

69  Angela Bourke, *The Burning of Bridget Cleary: A True Story*, Pimlico, 1999 is a modern scholarly work on this subject.

on a daily basis. And that was what farmers used to protect their good luck with the land and the crops and the harvest.

I'm sorry now but I have to go, there's someone at the door. We have a meeting this evening of the group who do the flowers in the Chapel.

*

It was a disorienting **Role-Reversal** when my interviewee started pointing out that my 'education' was so 'lacking' and my ideas were stuck in aspic, frozen in time from decades ago. Objectively, no-one could claim I lack university degrees. And wasn't it supposed to be me - the young one from the modern outside world - who was coming back to interview old timers about their old ways?!

But she was right, and in more ways than one. Firstly, this situation where I needed to be educated by her *is* the classic role of an ethnographer. If an ethnographer doesn't achieve that relationship with their interviewee, they've failed. That's the bar you mustn't fall below: that you are there for them to teach you what they are expert in and you are not, ie. their own worldview and the shared worldview of their community.

She was also right in another, deeper way, when she said that my views about the religion were 'stuck in aspic'. She was repeatedly trying to make me see that it's a **living thing** that doesn't stand still in one place just so that I could summarise it neatly in a book.

She had talked in very humorous ways about some of those 'evolutions' in the religion, like how even the zones of the spirit world had changed now to reflect what people need from them now, and what they no longer consider acceptable. As an example, she pointed out that the threat of Hell used to be 'rammed down our throats every day' while in fact people were living rather pious, innocent lives and were never the great sinners they were told they were.

Norma is quite right about me being stuck back there: that is definitely the religion that I remember, right up into the early 1990s. But she repeatedly pointed out that I had completely missed out on the next, and to her crucial, phase. That was the whole journey that got them to the more easy-going, positive, forgiving approach that she feels her Catholic Church has today, which to be honest is completely new to me. Because the old way was so fiercely imprinted on my memory, it took many conversations with her before I could even start to get a sense of that big shift.

Another thing I noted in this most recent recording was the sheer amount of **spiritual work** that the living did **for the dead** in our old religious culture. Other traditional cultures around the world tend more to just 'remember' their dead, for instance by having little shrines dedicated to them in the home or outdoors, whether all year round or at certain times of the year when there is a ritual emphasis on the dead. They may make offerings for them of flowers, incense or food. But it seems to me that few cultures put their back into it like rural Irish Catholics do. Our people used to do remarkably long, hard mental and spiritual work in prayer just to try to lighten the load in Purgatory of our loved ones who had already passed over.

Norma told me that her father, being a trained bookkeeper, had an orderly system for keeping track of this daily spiritual work that he did for the dead. He prayed daily for each deceased person for ten years, keeping their Mortuary Cards as reminders in his Prayer Book. But once their ten years were up (unless they were the closest of relatives), they would have to move out of his Prayer Book because otherwise there wouldn't be enough hours in the day to pray for those others who had departed this life in the meantime.

In this latest interview, I noted in Norma's approach another marker of being a mature spiritual practitioner. I had already seen that her spiritual maturity included being comfortable with change, and with others having different interpretations; not making any particular distinction between spiritual practices done by men and by women; seeing the difference between unchanging spirit and the outer trappings that can and perhaps must change; and seeing the natural and material world as a doorway to spirituality, not an obstacle.

But now she added that in her own mind, she also sees the spirit zones or dimensions as fundamentally '**states of mind**', not necessarily as physical places. In any of the world's religions, this is often another marker of a mature and adult approach to spirituality. This view doesn't make spiritual zones or experiences any less real or important. After all, to suffer intensely at the mental level - whether in this life or in an afterlife - is to suffer intensely, full stop. Having chosen my interviewee as a typical Crow Glen practitioner, not an exceptional one, I was left wondering now whether these characteristics of a particularly mature spirituality are also fairly typical of other Gleann practitioners around her. The only way to find out would be to do more interviews in a future project that listened directly to them.

# References

Bourke, Anglea, *The Burning of Bridget Cleary: A True Story*, Pimlico, 1999

Gaffin, Dennis, *Running with the Fairies: Towards a Transpersonal Anthropology of Religion*, Cambridge Scholars, 2013

*The New Scientist*, 'Vatican Admits Galileo was Right', 7-11-1992

# Chapter 8

# The Bards of Crow Glen
# and the Nagle Mountains

Images at the opening of this chapter:

~ An Irish Bard at work translating manuscripts
~ Original manuscript of fourteenth-century Bardic poetry from the Nagle
Mountains
~ Footbridge to ford the River Bride at Gleann an Phréacháin
~ Nano Nagles' house in Killavullen, restored as a modern retreat centre

# The Bards of Gleann an Phréacháin

Here is a fact that is little known or remembered today (I didn't know it myself before researching this book). In the seventeenth century, Gleann an Phréacháin produced a multi-lingual Gaelic Bard who is still recognised by scholars today as a leading national poet of his time!

He was Eoghan Ó Caoimh (O' Keefe in English), a member of the native Gaelic clan who held vast lands around Gleann before the English dispossessed them. This poet Ó Caoimh is described by scholars as 'born in Glenville, County Cork' in 1656. [70]  The area around Gleann was the last part of their lands left to them before the English drove them out entirely and installed their own settlers in Gleann - the Coppingers - around the 1730s. [71]

Working as a highly trained professional poet, Eoghan was the president of all the Bards in the North Cork area. The National Library at Maynooth and the Royal Irish Academy in Dublin hold eighteen of his manuscripts in Irish. And his poetry is included in the *Field Day Anthology of Irish Writing*, the definitive collection of the greatest Irish writers of all time. [72]

From his studies in the great Bardic Schools of the area's traditional Gaelic culture, Eoghan was highly educated in Irish, Latin and English, and was at least conversant with French. These North Cork Bards constantly translated and composed poetry and other writings between these four languages. His own work involved translating manuscripts all over Munster. For instance in 1692, records show that he was busy working in neighbouring Glanmire, 'translating manuscripts from Latin to Irish'. [73]

There are two folklore archives that say that the very placename of Gleann an Phréacháin or Glen of the Crow comes from this poet Ó Caoimh. With slight variations, both tell that he and a poet colleague were spending the night in the area now known as Crow Glen village, and put their horses in a field for safe keeping. In the morning, they saw a crow flying

---

70  Vincent Morley, *Dictionary of Irish Biography*, Royal Irish Academy with Cambridge University Press, available at https://dib.cambridge.org/viewReadPage.do?articleId=a6289
71  Norma Buckley has a document recording that the Coppingers had to officially swear in court that they were 'innocent Protestants' before the English Crown would grant them these lands that were confiscated from Irish Catholics.
72  Deane, Bourke & Carpenter (eds.), *The Field Day Anthology of Irish Writing*, Vol 4, Cork University Press, 2002
73  Vincent Morley, *Dictionary of Irish Biography,* as in Note 70

up from the head of Ó Caoimh's horse, who lay dead in the field. They composed spontaneous verses to record this striking moment, and folklorists say the place was henceforth called the Glen of the Crow. [74]

Since the middle ages, Ireland's Bardic Schools for professional poets had involved seven years of study and training in Greek, Latin and poetry composition, financed by patronage from the Gaelic clans. And in fact, some of the Bardic Schools' most famous, lasting compositions emerged from the area around Crow Glen and the Nagle Mountains to the north of it.

This Gleann poet Eoghan O' Keefe was happily married for 27 years to Eleanor Nagle from the Nagle Mountains. It was a marriage of love, but also an alliance of neighbouring Gaelic clans who were both major patrons of poetry and the Bards. Like the O' Keefes, the Nagles were one of the few Irish clans who had managed to hold onto some of their lands despite the English invasion and to co-exist with the occupiers, albeit as second-class citizens. Scholars have demonstrated that Gaelic Bardic Schools thrived on the Nagles' territory from around the year 1200 until the 1690s. [75]

At their homestead in Annakissy (now called Killavullen) beside the River Blackwater, they were renowned patrons of some of the most famous traditional Gaelic poets. Historians describe how across the middle ages, the Nagle family had long 'performed their role as Gaelic gentry, sponsoring music and poetry, dispensing profuse hospitality and patronising popular sports such as hunting, horse-racing, hurling and cock-fighting'. [76] You can see the ruins of the Nagles' small castle there to this day.

Sitting between the Bride River to the south and the bigger Blackwater River that runs parallel to it in the north, the Nagle Mountains form almost a hundred square miles of wild bogs, heathlands and forests. For nearly two thousand years, they have been a special place for the people who live around them. They are laid out like a skirt around a peak that the

---

74 Seán Ó Duinnshléibhe, *Gleann an Phréacháin - Béaloideas,* as in Note 32, and D. Ó Súilleabháin, *National Folklore Collection, Gleann an Phréacháin*, as in Note 22. Thanks to Máire Herbert, Prof. of Early and Medieval Irish at University College Cork, for translating the verse for me. In Chapter 1 we saw that the Village already had this name in colonial records almost a century earlier. It may have naturally acquired the name because of its many crows, with poet O' Caoimh formalising the name further after the incident with his horse.

75 Angela Bourke, *The Field Day Anthology of Irish Writing*, Cork University Press, Vol 2, 2002

76 Katherine O'Donnell, 'Edmund Burke's Political Poetics' in *Anáil an Bhéil Bheo: Orality and Modern Irish Culture*, Cambridge Scholars Publishing, Newcastle, 2009

people called *Suígh Finn* - 'Fionn's Seat' in the old language. This high point 'throne' of the legendary hero Fionn Mac Cumhaill looks south over the whole panorama of the Nagles, the Bride Valley and Gleann village beyond.

Scholars date back to the third century AD these oral stories about Fionn Mac Cumhaill and his band of warriors, the Fianna, that are told all over Ireland. One historian explains that the early kings of Ireland 'had in their service bodies of militia… at call like a standing army whenever the monarch required them. The most celebrated of these were… the Fianna who flourished in the third century. Though the accounts that have come down to us of these military organisations are much mixed up with romance and fable, there is sufficient evidence to show that they really existed and exercised great influence in their day'. [77]

He describes how the leaders of the Fianna 'had a passion for building great dúns or forts, many of which remain to this day'. The impressive earthworks for those famous ringforts, with raised perimeter rings, deep ditches and raised mounds inside them, are like much larger versions of Gleann's own little Holy Well ringfort at Doon. This scholar gives the example of 'the majestic fort of Dún Dalgain, Cúchulainn's residence, a mile west of the present town of Dundalk'. [77]

Back home in Gleann, our old folklore manuscripts tell the story of a day when Fionn and his right-hand man, Diarmuid, were on a boar-hunt that led them to *Suígh Finn*, the high point of our own Nagle Mountains. [78] When listening to these stories that we heard so casually as children, it is worth pausing to realise that we are hearing our local ancestors' voices coming down to us from the third century AD!

In this particular Crow Glen story, Fionn stopped to rest and get an overview of the terrain, thus forever giving the place its name of *Suígh Finn* or Fionn's Seat. However, this would be no ordinary boar-hunt. It had once been prophesied by a druid that the handsome, charismatic young Diarmuid would one day die from a boar-wound. And the ancestors round Gleann an Phréacháin used to tell that he was indeed wounded by the boar on this particular hunt near Gleann. Fionn went three times to get water from a healing spring nearby, which would have saved Diarmuid. But each time, before Fionn reached him, the water had trickled away through Fionn's fingers.

77  P.W. Joyce, *A Smaller Social History of Ancient Ireland*, Longmans, Green & Company, 1908
78  Ó Duinnshléibhe, as in Note 32

There's much more to this story than meets the eye. A sly meaning is hidden behind it, suggesting that if a person feels betrayed, they may wait a long time for their revenge, even if they seem to have forgotten about it. Those listening would have known the story of the previous adventures of these two hunting buddies. They included a long episode where Diarmuid had eloped with Fionn's fiancée, Gráinne, the daughter of the king of Ireland. It wasn't Diarmuid's fault: like so many women, she fell for the beautiful Diarmuid the moment she saw him. And she put a love-spell on him that *obliged* him to run away with her.

One whole earlier part of the Fionn Mac Cumhaill sagas is about Diarmuid and Gráinne's flight, hiding out in the hills, pursued by Fionn's men who eventually caught up with them and brought Gráinne back. On the surface, the matter had been sorted, but this story set in the Nagle Mountains shows that deep down, Fionn still felt some rancour about it much later. Before he made his third trip to the spring for the saving water, the dying Diarmuid begged him to just hold his hands tighter together. But for the third time, Fionn let the water trickle away between his fingers before reaching his friend. With typical Irish ambiguity, the Crow Glen version of the story doesn't quite spell out that Fionn did it deliberately. It leaves it to the teller to decide how to present the matter, or to the listener to mull it over for themselves.

When I first heard the Fionn Mac Cuhmaill sagas at school as a four-year-old girl, I was in no doubt about which bit interested me. Fionn was a big rough guy who was all about hunting, fighting, athletic feats and lots of manly shouting and running about. He didn't appeal to me at all. But our picture-books showed that the young Diarmuid was indeed, as the story told, extremely handsome and pretty. Above all, he had '*long blue-black hair*' which seemed truly irresistible. The pictures showed Diarmuid and Gráinne lying about romantically on the heather in their hideaway in the hills, eating wild blueberries that were the colour of Diarmuid's long locks. I knew only one place like that - the Nagle Mountains where my family went walking and picking wild blueberries whenever the weather was fine on a Sunday. As a tiny child I just assumed that that's where Diarmuid and Gráinne had gone together.

It was only while researching this book that I discovered that the locals around Gleann an Phréacháin in the first millennium AD had the same idea. They too had taken the national saga and situated it locally into their own landscape. According to their tradition, Diarmuid didn't just die *somewhere* around Ireland on a boar-hunt: it happened right here on our Nagle Mountains!

That may not be quite as far-fetched as it sounds. In 2017, a Celtic Studies academic published a book claiming to have found archaeological evidence that the actual grave of Diarmuid is in a place called Murragh near Bandon, about 30 miles south-west of Crow Glen. It claims that the Fianna warrior is buried in an ancient 'tumulus' or above-ground burial chamber, which has indeed been dated by the National Monument Service to the second or third century AD. [79]

*The Cork Examiner* quotes the authors of the study: 'We know that Diarmuid's tribe was from the West Munster area, which would probably have included West Cork... We also know that West Cork was a popular recruiting and training ground for the Fianna... We believe it very likely that his body was buried among his own people in West Cork.' [80] An expert on Ireland of the early centuries AD agrees that 'there is a strong possibility that the tumulus at Murragh is the burial site of Diarmuid'. [81]

In Gleann both my father and my younger brother, John and Patrick Buckley, have always been passionate about the Nagle Mountains, spending every spare minute of their lives exploring them. Each in turn, with a beloved dog, has been drawn to the place as if by a magnet. It has always sucked them out of their house in the Village, away from the womenfolk, heading north in beat-up trucks or on cross-country motorbikes, up past the Mass Rock, past Chimneyfield School and out at last onto the open mountain terrain that's called 'The Commons' where they can breathe easy, inhaling the scent of heather, peat and pine needles. Proper *Fionn Mac Cumhaill* air.

Patrick's hauntingly beautiful photography of the forests, streams, forgotten pathways and hidden places up there is probably the most extensive visual documentation there is of the Nagle Mountains.

I have always felt grateful that when I first went to school in the Village in 1970, Irish primary schools - at least in the countryside - had a policy of spending the first few months reading all the old Irish myths and legends to the children, before starting them on the tough task of learning to read

---

79  Ailín Quinlan, 'Burial site of legendary Diarmuid found, says historian', *The Cork Examiner*, 10-7-2017. The book is *Murragh; A Place of Graves*, Ballineen & Enniskeane Area Heritage Group, 2017.
80  *The Cork Examiner*, 'Is Fionn MacCumhail's wingman buried in West Cork?', 10-9-2015.
81  Daragh Smyth, *A Guide to Irish Mythology and Cú Chulainn, An Iron Age Hero*, Irish Academic Press, 2005

and write. Throughout the majority of human history, children have taken in complex oral sagas like this that were told to them without any need for writing. This first, archetypal layer of a child's mind was populated for us aged four or five by our Village scoolteacher reading to us the stories of Diarmuid and Gráinne eloping to the mountains. Oisín returning from Tír na nÓg. The Children of Lir being turned into swans to protect them. The boy Setanta excelling at hurling and becoming the national hero Cúchulainn. The young Fionn tasting the forbidden Salmon of Knowledge while cooking it for his druid teacher on the bank of a river...

At that time, I just assumed that all those events had happened around *our* locality, because I had no idea yet that there was a bigger world out there with lots of other places in it. Every Sunday for dinner we had salmon that my father or younger brother had caught in the Blackwater River. I saw the big fish coming into the house in a canvas fishing bag, and I saw my mother carefully cleaning it and cooking it for us. So the scene of young Fionn cooking a salmon for his teacher - and accidentally tasting the forbidden juice when he sucked on his burnt finger - made total sense to me. It seemed familiar, everyday, local stuff that could happen to anyone.

At age 4, I was too young yet to follow TV programmes, and we hadn't yet started to learn the religion, with all its divine characters and stories. So those Irish myths and legends were the very first layer of human information that was put into my mind from outside my home. I can still feel to this day that that those stories - like furniture coming into a new house - were the first material that went into the first layer of my imagination, with all other layers of information only going down on top of them later. Having spent my career working with writing, stories, narratives, conversation and dialogue, I feel those oral sagas gave me a wonderful start in that direction. [82] As we couldn't read yet, we four-year-olds received them entirely orally, exactly as our ancestors would have done 1,600 years before.

Along with mythology, story-telling and religion, the other activity that really animated Gleann's culture, traditionally as well as today, was sport. As a child in Gleann I had seen there a great deal of hurling, Gaelic football, hand-ball, road bowling, horse racing and cart-racing, as well as fishing and hunting competitions. Locals' accounts of memorable athletes and their great feats also pepper Gleann's old folklore records, especially

---

82  My work records present-day oral histories in order to listen to communities telling their own views and insights; I then work with local authorities to apply those insights in practical ways that help solve real-world problems in politics and society.

in athletics, hurling or Gaelic football. With one of these sporting battles that's recounted in the archives, it's hard to tell whether it's from the legendary realm of Fionn Mac Cumhaill, or whether it was an actual event.

The folklorist tells how the players of Ballyhooly, a village at the northern rim of the Nagle Mountains, played the Glean an Phréacháin men in a type of challenge that he calls 'Cross-Country Hurling'. The ball was thrown in at a mid-point between the two villages, and the match involved driving the other team back as far as possible towards their own village. The *sliotar* (the traditional leather hurling ball, in Irish) was driven back and forward for a while between the two territories before Ballyhooly finally got the upper hand and drove the Gleann lads back nearly all the way to Gleann village.

As a sporting version of clashes between warring clans, that version of the game sounds very ancient. It also sounds a lot like the oral legends about the great hero Cúchulainn. When he was still just the boy known as Setanta, he left his home to travel the long distance cross-country to the court of the king of Ireland, hitting his *sliotar* ahead in front of him all the way and running on to catch it. While researching this book, I learned that a similar kind of long-distance hurling called '*Poc Fada*' (the 'Long Shot') is being revived today around Ireland. Like a faster, wilder version of golf, today's *Poc Fada* championships require contestants to cover a set course of over three miles with the fewest shots possible of their *sliotar*.

As one archaeologist puts it, 'hurling is arguably the fastest field sport in the world, and quite possibly the oldest'. Cúchulainn's hurling feats date back to the oral sagas of the third century AD, but this archaeologist points out that a famous account of Ireland's Tuatha Dé Dannan warriors playing a bloody hurling match is set in the *eleventh century BC* ! He explains that hurling was an integral part of early Ireland's warrior culture: 'such stories often portray hurling as a form of martial training, and proficiency on the hurling field was equated with skill in battle'. [83]  Today, the Gaelic Athletic Association or GAA that runs the sport is considered the 'biggest amateur sporting association in the world with over 2,500 clubs, with over 800 outside of Ireland'. [84]

But here too, if we dig even deeper in the archival records, we find that both the history of hurling - and of Bards composing poems celebrating

---

83   Colm Moriarty, 'Hurling: Its Ancient History', *Irish Archaeology*, 3-9-2011
84   Rebel Óg Coaching, 'The History of Hurling', Páirc Uí Chaoimh, Cork, available at www.rebelogcoaching.com

feuds about hurling - come right down home into the very fields of Gleann an Phréacháin. Records show that 'the game was flourishing in the area' in 1741, when the Crow Glen townland of Glenagoul hosted the first ever inter-county match between Cork and Tipperary! Today 'the actual field of play on the roadside in Glenagoul is still pointed out' and Bride Rovers GAA Club visit it to celebrate their history there. [85]

This match in 1741 became famous and was recorded in verse by the Bards because the result was disputed. This dispute was fought out - in the Irish language of the time, of course - across a pair of renowned feud-poems composed by the Bards of each side. Present-day historians of the local Bride Rovers GAA club at Rathcormac explain that 'a Bard from Tipperary, who had obviously accompanied his team to Glenagoul, put it about and boasted that they had won. This was denied by the Cork side and Seán Ó Murchú na Raithíneach - one of the Gaelic poets of [neighbouring] Carrignavar - put down in verse a rebuke to the Tipperary poem'. The Bride Rovers Club give this extract from it, nicely translated into English by local Rathcormac historian Tom Barry. (Note that there were a lot of players called Barry on the Cork team.)

'Twas improper of the Northern party
to boast their feats in lasting poetry.
Whatever result they bandied about,
'twas the Barrys won without a doubt.

Mistaken was the team that came
loudly boasting of their hurling fame
in the fearsome gap of Glenagoul
to find that we instead prevail.

Before McAdam, leader of the district,
and every noble at the conflict,
with skill we wrung the match ahead
to leave your verses lame and dead.

This winning band, not easily swept away,
this fighting band, untiring in the fray,

85 *Bride Rovers GAA Club*, 'The Early Years'; verses translated by Tom Barry, available at www.briderovers.ie/contentPage/203813/early_years

this band able open any lock
beware these men from Ballinagloch! [86]

The Nagle Mountains north of Crow Glen may look relatively wild now. But in fact, a poetry collection of national renown came from a sophisticated Bardic School in the Nagle Mountains in the fourteenth and fifteenth centuries. This poetry book is named for the nearby town of Fermoy at the eastern end of the Nagles. As scholars put it, 'the *Book of Fermoy* contains 30 syllabic poems attributed to Gearóid Iarla Mac Gearailt'. Living from 1338 to 1398, he is 'the earliest recorded writer of courtly love lyrics in Irish'. [87]

Another historian explains that Mac Gearailt, a professional writer around the Nagles and Blackwater area, was bilingual in French and Irish. As one scholar puts it: 'Acquainted with both the French tradition of *amour courtois* and the Irish tradition of Bardic poetry, authors like Gearóid Iarla were admirably placed for introducing courtly love into Irish verse'. [88]

Amazingly, the original manuscript book of those poems composed in the fourteenth century around the Nagle Mountains and the Blackwater Valley in beautiful Gaelic calligraphy can still be viewed by anyone today, on the website of the Royal Irish Academy. As was typical of this new 'courtly love' style, the Royal Academy points out that 'among the features of (the Fermoy poems) is the involvement of women as literary patrons and as the subjects of poems'. [89]

Originating in France and spreading around Europe, this poetry style called *courtly love* shifted away from earlier poems that focused only on the fierce, *macho* values of warfare and warriors. Instead, courtly love poems now gave new attention to gentler themes like love, beauty, soulfulness and a dialogue with women. These earliest Irish courtly poems by Gearóid Iarla were composed 'mainly for members of the Roche family of Castletownroche', whose lands, perched over the Blackwater River, interwove with those of the Nagles to the north of Gleann an Phréacháin. [90] (The *Avondhu Blackwater Partnership*, the community development agency

---

86   Bride Rovers, as in Note 85
87   Angela Bourke, as in Note 75
88   John Koch, *The Celts: History, Life and Culture*, Vol 1, ABC-Clio, Oxford, 2012
89   Royal Irish Academy, 'Cultural Artefacts from Sixteenth-Century Ireland' at
www.ria.ie/another-view-gaelic-manuscript-culture-edmund-spensers-ireland and *The Book of Fermoy*, RIA MS 23 E 29 (Cat. no. 1134) at www.ria.ie/another-view-gaelic-manuscript-culture-edmund-spensers-ireland
90   Angela Bourke, as in Note 75

who were partners in producing this book that is in your hands, have their headquarters today in the beautifully restored old mill of Castletownroche.)

Gearóid, clearly a feminist before his time, was a keen and early practitioner of this courtly love approach imported from the French language, which he spoke like a native Frenchman. One of his most famous poems, composed around 1370, is 'Speak Not Ill of Womankind':

Speak not ill of womankind,
it's no wisdom if you do.
You that fault in women find,
I would not be praising you.

Sweetly speaking, witty and clear,
a tribe most lovely to my mind,
blame on them I hate to hear.
Speak not ill of womankind.

Bloody treason, murderous act,
it's not by women they're designed,
nor bells o'erthrown nor church ransacked.
Oh, speak not ill of womankind.

Bishop or king upon his throne,
great leaders who can free or bind,
they're sprung from women, every one!
Oh, speak not ill of womankind. [91]

At the back of this book you can see the original Irish versions of all the local Bardic verses quoted in this chapter. Even when we don't understand them, it is worth casting our eye over those native words that sprung up directly out of Gleann an Phreachain's own soil - and had been springing from it for thousands of years until English replaced them only in the mid-nineteenth century.

That replacement of the local language is very recent, really, compared to the millennia of Crow Glen history that we are overviewing in this book. Irish was spoken and written in Gleann for thousands of years, and

---

91 'Speak Not Ill of Womankind', translated by U. Cronin at *Get behind the Muse,* available at https://ucronin.wordpress.com/2017/09/17/gearoid-iarla-and-ennis

English has been there for only about 170 years. It's just the same length of time between when the Carneys took the coffin ship in 1847, and their descendants came back on the silver bus in 2017. Even if we don't know the language now, most of us can recognise a word of it here and there. And like precious pieces of archaeology or old tools, those words are our birthright, our heritage. They still lie all around us in Gleann's placenames, like crusty jewels hidden just under the rich black soil. By reading now these verses of our own ancient local Bards, we enable their voices to get back up again from under that soil and be heard once more, sounding out in the bright light of day.

Through a well-aimed blow from the Penal Laws, our Bards in Gleann, the Blackwater Valley and the Nagle Mountains were hit so hard that scholars call that moment 'the collapse of the Gaelic world'. [92] The British would no longer tolerate the robust Gaelic culture and learning fostered by the remaining Irish clans. As we know, in 1649 Cromwell was sent to invade Ireland and 're-conquer it for the British', this time banning the native Irish from owning land, receiving a Gaelic education or practicing their Catholicism.

The Penal Laws that outlawed Catholicism also struck deliberately at the Bardic School system. [93] By 1695, all forms of education for Catholics were illegal. As intended, this put an end to the Irish Bardic Schools. But holding out a full century against the mighty Penal Laws, the Nagle family secretly maintained their Gaelic culture, language and learning at their home in Killavullen to the north of Gleann. For instance, scholars have demonstrated that as late as 'in the 1760s, the last great Gaelic poet of eighteenth-century Ireland, Eoghan Rua O Súilleabháin (1748-1784), was tutor to the Annakissy Nagles' there. [94]

Nicknamed Eoghan an Bhéil Bhinn ('Eoghan of the Sweet Mouth'), this Bard who worked in the Nagle Mountains was reknowned for his 'fluency and learning in Gaelic, English, Latin and Greek'. [95] He was a lively character who travelled and worked all over Munster. But as one of his biographers puts it, he 'lived at the worst time in history for an Irish poet, when the Penal Laws were killing the ancient way of life and Catholics had

92 Michelle O' Riordan, *The Gaelic Mind and the Collapse of the Gaelic World*, Cork University Press, 1990
93 Michelle O' Riordan, as in Note 92
94 Katherine O' Donnell, as in Note 76
95 Pádraig Ó Cearúill, 'Eoghán Rua Ó Suilleabháin: A True Exponent of the Bardic Legacy' in *Proceedings of the Barra Ó Donnabháin Symposium*, New York University, 2007

no legal way to make a professional living'. [96]  Describing having to move from place to place to find work as a writer or poet, one of Eoghan Rua's poems describes his status as a dangerous outsider:

> When I visit a village as others do
> in hostile mood my ways they view.
> The gossip-women have something new:
> *Oh, whence? Who is he? From where has he been removed?* [97]

On the internet, you can watch Seán Garvey, an All-Ireland champion of the *sean-nós* song tradition, singing this verse and the rest of this poem in the original Irish. [98]  Eoghan Rua's life - adventurous but not easy - ended at just 36 after a brawl. People he had satirised in a poem hit him over the head with a fire-iron, and he died from the injury a few days later. He is said to have been writing a poem in his sick-bed when he died, but he had completed only these two famous lines of it, which were carved on his early gravestone. They reflect the demise of the Bards under the Penal Laws, as well as Eoghan Rua's own demise:

> See here a weakened poet,
> feeble now the pen has fallen from his hand... [99]

Eoghan Rua's patrons, the Nagle family, insisted upon education for their daughters as well as for their sons. Around 1735, they smuggled their daughter Honora abroad to France for further education there. Under the Penal Laws it was illegal and hence dangerous to send Irish Catholic youth abroad for schooling. [100]  But Honora (nicknamed Nano by her doting father) and her sister got to enjoy Parisian high society alongside their

---

96  George Petrie (ed.), *The Petrie Collection of the Ancient Music of Ireland,* Gill, Dublin, 1855
97  Séamas Ó Domhnaill, 'Eoghan Ruadh Ó Súilleabháin: Aspects of his Life and Work' in *Church and State, Fourth Quarter, Lux Occulta* website, 2010
98  Seán Garvey sings Eoghan Rua's 'Slán le Máigh' on Trad TG4 TV, 26-8-2017, available at www.youtube.com/watch?reload=9&v=JliwjO90EjI; also gives the original lyrics in Irish
99  'Sin é file go fann, Nuair thuiteann an peann as a láimh…'; translated by Marella Hoffman
100  The eighteenth-century Nagle homestead has been renovated as an attractive Catholic retreat centre with a programme of ecological activities, set on its own organic farm. Visit www.nanonaglebirthplace.ie

studies. In 1758, the *Cork Evening Post* described one of her sisters, Elizabeth, as 'an agreeable lady with a fortune of £12,000'. [101]

But it was the sudden deaths of her beloved parents and a sister that brought the young socialite Nano to a spiritual epiphany. She returned home and devoted the rest of her life to assisting and illegally educating the Irish Catholic poor, and girls in particular. By her late twenties, she was running six illegal schools for poor Catholic children in Cork city - two for boys and four for girls. As one reporter recently put it, 'once voted Ireland's greatest ever woman…, a case could be made for Nano Nagle as the most influential person in (Irish) education of the past three centuries'. [102]

It was a similarly painful bereavement that secured centuries of fame for Gleann an Phréacháin poet Eoghan Ó Caoimh, whom we met at the start of this chapter. His wife, Eleanor Nagle (a relative of Nano's), died in 1707 after twenty-seven years of marriage. Ó Caoimh was distraught, and the heart-wrenching lament that he wrote for her has become his most famous work. I am no expert in high-brow medieval Irish but having written a PhD thesis on poetry, I can see that in the original Irish, this lament by Ó Caoimh of Gleann an Phréacháin is a poem of extreme beauty and complex language, equal to any of the world's great poetry, ancient or modern. [103] As a love poem, it is of course a fine example of the 'courtly love' tradition that the Nagle and Crow Glen Bards so keenly imported from France. It addresses his wife as his intelligent equal, a 'friend or ally' with 'flawless speech'.

This book in your hands is a meeting place of many voices. So although Eoghan's voice here is a sad one, why would we not listen here to the golden lament of this famous son of Gleann an Phréacháin, and restore

---

101 *Blake of Ballyglunin Papers, 1770-1830*, Archive ref. IE JHL/LE007, Archives of National University of Ireland Galway

102 *The Irish Independent*, 'Nano Nagle remains an influential educator', 29-4-2009. Pope Francis recognised Nano as 'Venerable' in 2013. But she will have to produce two Church-recognised miracles before she can be canonised a saint. Patsy McGarry, 'Cork-born founder of Presentation Sisters declared 'Venerable'', *The Irish Times*, 1-11-2013.

103 It is known in Irish by its first line, 'Mo chás cumha, mo chumhgach, mo chogadh, mo chreach'. Deane, Bourke & Carpenter (eds.), *The Field Day Anthology of Irish Writing*, Vol 4, Cork University Press, 2002

him to the Village memory where he belongs? At the beginning of his own handwritten manuscript of this poem, he added a note apologising that it's not in the elaborate rhyming form that the Bards usually used. He says he had to use plainer speech to cry for her 'since I feel her loss so grievously and am bereft without her':

Oh source of my ruin, root of my grief, ground of my woe -
that fatal day, thief of my joy! How my eyes flow
for my girl who died this day and lies below,
buried in Brosna, while I break down in cries.

Your blue eyes drowned in clay.
Your sighs of love
gone from me.
Your flawless speech, your cries,

Your foam-white breast,
extinct under stone.
And I am mute, marooned,
without friends or allies.

Stifled in clay you, my eternal love,
who never ignored or forgot the poor,
since I will not see your face again, not ever,
may God on the last day open to you his door.

And may the blackest loathing of the hatred of the whole region
afflict *you* - shrivelled Death!
You importunate wretch who scythes down the living in legions,
You took my wife and left me desolate, unfortunate.

We saw that due to the Penal Laws outlawing education for the native Irish, the Gaelic clans of the time used to send their children to France for further education. Eoghan had duly sent his beloved son Arthur there to train to be a priest. And when Arthur died in France just a month after getting there, this second loss caused Eoghan to give up worldly life completely and himself become a parish priest in neighbouring Doneraile until his death in 1726.

In the Bardic tradition, a person's moments and messages of greatest meaning were always expressed through poetry, not through ordinary language, at times when normal words just didn't feel powerful enough. So when his son died, the heartbroken Eoghan let his own best friend know what had happened by sending him the message in verse. The friend, one William McCurtin in nearby Whitechurch, acknowledged and replied to the message in verse with a eulogy for Arthur, expressing in poetry his sympathy and horror at the young man's early death. [104]

We saw that under the Penal Laws, the Irish had moved their Masses to secret places outdoors. In the countryside they also moved their secret schools to concealed, mobile outdoor spaces where teacher and pupils could quickly disband if at risk of being spotted by the English authorities. These so-called 'hedge schools' originally took place in barns and sheds, and the young Honora Nagle attended one in the Nagle Mountains before moving on to her further schooling in France. But as the Irish clans got poorer and weaker over the ensuing century, the schools moved fully outdoors to meet only in groves, under trees and beside hedges, thus truly earning the name 'hedge schools'.

As one scholar puts it, 'the medieval bardic schools deteriorated into hedge schools', though the latter 'continued to flourish, reaching a peak in the 1820s'. [105] When I was a child, we were familiar with the nineteenth-century drawings of barefoot, ragged hedge-school 'teachers' who looked to us like homeless people, with what looked like street-urchins sitting at their feet. Those teachers were sustained by the few pennies that local native farmers could give to ensure their children would receive at least some basic level of instruction.

# The calligrapher of Chimneyfield

Chimneyfield School sits atop the northern slope of the Bride River Valley. Until classes were moved into the Village in the 1960s, the school had served children from the Valley and all over the mountainous Nagle area that stretches away from it to the north.[106] With what we now know about the Bardic School of the Nagle Mountains, we realise that that old

---

104 'Eoghan O'Keeffe, 1656-1726', *O'Keeffe Clan Gathering and Rally*, 2016, available at http://okeeffeclans.com/fathereoghanokeeffe.html
105 Diarmuid Mac Giolla Chríost, *The Irish Language in Ireland: From Goídel to Globalisation*, Routledge, London, 2004
106 In 1968 this school was moved to a modern building in the Village where we were taught by Batt Dunlea, the son of this Chimneyfield teacher Seán Ó Duinnshléibhe.

stone building backs onto what had been a terrain of teaching and learning for centuries.

It was up there in the late 1920s that the last of centuries of those teachers, Seán Ó Duinnshléibhe, sat at his desk, writing out in his beautiful Gaelic calligraphy the 234 pages of folklore that he collected from the farms and townlands around him, and later donated to the National Folklore Collection in Dublin. [107] Some of his document is in Irish, some in English, but all is in the same elegant, hand-drawn calligraphy.

In it, he describes the hedge school that existed in Chimneyfield before his own school was built there in 1833. He explains that it was 'taught by O' Leary who lived in a small house in Bunaglanna', perched on the north slope of the Bride Valley. Ó Duinnshléibhe himself saw the outlines of O' Leary's 'house' on the ground there. Testifying to the poverty of hedge-school teachers, he says it measured just '10 feet by 8 feet', or about 6.5 square metres, like a small garden shed or a big cupboard.

By the mid-nineteenth century, the native Irish language was being eroded in North Cork. [108] The area was so fertile, and the produce so exportable through Cork harbour, that it had long been an intense focus of British occupation and anglicisation (whereas in parts of West Cork where the land is barren, Irish is still spoken to this day). But Ó Duinnshléibhe records that when his Chimneyfield School was founded in 1833, 'Irish was the spoken language' and the local 'pupils were illiterate as far as English was concerned'.

One of the purposes of these so-called 'National Schools' established all over Ireland in the 1830s by the English authorities was to formally suppress the Irish language, educating the natives to become English-speakers. Ó Duinnshléibhe details the physical punishments that methodically stopped the children speaking any Irish words during the school day.

---

107  Seán Ó Duinnshléibhe, *Gleann an Phréacháin - Béaloideas,* as in Note 32. In the 1930s the Irish government completed this massive collection of folklore gathered from all over the country. Over a million pages long, it sits in the archives of University College Dublin, where I spent many a happy afternoon reading the books of it on Gleann an Phréacháin.
108  Mac Giolla Chríost explains that Britain's Ordinance Survey mapping of Ireland (1825-1841) was done primarily to ensure maximum efficiency in collecting taxes from Irish tenant farmers. But he points out that it also struck a definitive blow against the Irish language by anglicising the country's placenames. It's no coincidence that this anglicising of Irish placenames occurred at the same time as the creation of 'National Schools' to eliminate Irish-speaking among the young.

He explains that by 1898, just 65 years later, Irish was allowed to be taught in Chimneyfield School again. But he laments that the formal suppression of it through the 'National Schools' had been so dismally successful that when it was legalised again in Chimneyfield School in 1898, it had to be relearned from scratch as a second language! Nonetheless, a census in 1891 records that there were still no fewer than 'six hedge schools' in the parish around Gleann an Phréacháin. [109]

Ó Duinnshléibhe introduces, explains and signs his manuscript in Irish, sounding as if that were his 'home position'. Some of the oldest mountain people whose interviews he transcribes gave him their evidence in their native Irish. He includes lots of effortless English too, being bilingual like all country teachers of his time. But you can see by a shift in his handwriting that the passages in Irish are where he feels more free-flowing, enthusiastic and authoritative.

Part of that first generation of teachers who represented the values of the new Irish Republic, he enthusiastically records a whole glossary of quaint terms in Irish that had been very local to, or perhaps even exclusive to, Gleann an Phréacháin when Irish was the native language there until near the middle of the nineteenth century. My own favourite is '*básachan*', apparently the term for 'a death-like youth' - not an expression you'd expect to use often. And, no doubt in more common usage, to be '*ag raimseál*' meant to be 'ramming potatoes in a tub with a stick'.

More importantly, he also points out the crucial layers of local meaning and heritage that were lost when the English forcibly anglicised all the placenames of the Irish countryside. Without stepping outside his door, Seán can give the immediate example of his school's location, 'Chimneyfield'. He shows how it's a typical anglicisation that drains away the meaning out of the placename. He explains that there have never been any significant 'chimneys' in the area. Rather, the placename in Irish was '*Páirc na Seimhne*' meaning 'Field of the Bulrushes'. 'Seimhne' was anglicised as 'chimney' just because the English reckoned the word looked like the English word 'chimney'!

Seán's manuscript makes a start at restoring for us this rich blanket of meanings that lie embedded in the ground all over the parish of Gleann an Phréacháin, hidden in the original names of our townlands. It is a rewarding task that we can now carry forward today. From Baile na

---

109 The registers of the English named Crow Glen at that time as being within a larger parish called Ardnageehy. *Lewis's topographical Dictionary of Ireland, 1837*

gCloch (Townland of the Stones, or Stone Buildings) to Inse na nEach (the Water-Meadow of the Horses), from Árd na Gaoithe (Windy Height) to Tuar Garbh (The Rough Pasture), he started reconstructing this map of knowledge that our ancestors stored in the land when they individually named every single little field, not just townlands! As an example, Seán gives the range of rich Irish names for every single *field* on one farm, to show how densely this carpet of micro-naming lies across our parish. I hope that the community will be able to record and translate all our Crow Glen placenames before they are lost entirely.

Meanwhile, let's take a walk around some of those townlands. We can take the current placenames, trace them back to their original meaning in Irish, and as we walk, the landscape itself will talk back to us, revealing its original meanings and messages about how people lived in it. For instance at *Lyre* - meaning **Ladhar** or Fork in Irish - we will indeed meet a fork in the road. And at *Lyravarrig* (real name in Irish **Ladhar an Bharraigh**, or Barry's Fork), there is a fork in the little riverbed there.

But my own personal favourite by far is the place that we still today call *Lyrenamon*. Its real name in Irish is **Ladhar na mBan**, meaning **The Women's Fork in the Road**. The earliest written record of it shows it was already called that in 1699 - but who knows for how many centuries before that? [110] Oh, how we would love to know what those ladies of Lyrenamon used to talk about - in their native Irish, of course - when they gathered there after the day's work was done!

At Mullanabowree - real name **Muileann na Buaraí**, The Mill of the Cattle - you will come across a rushing stream tumbling down a slope with an old building against the bottom of the river-course. Presumably this is where the old watermill captured the falling water. The familiar placename *Ardarou*, less than a mile north of the Village, is especially interesting too. The records say that Ardarou in Irish is **Árd an Rabhaidh**, meaning The Height with the Fire-Beacon, or Warning-Signal.

As the first high point between the Bride River Valley below and the Nagle Mountains to the north, it would have been an ideal spot for a warning beacon - which in previous centuries would of course have had to be an actual fire lit as a recognised message of warning. It seems logical to assume that that practice dated back to when organised defences were

---

110   In 'Abstracts of The Conveyances from the Trustees of the Forfeited Estates and Interests in Ireland in 1688', *Fifteenth Annual Report from the Commissioners of Public Records of Ireland*, London, 1825

needed against warring and raiding clans, which would have been in the first millennium AD. But in the next two chapters, we will see how Ardarou - at the Hegarty homestead up there - again became a strategic point for locals passing secret military signals to each other, just a hundred years ago. [111]

As a community, we could map out some interesting walks or tours through our whole local landscape as it speaks to us like this in its native Irish. We don't have to be Irish speakers to do it. An *Ordinance Survey* map, the online *Placenames Database* given in the footnotes below, and an Irish-language dictionary are enough to get the landscape talking to you again as you walk it step by step. Overleaf are my own first efforts at listening to Gleann's placenames in this way. I've retrieved the original Irish spellings, given their meanings in English, and positioned them approximately onto a map of the locality. There are lots more local placenames waiting for this sort of attention.

---

111 I retrieved these Irish-language placenames from the 'Glossary and Distribution Maps' of the excellent *Placenames Database of Ireland*, available at www.logainm.ie  The recent book *Thirty-Two Words for Field: Lost Words of the Irish Landscape* (Gill, 2020) by Manchán Mangan is a great inspiration for this kind of listening to your own local landscape.

Ardarou, **Árd an Rabhaidh**, Height with Fire-Beacon or Warning-signal

Ardnageeha, **Árd na Gaoithe**, Windy Height

Ballinamadree, **Baile na Madraí**, Townland of the Dogs

Ballinagloch, **Baile na gCloch**, Townland of the Stones or Stone Buildings

Ballybrack, **Baile Breac**, The Speckled Townland

Ballynabortagh, **Baile na bPortaigh**, Townland of the Turf-Bogs

Beenaskeha, **Binn na Scéithe**, The Peak of the Hawthorns

Bridestown, **Baile na Bríde**, Townland of the River Bride

Bunaglanna, **Bun an Ghleanna**, End of the Valley

Cumar, **Cumar na Sagairt**, Ravine of the Priests

Coolea, **Cuaille**, The Marking-Post

Coome, **Com**, The Hollows

Doon, **Dún**, The Ringfort

Glannasock, **Gleann na Sac**, Glen of the Sacks (eg. of oats)

Glashaboy, **Glas Buí**, The Yellow Stream

Glenagoul, **Gleann an Ghaill**, Glen of the Standing-Stone, or of the Foreigner

Graigue, **Ghráig**, The Village or Hamlet

Inshannach, **Inse na nEach**, The Horses' Water-Meadow

Keame, **Céim**, The Stepping-Stone

Kildinan, **Cill Daighnín**, The Church of Daighnín

Killuntin, **Cill Fhiontain**, Fintan's Church

Knocknacaheragh, **Cnoc na Cathrach**, City Hill

Knoppogue, **Chnapóg**, The Little Rise in the Ground

Lackendarragh, **Leacain Darach**, The Hillside of the Oaks

Lyravarrig, **Ladhar an Bharraigh**, Barry's Fork in the River

Lyre, **Ladhar**, The Fork in the Road

Lyrenamon, **Ladhar na mBan**, The Women's Fork in the Road

Mullanabowree, **Muileann na Buaraí**, The Mill of the Cattle (or Mill where cattle were scoured by vets)

Tooreen, **Tuairín**, The Small Pasture

Toorgariffe, **Tuar Garbh**, The Rough Pasture

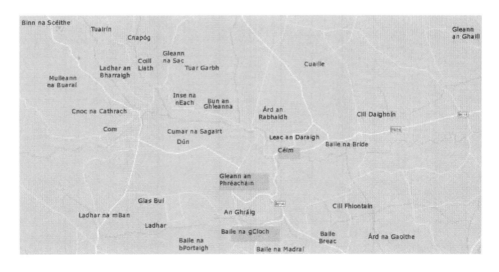

192

Looking out from his own schoolhouse, Ó Duinnshléibhe was well aware of the centuries of name-making and Bardic culture embedded in the wild-looking area stretching away from him to the north, as well as in the fertile Bride River Valley and around the village of Gleann an Phréacháin to the south. In his folklore records, it's clear that composing songs and poems remained a routine tradition among ordinary farming people in the area throughout the eighteenth and nineteenth centuries. His manuscript is studded with a range of songs and poems composed, performed and passed back and forth by the ordinary people of the Nagle Mountains, Bride Valley and Crow Glen areas.

In fact, his manuscript shows that the medieval tradition of composing songs and poetry still thrived among ordinary local people right into the early twentieth century. For instance, he puts into writing, probably for the first time, the song of praise below for the River Bride. It was performed for Ó Duinnshléibhe in the 1920s by 14-year-old John Glavin from the Gleann townland of Inshannach, who had learned it from his father, William Glavin, born there around 1860.

The fact that this song closes by describing Ireland as 'yonder green isle' and bidding 'farewell' to Gleann suggests that it was composed by emigrants looking back in memory at the Bride River, from their far-off exile. As an emotional connection between emigrants and those who had stayed at home, such emigrant songs - composed in places like New York, Liverpool or Newfoundland - often travelled back to the home-place to be performed there by neighbours who had never left home at all, as was the case with John and Willie Glavin of Inshannach:

All you that are prone to sport and to pleasure
come roam by the sweet Bride's side.
'Tis there you'll be amused by the youths when collected,
no grief there to trouble their minds.

Where the pipers and fiddlers with pleasure do play
and the songbirds do tune their sweet notes on each tree,
joining in chorus in praises all day
of the lovely sweet banks of the Bride.

'Tis down by charming Glenville and Pete Driscoll's inn
the waters do gently glide,
where numbers in coaches cross over Keame Bridge

with a sporting laugh and a smile,

Where the trout and the salmon do jump with joy
and the long-snouted otters do gently dive,
the flat fish and eel no closer can lie
by the lovely sweet banks of the Bride.

Where the hare is on his seat, and the rabbit in his burrow,
the fox well secured with his den well covered.
The ducks wild and tame in the streams they do flutter
by the lovely sweet banks of the Bride.

Where the water glides is a fine situation,
its equals are scarce to be found,
there's a wholesome air and the plains, they are bounded
all spangled with sweet scented flowers.

Farwell, charming Glenville, I never can forget thee,
where my forefathers lived at their ease,
and the Hon Sir Edward Kinahan, he lived in great splendour,
may his offspring be always the same.

There is a spring well in yonder green isle
It cures the lame, the dumb and the blind.
They have forgotten their crutches and left them behind
by the lovely sweet banks of the Bride.

Ó Duinnshléibhe's folklore manuscript gives another interesting example of how locals in Gleann, like amateur bards, composed spontaneous songs among themselves for all sorts of occasions. In the medieval Bardic tradition, bards were feared as well as respected because - a bit like the media today - they could either make or break a clan's reputation, with a satirical song or a song of praise. The Crow Glen song below was composed in 1890 by an ordinary local person, to strike a satirical blow during a feud with a neighbour over land.

Ó Duinnshléibhe explains that a certain Davy Power, back in the wild, mountainous Crow Glen townland of Tourgarriffe, used to spend much of his time away in Dublin. Certain poorer locals trespassed on his land, using it to grow food or pasture animals in his absence, and he took them to court over it or 'summoned' them, as the expression went at the time.

The trespassers may not have had the money to fight back in the courts, but in the following verses they took considerable revenge through poetry! (To help guide you through them, note that in Irish a *banbh* is a piglet and a *leanbh* is a child.)

Oh, Davy Power is in law with his neighbours.
That same is not a bad plan.
But he's gone to the devil, be-jeepers,
and what will become of that man?

He was once a man of great honour.
He would spend a pound in an hour.
And now he is going by the ditches.
Misfortune overtook Davy Power.

He summoned Owen Curtain's blind *banbh*.
He summoned Lord Graddy's dead goose.
He would summon yourself or a *leanbh*
if he thought it would be any use.

Oh, he brought a madam from Dublin
to comfort his bones, it is said.
But I do not know, sure, from Adam,
what good is that creature in bed.

I'd rather sleep with a ladder.
I'd rather embrace an old plough.
I'm sure I'd be dying if I had her
but sure, I'd be dying anyhow.

For she's as bare as the devil could make her
and her bones would cut meat like a knife.
Well, hurray for the relic of honour!
Don't know how much he got for it, or how long it will last.

My memory is that saucy lyrics were not a part of our culture when I was growing up in Crow Glen, and I'm surprised to see them here in English. However, all over the country, the tradition of poems and songs in Irish has always been much more earthy, with lots of vulgar references and jokes since the earliest records. There is a fascinating new book about the

Irish language called *Thirty-Two Words for Field: Lost Words of the Irish Landscape*. Written to interest readers who don't speak Irish as much as those who do, it goes so far as to claim that 'sex in Irish was dealt with in a less prudish and more honourable way than in other cultures'. [112]

## Life around the Bride River Valley

While I was preparing to visit the old homestead in Doon with the Americans, I had thought a lot about the life that my grandmother Nell had lived there as a child. Nestled below the Nagle foothills, the Valley was then a lush, fun and peaceful place to grow up in. [113] The Famine was sixty years behind them, and every decade was now bringing a new push or uprising around the country towards the dream of a democratic, decolonised Republic of their own.

Set away from the Village, the Bride Valley was the much older centre, where people had lived the Gaelic homesteaders' lifestyle for millennia. That's why its slopes and the mountainous territory stretching away from it to the north hold the oldest sacred and cultural sites of Crow Glen.

The Village, by contrast, was only built much more recently by the colonisers for their own convenience. The native Irish had no cause to live in a village before that, as their subsistence farms were dispersed evenly across the landscape. The colonisers built the Manor House, and the Village was built to house Irish staff allowed back in to work for the estate, which would need huge amounts of local labour. In 1779, the first colonials there, the Coppingers, sold their Manor and its estate to the Hudsons, who later put Pat and Johanna Carney on the coffin ship in 1847.

Before the creation of the Manor and the estate, the spot where the Village stands beside them had not been a focus of habitation. The homesteads of the local Irish were congregated in townlands to the south of it and to the north, on and above the slopes of the Bride River Valley. That Valley and its hinterlands to the north had already been a special place for nearly two thousand years before my ancestors moved in there

---

112 Manchán Magan, *Thirty-Two Words for Field: Lost Words of the Irish Landscape,* Gill, 2020
113 As mentioned in a previous chapter, it is now protected from further development as a Site of Scientific Interest with a rare flora, fauna, quality of environment and heritage. Cork County Council, *Local Area Plan, Cobh Municipal District,* Vol 1, Section 4, 'Main Policy Material', available at http://corklocalareaplans.com/cobh-municipal-district

around 1848. They contained the Fionn Mac Cumhaill legends, the Holy Well, the Mass Rock, the 'hedge school' where Irish was natively spoken and taught into the nineteenth century, and before that the great Bardic Schools where the native Gaelic culture of poetry and learning still thrived. [114]

It was in this culturally rich environment that Nell and her three siblings grew up, their faces turned north towards all those sites around and beyond the Valley, rather than south to the less interesting Village where they went to get provisions. They enjoyed a thriving social life on both slopes of the Valley. Visiting (*'ag cuairteoireacht'* in the old language up to the mid-nineteenth century) was the main entertainment. People would trot down either slope of the Valley, ford the river over the boulders placed in it for that purpose, and make their way up through the hazel woods that bordered the river to sit out the evening by each other's firesides telling stories, exchanging news and getting to know each other ever better.

As youngsters, Nell, her two sisters and her beloved brother Patrick (named for his grandfather, the first gamekeeper) spent all their free time skipping across the Valley to visit neighbours. Nell once told me that she had at that time a pair of shoes that she really treasured. The sisters only wore shoes on special occasions or to walk long distances. One Sunday, she went down to the river to go visiting on the other side. But as she jumped between the boulders, shoes in hand, Nell slipped and dropped one of her precious Sunday shoes in the river. It bobbed away from her on the shallow, fast-moving Bride. Trying to run after it in the stony river, she could not catch up and she never saw the shoe again. Later, when we used to play in the river as children, I always half-expected to see Nell's Sunday shoe bobbing along permanently on its silvery, glinting waters.

In Nell's day it was still customary to marry across the Valley, and the young people did not seem dissatisfied with the choice of partners available. The women were free and independent, choosing their own paths in life. Norah, Nell's older sister, was a quiet, modest, extremely sweet-natured person. When I knew her in her old age, just to sit by her was like a country balm. Yet, along with their other sister, Kathleen, the unassuming Norah had taken herself off on an adventure to Australia in the 1920s where they enjoyed training, qualifying and working as nurses for two periods of several years. They travelled home in the interim to

---

114 Katherine O'Donnell, as in Note 76

visit on a vast, slow, comfortable cruise-ship. We have photos of the sisters reclining luxuriously in the sun on the liner's deckchairs.

But on her second visit home, Norah unexpectedly decided that she would stay. She stayed to marry tall, gentle Jim O' Mahoney from the nearest homestead across the Valley. She settled into his well-appointed farm and their son, as if passing the ball back, later married a particularly beautiful young woman called Josie, from the opposite slope where his mother had come from. O' Mahoneys' farm continues to thrive and expand today. A hundred and sixty years after people starved to death on those slopes, their son is an international lecturer in Food Science at the National University of Ireland, and their niece a busy country doctor.

We used to visit that farm often when I was a child. They had all the modern conveniences but in layout, their house in the early 1970s chose to remain traditional. At the centre of a big, welcoming room stood a huge stone fireplace. It was big enough for the two elderly people to sit inside either end of it on stone ledges where they could keep the fire going all day, as well as keeping themselves warm and at the centre of things. Though she had a modern kitchen if she wanted to use it, Norah sometimes still chose to cook over the fire in black, cast-iron pots. They hung on black iron arms three feet long, which the cook could swivel to move the pot directly over the flames, and swivel away again when the food was cooked.

I once went there every day for a week to help harvest their potatoes as a summer job. It was a crop that they were renowned for, and sold very profitably. The main meal, as was the tradition, was in the middle of the working day. The men of the house, the farm laborers and myself came in from the fields at midday. We sat beside the very long dining table in the kitchen, on two comfortable benches that ran down either side of it. The table was covered with an oilcloth that was constantly wiped clean by the women of the house. We each had our own plate, cutlery and glass. There was a generous slab of the farm's own butter, as well as a traditional ceramic jug of their milk, unpasteurised from the cow that morning.

Norah had boiled over the fire a black pot of the potatoes that we were picking. And this time, she chose to serve them in a very old way, by standing at the top of the table and spilling them out along it, as if pouring out a crock of gold. A popular type of potato at the time was in fact called *Golden Wonder*, and they did pour down the centre of the table in front of us like a river of gold.

I will never forget the relish with which we ate those new potatoes, melting the farm's butter onto them, after the morning's hard work in the fields. They could have been caviar. I later had the chance to enjoy caviar as an adult abroad. It was at one of France's finest Michelin-starred restaurants where, accompanied by Bordeaux wines, you paid 250 euros for your dinner. It was nice, but it did not taste as good as that dinner at the table of Norah O' Mahoney on the northern slope of the Bride River Valley.

Walking back home to the Village at the end of that day's work, I stopped to dangle my feet in the Bride's silvery waters. It's strange to think now how little I really knew at the time about our heritage in all those historic places that those waters were flowing from.

## References

Ballineen & Enniskeane Area Heritage Group, *Murragh: A Place of Graves*, 2017

*Blake of Ballyglunin Papers, 1770-1830*, Archive ref. IE JHL/LE007, Archives of National University of Ireland Galway

Bourke, Angela, *The Field Day Anthology of Irish Writing*, Vol 2, Cork University Press, Cork, 2002

Coppinger, W.A., *History of the Coppinger Family of County Cork*, Sotherton, London, 1884

Cork County Council, *Local Area Plan, Cobh Municipal District*, Vol 1, Section 4, 'Main Policy Material', available at http://corklocalareaplans.com/cobh-municipal-district

Cronin, U., 'Speak Not Ill of Womankind', translation at *Get behind the Muse*, available at https://ucronin.wordpress.com/2017/09/17/gearoid-iarla-and-ennis

Deane, Bourke & Carpenter (eds.), *The Field Day Anthology of Irish Writing*, Vol 4, Cork University Press, 2002

*Fifteenth Annual Report from the Commissioners of Public Records of Ireland*, 'Abstracts of The Conveyances from the Trustees of the Forfeited Estates and Interests in Ireland in 1688', London, 1825

Joyce, P.W., *A Smaller Social History of Ancient Ireland*, Longmans, Green & Company, 1908

Koch, John, *The Celts: History, Life and Culture*, Vol 1, ABC-Clio, Oxford, 2012

Mac Giolla Chríost, Diarmuid, *The Irish Language in Ireland: From Goídel to Globalisation*, Routledge, London, 2004

McGarry, Patsy, 'Cork-born founder of Presentation Sisters declared 'Venerable'', *The Irish Times*, 1-11-2013

*Military Service Pensions Collection*, available at www.militaryarchives.ie

Magan, Manchán, *Thirty-Two Words for Field: Lost Words of the Irish Landscape*, Gill, 2020

Morley, Vincent *Dictionary of Irish Biography*, Royal Irish Academy with Cambridge University Press, available at
https://dib.cambridge.org/viewReadPage.do?articleId=a6289

Ó Cearúill Pádraig, 'Eoghán Rua Ó Suilleabháin: A True Exponent of the Bardic Legacy' in *Proceedings of the Barra Ó Donnabháin Symposium*, New York University, 2007

Ó Domhnaill, Séamas, 'Eoghan Ruadh Ó Súilleabháin: Aspects of his Life and Work' in *Church and State, Fourth Quarter, Lux Occulta* website, 2010

O' Donnell, Katherine, 'Edmund Burke's Political Poetics' in *Anáil an Bhéil Bheo: Orality and Modern Irish Culture*, Cambridge Scholars Publishing, Newcastle, 2009

Ó Duinnshléibhe, Seán, National Folklore Collection, Roll No. 12542, p. 221-467. *The School Collection, Volume 0382: Áth Dúna, Gleann an Phréacháin, Mainistir Fhearmuighe - Béaloideas,* viewable at www.duchas.ie/en/cbes/4921859/4896737/5190225?ChapterID=4921859

*O'Keeffe Clan Gathering and Rally*, 2016, available at http://okeeffeclans.com/fathereoghanokeeffe.html

O' Riordan, Michelle, *The Gaelic Mind and the Collapse of the Gaelic World*, Cork University Press, 1990

Ó Súilleabháin, D., National Folklore Collection, Gleann an Phréacháin, Roll No. 450, p. 148, available at https://www.duchas.ie/en/cbes/4921858/4896707

Petrie, George (ed.), *The Petrie Collection of the Ancient Music of Ireland,* Gill, Dublin, 1855

*Placenames Database of Ireland*, 'Glossary and Distribution Maps', available at www.logainm.ie

Quinlan, Ailín, 'Burial Site of Legendary Diarmuid Found, Says Historian', *The Cork Examiner*, 10-7-2017

Royal Irish Academy, 'Cultural Artefacts from Sixteenth-Century Ireland' at www.ria.ie/another-view-gaelic-manuscript-culture-edmund-spensers-ireland

Royal Irish Academy, *The Book of Fermoy*, RIA MS 23 E 29 (Cat. no. 1134)

Smyth, Daragh, *Cú Chulainn: An Iron Age Hero*, Irish Academic Press, 2005

Smyth, Daragh, *A Guide to Irish Mythology*, Irish Academic Press, 1998

*The Cork Examiner*, 'Is Fionn MacCumhail's Wingman Buried in West Cork?', 10-9-2015

# Chapter 9

# Hide the weapons

Images at the start of this chapter:

~ IRA General Michael Collins, who held a major strategy meeting at
Kate Hickey's house in Gleann an Phréacháin in 1921
~ Bridge over the Bride River Valley, as it was during the War of
Independence and is today
~ Liam Lynch, Commander of the IRA's Cork No. 2 Brigade in North
Cork, later the IRA's Chief of Staff nationwide, who was headquartered at
Kate Hickey's house, Gleann, in the first half of the War of Independence
~ National IRA leader Ernie O' Malley, a former medical student, who
taught a three-week training camp for IRA fighters in Crow Glen during
the War of Independence in 1920

# A secret told

On the day that the Americans' silver bus took us to visit the site of Pat and Johanna Carney's homestead, we were leaving Doon in the bus when Norma pointed down the green sloping field into the valley. Leaning over to me, she said: 'That's where your people used to hide the weapons'. Then she turned away to continue chatting with the Carneys. This bizarre message buzzed at the back of my mind until the visitors had left the Village at the end of the day. I went back to her house then and asked her what she had meant.

She said it was finally time that I could be told that there, in the Doon homestead, my ancestors, the Sweeneys, had been very active in the Irish armed effort during the War of Independence that raged from 1919 to 1921. She said they stored the IRA's weapons in a special dugout on their land. [115] That my grandmother Nell - the one I had grown up beside in the Village - had, at age 11, been a look-out, hidden at the end of the lane. Apparently, the role of her and her brother Patrick was to watch the lane night and day for the inevitable British Army patrols and raids, and to forewarn their people at the homestead.

My first reaction was anger towards Norma. Why hadn't she told me this before, during our many local history discussions by her fireside over the years? Infuriatingly, she said: 'Ah, you can't be telling young people those things'.

Initially, I found it hard to believe that the War of Independence could ever have made its way to quiet little old Crow Glen, hidden away from everywhere. But as I questioned her about it, I began to understand two things: first, that Gleann's remote, hidden quality made it ideal for the task; and second, that preparations had been secretly laid there for decades, back in Doon, long before the War of Independence actually began.

In earlier chapters we saw Henry Hudson, the landlord from the Manor House, putting Johanna and Pat Carney and their children out of their homestead in 1847, in exchange for a one-way ticket on the coffin ship. He had plans for their place. Once they were gone, he built a substantial farmhouse there, to help attract an important new employee that he was

---

115 The Irish Republican Army (IRA) was the name of the official citizen army of 'Volunteer' Irish people who successfully fought to end the British occupation of Ireland between 1916 and 1921.

taking on for his estate: a gamekeeper. Hudson wanted a gamekeeper because he had ambitions to host the kind of international shooting parties that were fashionable among the British gentry at the time. Aristocratic guests would come from other European countries too, as well as from Britain.

The new gamekeeper's role would be to stock the estate well with game and to set up the infrastructure for those shooting parties. That man, Patrick Sweeney, was my great-great-grandfather who came from the neighbouring county of Limerick around 1848, with recommendations from a similar estate there. He moved into what was by then a comfortable house in Doon that came with forty acres of rich pasture that he could farm profitably on the side alongside his main job.

One of the roles of this gamekeeper was, with the assistance of the British police who kept a small barracks in the Village, to prevent the locals from poaching the estate's game. He had under him a small team of rangers who prevented poaching farther out on the peripheries of the estate's lands. In all, this man ended up being very familiar with guns; with managing teams of armed men out on the farthest terrains of Gleann an Phréacháin; with the workings of the occupying police force; and with the habits and mentality of the upper class colonisers. His son would go on to inherit his gamekeeper job and all those forms of knowledge that went with it. And they would serve him well for the very different pursuits that his family would undertake years later.

Once he was well established in the role and well liked at the Manor, what Patrick Sweeney did next was to start secretly laying down decades of preparations for the cause of Irish independence. But he wasn't alone in these activities: he had the most unlikely co-conspirator. Gamekeeper Sweeney developed an unusually close working relationship with one of the sons of the Manor House, Elliot Hudson. Elliot was a prominent barrister in Dublin who also spent a lot of time at his childhood estate in Gleann.

The friendship was unlikely in the first place due to the chasm of class that gaped between them. But it took a further unexpected twist when Hudson one day shot Patrick Sweeney, albeit accidentally, in the course of a shooting party. The wound was not too serious, but it permanently shifted the ground under what now became the closest of friendships. As if cutting through the barriers of class, that accidental bullet left the two men speaking to each other as equals for the rest of their lives.

This unlikely bond drew Hudson farther and farther away from the values of the colonising class that he had been born into. He had already become active in the *Young Irelanders*, the 1840s independence movement founded by his close friend, fellow barrister and political activist Thomas Davis. Thomas was born in Mallow, on the Blackwater River just across the Nagle Mountains from Gleann an Phréacháin. His *Young Irelanders* movement was close with Daniel O' Connell; later influenced the Fenians and Parnell; and bequeathed to the cause the tricolour flag that represents the Irish Republic today. As one scholar puts it, they 'advocated the study of Irish history and the revival of the Irish language as a means of developing Irish nationalism and achieving independence... In 1848 the movement came to an end when a revolt led by the radical wing of the Young Irelanders was suppressed.' [116]

The fatherless Thomas Davis, whose dad died before he was born, himself went on to die of scarlet fever at just 30. He wrote the famous rebel songs 'The West's Asleep' and 'A Nation Once Again', whose haunting melodies outlive him today by nearly two centuries. Daniel O' Connell is described as having been 'distraught' at his death. A statue of Thomas overlooks Davis Street in his hometown of Mallow, and Cork harbour is guarded by Fort Davis. But he is worth remembering in more modern, psychological ways too, because this amazing son of the Blackwater Valley has an extraordinary link with our way of our life today.

Back in the 1840s, he was the first person ever to call publicly for the kind of *inclusive* Irish identity that we expect and enjoy now. For Davis, ethnicity and religion were irrelevant. He was the first to argue that Irish nationality should be neither genetic, nor class-based (for example, not for the Protestant 'Ascendancy' elites only), nor religion-based (that is, not for the Catholic 'natives' only). Instead, he defined it - for the first time ever - as a collective belonging based on shared culture, values and location. Davis drew on the unusually secular ideas of the United Irishmen's Rebellion of 1798. And he supported Daniel O' Connell's early nineteenth-century movement, but went beyond its Catholicism. Instead, Davis - like Elliot Hudson, his friend at the Crow Glen Manor - promoted the Irish language and distinctly Irish culture as that of a 'rising, not declining, people', separate from Britain. [117]

---

116 *Encyclopedia Britannica*, 'Young Ireland - Irish Nationalist Movement', available at www.britannica.com/topic/Young-Ireland
117 Fintan Cullen, *Sources in Irish Art: A Reader*, Cork University Press, 2000

Elliot Hudson contributed his skills as a lawyer to help with the defence of Davis' Young Irelander colleagues Thomas Francis Meagher and William Smith O'Brien, after their failed rebellion in 1848. [118] Continuing this legacy of activism towards Irish independence until his own early death due to tuberculosis in 1853, Elliot was ostracised by his colonial family at the Gleann Manor. Months before his death, he converted to Catholicism. When he died, his family refused to allow his body into the Manor's cemetery. Instead, he was received by the Sweeneys and tenderly buried in their plot. So Elliot Hudson found his rest in the tiny, thousand-year-old burial ground at the Holy Well on the old land in Doon, where Patrick Sweeney would join him years later, lying shoulder to shoulder. You can still see the two friends' adjacent headstones there today.

Soon after he had first arrived in Gleann, Patrick, as the new gamekeeper, had settled down and married a local girl from across the Bride River Valley. They raised a family and their son, Michael, was trained up to take on Patrick's role as estate gamekeeper when Patrick retired. At some stage - presumably before Elliot died in 1853 - Patrick's friendship with this son of the Manor was significant enough that the estate signed over the fine house and lush farm in Doon to become the gamekeeper's own private property from then on.

I was already well into my investigations for this chapter when Norma Buckley revealed to me that the gamekeeper and his friend Elliot Hudson from the Manor House do not lie alone in their grave beside the Holy Well in Doon. In fact, another man lies there with them, because the three had made a pact to be buried there together as soul-brothers, shoulder to shoulder. And now Norma gave me his name: Dónal Fagan. He was Gleann an Phréacháin's very last hedge-school teacher. And it turns out that this man - the penniless practitioner of an impossible profession - had a significant, singlehanded effect on the War of Independence in Crow Glen.

The friendship between these three men was like the confluence of three rivers coming from very different directions, converging in a shared dedication to the cause of Irish independence. Hudson, as a colonial elite, was the most unlikely candidate for that mission. And Sweeney, enjoying a comfortable role collaborating with the colonial estate, was unlikely too.

---

118 'The Hermitage, Rathfarnham', *Buildings*, Ireland XO, available at https://irelandxo.com/ireland-xo/history-and-genealogy/buildings-database/hermitage-rathfarnham

But Norma finally yielded the key to this mystery by revealing the pivotal influence that Dónal Fagan had on them.

Fagan was the last survivor of that line of Gaelic learning and culture that stretched back for centuries to the north of Gleann, back through the Chimneyfield hedge school and the medieval Bardic School of the Nagle mountains. He was looking behind him at the 'collapse of the Gaelic world', imposed so effectively by the Penal Laws and the suppression of the Irish language. [119] England's thorough colonisation of his world had left him a deeply marginalised, discarded person with no resources other than those he carried inside himself. But like Johanna Carney when faced with her ticket for the coffin ship, he saw one small remaining margin of action available to him, and he took it.

What Fagan did was to befriend the new gamekeeper who had moved into the Bride River Valley. Fagan must have sensed that there were spaces inside this newcomer that were open to values other than the bourgeois comforts he enjoyed as a senior employee of the Manor. Over time, with Fagan visiting constantly in the privacy of the gamekeeper's homestead at Doon, the two became close. And it all made so much more sense when Norma explained that it was Fagan who 'turned' the gamekeeper to risk everything for the fight for an Irish Republic. The gamekeeper didn't think all that up by himself. With the eloquence of five hundred years of his own lineage of teachers speaking through him, the silver-tongued Fagan could describe to the gamekeeper a vision of a free, confident, independent Ireland. And Fagan built up in him enough passion about it for the gamekeeper to share that vision with the son of the Manor house too. Without Fagan's influence, the homestead in Doon might never have taken the risks it later did to assist the IRA's War of Independence.

In 2018, Norma Buckley honoured Dónal Fagan's pivotal role in the history of Crow Glen by hiring a stonemason to add his name to the trio's grave at the Holy Well. The inner wealth and confidence that drove his vision of a free Irish Republic had poured down through the centuries in the learned traditions carried by Fagan. But when he followed his two soul-brothers into the grave at Doon, Fagan had no outer wealth in his pocket to pay for the carving of his grave-name.

Meanwhile, Irish independence movements simmered away in Dublin and in the USA over the coming decades. The second-generation gamekeeper, Michael Sweeney, skilfully continued both sides of his father's legacy. On

---

119  Michelle O' Riordan, as in Note 92

the one hand, he remained well-liked and trusted as the Manor's second-generation gamekeeper. And on the other, hidden away at his home in Doon, he secretly supported and held meetings for movements like the Fenians, the Irish Republican Brotherhood, the Land League and the cause of Charles Stewart Parnell - all unacceptable, enemy causes in the eyes of his colonial employers, the Hudsons.

In 1880 the *Cork Examiner* published a lengthy article about a new branch of the Land League that had recently been formed in Gleann an Phréacháin to oppose the cruel practices of what the *Cork Examiner* called the 'rack-renter' landlord Henry Hudson. The newspaper went so far as to denounce what it called 'The extermination of Glenville tenants by the Hudons'. [120]

Local tenants like Mr Hickey of Badger's Hill (whose family would later play the key role in Gleann's War of Independence) were praised by the newspaper for their active resistance and organisation against Hudson's system in 1880. The article points out that 'despite local influences', the attendance at the inaugural meeting of Gleann's Land League branch 'was extremely large', and gathered in front of 'a banner bearing the words *Down with Tyranny*'.

The article gives a damning account of Hudson's behaviour during the Famine. It explains that in 1847 Hudson, 'seeing that the lands were not fruitful… set the crowbar brigade to work and evicted about 30 families [in Gleann]. He hired a ship to transport the evicted families to a foreign land. [On] the stormy waters of the Atlantic, pestilence fell among them and famine did its work, for the ship was poorly provisioned, and the result was that scarcely a man survived to tell the tale.' [121] Presumably the ship in question is The Avon, the one that Hudson put Pat and Johanna Carney and their eight children on in 1847.

As well as Parnell's Land League, the Fenians too apparently had an active branch in Gleann. With information gathered around the 1900s, Gleann's keeper of local records and folklore, Seán Ó Duinnshléibhe, records that at the crossroads of Killeagh, a couple of miles north of the Bride River Valley, 'tradition says that there are two cartloads of arms buried in this

120 'Land Meeting in Glenville', *The Cork Examiner*, 29-12-1880; article supplied to the author by Keith Carney
121 *The Cork Examiner,* as in Note 120 above. Henry Hudson published a note in the *Examiner* the following day confirming that together with another colonial landlord (the British aristocrat called Lord Fermoy), the Hudsons had indeed chartered such a famine ship in 1847, but Hudson argued that it was an act of 'benevolence'.

townland by the Fenians', and that 'Déimhis Foley was the local Fenian'. [122]

This name *Déimhis* is interesting. At a time when local Irish people were named from a limited range of local options, Déimhis was an extremely unusual forename. I have not been able to find another example of it anywhere, in either Irish-language or English sources. It's clearly an Irish spelling of the English-language surname Davis, and would be pronounced in the same way. So I would speculate that this man, from that remote place north of the Bride River Valley, did indeed come from a family who were active in the cause of Irish independence. They seem to have taken the surname of the independence visionary Thomas Davis who was born nearby in the Blackwater Valley. They patriotically transcribed it into an Irish-language spelling, and gave it as a forename to their own newborn son. And he apparently went on to become Gleann's local Fenian leader, as his forename predestined him to do.

Perhaps Patrick Sweeney, the first gamekeeper in Doon, helped the Gleann Fenians to manage their weapons cache in the 1860s just as his son did the IRA one on his own land in 1919. But unlike their friend Elliot Hudson, the two generations of gamekeepers excelled, by necessity, at keeping their political activism entirely secret and separate from their day job at the Manor.

And so things continued. The second-generation gamekeeper, Michael Sweeney, married the beautiful Hanora Martin from across the Bride River Valley. And Nell, my grandmother, was born to them in 1909. But seven years later in 1916, when the Irish revolutionaries declared the Proclamation of Irish Independence at their armed uprising in Dublin, the Sweeneys, like so many others around the country, stood more than ready to respond. They had been preparing for decades and would support the coming independence struggle in any way they could.

## War in Crow Glen

After decades of preparation through the movements and rebellions of the nineteenth century, Ireland's War of Independence finally broke out on the 21st of January, 1919. On that chilly day, Seán Ó Duinnshléibhe would

---

122 Seán Ó Duinnshléibhe, *Gleann an Phréacháin - Béaloideas,* as in Note 32

have been sitting at his desk near the fireplace in Chimneyfield School, teaching the farm children Irish, writing, maths, poetry and folklore.

Hidden away from the Village, the Bride Valley homesteads below him swung silently into action. The Doon homestead of Nell's family and Hickeys and Hegartys, two other farms that triangulated it across the Valley, would soon be core helpers for the Irish armed effort in the area.

Hegarty's house stood opposite Nell's on the north side of the Valley and Hickey's land, where the Mass Rock stood, was at the west end of the Valley. Both Hickeys and Hegartys provided sons who, at stages during the war, became Commanding Officers for the IRA branch in the Glen of the Crow, called the Glenville Company. Nell's father, Michael, was too old now for active combat and his only son was still too young.

Basically, that was all that Norma Buckley told me about the War in Gleann. It was up to me to go and find out the rest. After her revelation, I spent the following days and weeks in libraries poring over the official records and archives, which I found are in fact very extensive and transparently available. One 'lead' led to another, as if assembling the lost pieces of a mosaic.

I discovered that rural North Cork became an intense focus for the war as it progressed. IRA activities were shared out carefully between the three homesteads in the Valley. They lived as soul brothers and sisters through those two and a half years of putting their lives in each other's hands. The main weapons-cache was in a special dugout on the Sweeney farm. Rank and file IRA men passed through there for weapons, sometimes meeting there. And the men of the Hegarty household were extremely active as fighting leaders.

But Hickeys house became the core HQ where national-level IRA Brigade leaders lived hidden for months at a time. [123] By mid-1920, Kate Hickey's house in Badger's Hill, Gleann, would have been one of the most hunted, sought-after locations in the county for the British Army, if only they could find it. This intense and perilous role was taken on by Kate, that extraordinary woman of the Hickey household. The youngest of Kate's children were just two and six years old. Her husband had died recently, when she was 35. She was left with the job of farming and raising their family on her own. All this would seem challenging enough but the young Kate decided that she also had another mission in life, and that she would

---

123  Peter Hart, *The IRA and its Enemies: Violence and Community in Cork*, Oxford University Press, Oxford, 1998

embrace it fully. She took the decision that as well as raising her family, she personally would also hide, protect, feed and lodge in her home the national-level leaders of the IRA effort in North Cork, as well as enabling them to hold national-level strategy meetings and training sessions there. And that is what Kate did.

Senior leaders billeted at her house for months at a time, using it as the headquarters for the entire North Cork Brigade of the IRA - which *numbered 2,318 armed, fighting men!* The British Army had orders to burn to the ground any homes or farms that harboured even one lowly IRA man for even one night. But as well as the destruction of her home, farm and livelihood, the punishment for Kate's level of activity would have been execution, if she were a man. Perhaps softened to life imprisonment as a woman? [124]

Fortunately, Kate Hickey went on to live to the fine old age of 94, and her contribution to the birth of the Irish Republic earned her an obituary in Cork's *Evening Echo* newspaper. The article points out that though 'she bore many crosses' in her long lifetime, 'they never put a damper on her national spirit'. It confirms that 'during the critical years between 1918 and 1921, her home and all the hospitality it provided were at the disposal of the national leaders. Liam Lynch was her guest for many months.' It adds that IRA fighter 'Seán Moylan, when on the run from British forces, availed of her hospitality and safe custody for many months. As a Minister of State in later years he visited her occasionally to express his undying gratitude.'

The article concludes that 'it was not surprising to witness the unprecedented crowds that turned out to the removal of her remains and her funeral. She was extensively known and admired for her deep patriotism and made a noble contribution to a noble cause.' [125]

It is significant that this obituary for Kate Hickey appeared in 1978 in the most widely read Cork newspaper. It shows - to my great surprise - that in the late 1970s it was still popular knowledge that Gleann an Phréacháin had been an important focus of national-level IRA activity in the War of Independence. The article makes clear that the community was still well aware of the fact at that point, and at least some were proud of it and

---

124  But being a woman also left one exposed to extra risks compared to men, as described by recent scholars of physical and sexual violence against women by both sides during the Irish Revolution. See the documentary *Cogadh ar Mhná / A War on Women* by Ciara Hylan, broadcast by TG4 on 14-10-2020
125  *The Evening Echo*, 'Late Mrs K. Hickey, Glenville', 5-6-1978

grateful for it. I don't know what changes in society from the 1980s onwards caused this important tranche of local history to be wiped from the collective memory of Crow Glen. But at least we can restore these memories now, in time for the centenary celebration of them in 2021.

The same as for the Famine, for the War of Independence too I grew up believing it had happened *elsewhere* around Ireland. No-one had ever told me otherwise. But in fact, the archives of the Irish government and the National University of Ireland do tell the vivid story of Crow Glen's War of Independence in full, for those who care to hear it. In the archives, I sat in total incomprehension when I saw that our Village, its heritage industry and the local school system had all covered Gleann's intense activity in the War of Independence with a blanket of silence, wiping it out as if it had never happened.

I did the research for this book in order to educate myself out of that ignorance that had been imposed on us. And I am publishing it to honour the astounding sacrifices that so many people around Crow Glen made for us - us who blithely live now in the decolonised, democratic future that they risked everything to attain for us. It's easy to scoff or dismiss their memory, but if *someone* had not done that for us at some point in the meantime, Ireland would still be occupied by Britain and the yellow-haired Boris Johnson would be our leader as we face the challenges of the twenty-first century. [126]

The 11-year-old Nell Sweeney, shivering in her look-out hide, was with me, over my shoulder, through every minute of those days while I sifted through the old records. And as I learned more - with layers peeling off to reveal new layers below - I felt her shivers intensify. I increasingly saw, laid bare before my eyes on those yellowed library papers, all that she had to fear and to lose.

While the war raged in 1921, the British forces fighting in Ireland numbered about 73,800. During 1920, they had flooded into County Cork and the surrounding area, which saw some of the fiercest fighting. The British imposed martial law there. And they had a major military garrison in the town nearest to Gleann called Fermoy, about twelve miles to the north east.

---

126  To consider in detail what that would be like, see this widely read article by Séamas O' Reilly in *The Guardian*, 29-7-2020: 'Ireland isn't Really a Utopia, It's Just its Neighbour is a Gurning Claptrapocracy - The Country's Mild Competency over Coronavirus Can Appear to be Stone-Cold Genius Compared with the UK's Blundering Mess'.

From their barracks at Fermoy, British forces made wary sorties along the main roads. Minor roads were constantly being destroyed or ambushed by IRA men, who then disappeared back into the open countryside. Gleann an Phréacháin became important because the mountainous terrain between it and Fermoy is wild, unpopulated territory where the local IRA moved easily but the British didn't. And the whole terrain around the Village itself is, even to this day, accessible only by tiny, twisting roads that were easily sabotaged or ambushed.

Military engagements by and with the British Army were quite fierce in the triangle that is formed by the towns of Fermoy to the north-east, Mallow to the north-west and Cork, to the south. By September 1919, Fermoy was already being ransacked by British forces in reprisals against local IRA activity. A year later, the infamous 'Wreck of Mallow' followed the same pattern. And Cork city was burned by the British in one of the War's biggest reprisals the following December.

Glen of the Crow happened to sit remote, isolated and difficult to access at the exact centre of that triangle. The Village had its own armed branch of the IRA, called the Glenville Company. They numbered 57 officially enlisted men. [127] But we saw above that for the first half of the War of Independence, Crow Glen was not just a routinely active branch of the IRA. It was also the headquarters for the IRA's Cork No. 2 Brigade which numbered 2,318 men, covered all of north County Cork, and saw some of the most intense combat in the country. [128] Liam Lynch (pictured at the start of this chapter) was the Commanding Officer of this Brigade. Before the war he lived and worked in Fermoy and in the war's second half, he became the national IRA's Chief of Staff or main commanding officer.

During the first half of the war, Liam Lynch had his headquarters in Kate Hickey's house in Gleann an Phréacháin, on the slopes of the Bride River Valley that stretched away from the Sweeney homestead in Doon.[129] This

127 'The average strength of the companies would be around the 50 mark', remarks IRA fighter Con Leddy in his testimony to the Bureau of Military History (No. BMH WHS756). The Watergrasshill Company was made up of 69 men.

128 John Borgonovo, 'Atlas of the Irish Revolution, The War in Cork and Kerry', 18-9-2017, IrishExaminer.com The IRA's forces in County Cork numbered almost 18,000 - almost 20% of their total around the country. The IRA had only 1,379 full-time fighters around the country, but over a third of them were in County Cork.

129 IRA officer George Power's explains: 'With Liam Lynch on the run and able to devote himself full-time to the Brigade organisation, the efficiency of the Brigade developed. Brigade headquarters was now established at Glenville, about nine miles south-west of Fermoy'.' From George Power's testimony at Irish Bureau of Military History, BMH WS0451, available at www.bureauofmilitaryhistory.ie. And on page 60 of No Other Law: The Story of Liam Lynch and

nationally important, life-and-death activity of hiding him and his Brigade was hosted in Kate's house, and the secret was guarded by the families dotted around the Valley, who could see signals from each other's homesteads. The Hickey family had in fact two houses at the west end of the Valley, in neighbouring fields. One was Kate's - the IRA headquarters - and the other supplied the leader of Gleann's IRA fighting Company, Denis Hickey. When Denis was captured and interned by the British, his neighbour Denis Hegarty across the Valley took on that role.

In mid-1920, the IRA in the area around Gleann captured a leading figure of the British Army, General Cuthbert Lucas, during a daring raid in Fermoy, that garrison town twelve miles north east of Gleann. Amidst national consternation in the British press, they secretly moved the captured VIP 'via Glenville [meaning Crow Glen] to Mallow'. [130]

The IRA HQ at Gleann also hosted major strategy meetings of the national IRA leaders. In September 1920, it hosted a three-week training camp that created a Flying Column, an elite formation of up to 15 full-time fighters who lived permanently 'on the run', making lightning strikes on the enemy. IRA Commandant Patrick O'Brien describes how they first 'spent a week in training under Liam Lynch in Glenville. This training mainly consisted of musketry, rifle marksmanship, fire control and minor tactical training, including field signals. After about a week Ernie O' Malley joined us.' [131] They were trained intensively for three weeks at Gleann by Ernie O'Malley, another national leader of the IRA.[132]

Unlike Liam Lynch, Ernie O' Malley (also pictured at the start of this chapter) only visited the Crow Glen HQ for strategy meetings and to give advanced trainings. A Dublin medical student who resumed his studies after the War and became a well-known man of letters internationally, he

---

the Irish Republican Army, 1916-1923, Florence O' Donoghue describes when Lynch 'began the period of full-time active service which terminated only with his death. When he returned to his Brigade area, he set up his headquarters at Glenville, about 10 miles south-west of Fermoy'.
130 Military Service Pensions Collection, record of Eoin (also spelled Owen) Curtain, available at www.militaryarchives.ie
131 Patrick O' Brien, testimony at Irish Bureau of Military History, BMH WHS0764, available at www.bureauofmilitaryhistory.ie
132 In Rebel Heart: George Lennon, Flying Column Commander, Terence O' Reilly states: 'As the first step to forming the North Cork Flying Column, a training camp was organised near Glenville in County Cork. The local Sinn Fein council funded this venture by providing £400 for equipment, clothing and rations. Participants included Liam Lynch and George Lennon and the supervising officer was Ernie O'Malley who later recalled: 'I trained the column in fieldwork for over three weeks… ; at night the men attended lectures I gave to officers of the local battalion.' George Lennon adds that 'I had helped to train a column for him at Glenville in the Nagle Mountains'.

is an interesting figure, described by one of his biographers as an 'IRA intellectual'. [133] Living on the run, he was wounded, imprisoned and tortured for information by the British in Dublin Castle. Despite the lifelong injuries that resulted, O' Malley survived - unlike many of his contemporaries - to return to his intellectual life after Irish Independence.

As one biographer explains: 'severely weakened by gunshot wounds, hunger strike and the lasting effects of torture in Dublin Castle, O'Malley was told by doctors in 1923 that he would never walk properly again; he promptly took himself on a walking tour of Europe'. [134] That journey was spiritually as well as physically restorative; he learned, as he put it, 'to use my eyes again in a new way'. He became a respected writer in the 1940s and 50s, often living and lecturing abroad.

Historians describe how many of the IRA leaders and officers were keen readers of international, as well as Irish, literature and politics. [135] Long hours lying hidden in ditches or outhouses while 'on the run' could be passed as reading time, if the book was small and light enough to carry. For O' Malley, like many leaders of the Irish independence effort over the decades, 'books remained at the centre of his life' and 'he amassed an impressive collection', numbering many thousands. [136] The *New York Times* described O' Malley's own book on his War of Independence experiences, *On Another Man's Wound,* as 'a stirring and beautiful account of a deeply felt experience'. [137] The *New York Herald Tribune* praised it as 'a tale of heroic adventure told without rancour or rhetoric'. [138]

In recent years, O' Malley's autobiographical works were the main inspiration behind the 2006 film of Ken Loach, *The Wind That Shakes the Barley*, which depicts the War of Independence in County Cork. It won the much-coveted *Palme d'Or* prize at the 2006 Cannes Film Festival, becoming Loach's biggest box office success and Ireland's highest-grossing independent film to date. [139] Even if you considered that O' Malley was wrong to lead an armed conflict to achieve decolonisation, his

133  Richard English, *Ernie O' Malley: IRA Intellectual*, Clarendon Press, 1999
134  Richard English, as in Note 133
135  See Kieran Allen, *1916: Ireland's Revolutionary Tradition*, Pluto Press, 2016; Maurice Walsh, *Bitter Freedom: Ireland in a Revolutionary World*, Liveright, 2016; and Richard English, *Ernie O' Malley: IRA Intellectual*, Clarendon Press, 1999
136  Caoimhe Nic Dháibhéid, 'Portrait of a Revolutionary Afterlife', *The Irish Times*, 12-11-2011
137  Ernie O' Malley, *On Another Man's Wound*, Mercier Press, Cork, 2013.
138  Cormac O'Malley, 'The Publication History of *On Another Man's Wound*', *New Hibernia Review*, Autumn 2003
139  Ken Loach, feature film *The Wind that Strikes the Barley*, Sixteen Films Matador Pictures, 2006

book on his War of Independence experiences reveals a profound philosophical mind of great intelligence. I cannot understand why activities in Gleann an Phréacháin by a figure of such international standing should be written out of our local history.

In March 1921, there was what the archives go on to describe as 'at Glenville, a meeting of Munster IRA leaders' for another discussion on strategy.[140] This is described as 'the second conference of IRA southern Brigades at Glenville, spending the previous night in Cork city before proceeding to the meeting.' [141] In the government archives, IRA fighter Paddy Paul recalls: 'The meeting was called by Liam Lynch, apparently for the purpose of a general survey of the position and... we were informed of the projected landing of an Italian cargo of arms that was expected to take place on the south coast in the immediate future.' [142]

A 'second purchase in Germany' of arms also involved 'a meeting in Hickeys of Glenville to arrange'. [143] Again, this was the home of the young widow Kate Hickey and her children. Kate's obituary in Cork's *Evening Echo* in 1978 records that 'General Michael Collins held a meeting of his chief County Cork collaborators in her home in early 1921 - a day of great activity for the local Volunteer companies'. [144]

Also in March 1921, Dan Breen, an important IRA fighter around the south of Ireland, is known to have been hidden in Crow Glen. Having escaped a British Army raid in nearby Conna in which an Irish civilian was shot dead, Breen was 'driven to Glenville in a horse and trap and from there he was taken to Burnfort by some members of the Glenville company'. [145]

At the time, the British were offering an amazing £1,000 reward for a word of confidential information that would lead to the arrest of Dan Breen. Yet they were unsuccessful. No-one was tempted in Gleann as Breen made his way through the 'safe houses' there. Like a cat with nine lives, Breen was particularly tough. Despite being shot no fewer than six

---

140   Ernie O' Malley (eds. Ó Ruairc, P., Borgonovo, J. & Bielenberg, A.), *The Men Will Talk to Me*, Ernie O'Malley Series, West Cork Brigade, Mercier Press, Cork & London, 2015
141   Terence O' Reilly, *Rebel Heart*, as in Note 132
142   Terence O' Reilly, as in Note 132
143   Ernie O' Malley, as in Note 140
144   *The Evening Echo*, 'Late Mrs K. Hickey, Glenville', 5-6-1978
145   Cork County Council, *Centenary Timeline for the County of Cork (1920 – 1923): War of Independence and Civil War*, available at www.corkcoco.ie/sites/default/files/2020-02/centenary-timeline-for-the-county-of-cork-1920-to-1924.pdf   Also in Barry Keane, *Cork's Revolutionary Dead*, Mercier Press, Cork, 2017

times, he too was one of the IRA leaders who survived both the Independence and Civil Wars. He lived to become an elected politician of the new Republic and to publish his best-selling account *My Fight for Irish Freedom*, where he points out 'How many men were wounded and suffered as much as I did? How many were wounded six times and still came back for more?' [146]

Next, the archives state that 'in the month of May 1921, an intensive push was made by the enemy in the (Gleann) Battalion area'. [147] This included an intensification of spying activity on both sides as the British desperately sought to locate the area's IRA HQ, which was giving so much trouble to their garrison in Fermoy. On 16 May 1921, an alleged British spy, David Walsh, was captured in Crow Glen by the IRA's Glenville Company. He was interrogated there by higher level IRA officers who came in for the purpose. He was tried and executed there. [148] This spy was of national importance because he was judged to be responsible for one of the war's most infamous massacres of IRA people, at a neighbouring village called Clonmult. [149]

Just a week later, on 24 May 1921, Lieutenant Seymour Lewington Vincent of the British Army Intelligence Staff met the same fate at 'Coome East near Glenville'. [150] The archives explain that 'he was arrested by members of the Glenville-Watergrasshill Company and it was subsequently discovered that he was a… British Intelligence Officer from the Fermoy garrison.' [151] In Vincent's bag the IRA 'found a revolver, a Sam Browne belt, a camera…and a note book containing a list of names

---

146 Dan Breen, *My Fight for Irish Freedom*, Anvil Press, 1993
147 Con Leddy, testimony at Irish Bureau of Military History, BMH WS0576, available at www.bureauofmilitaryhistory.ie
148 In his testimony in the Irish Bureau of Military History Archive (BMH WS 1009), p. 21, William Buckley explains: 'David Walsh of Shanagarry was a former British soldier suspected of having given information that led to the Clonmult disaster for the IRA. He was arrested by the Glenville Company and detained. Walsh allegedly admitted to having been paid £1 a week as a British spy, and gave the names of other spies. He was tried by members of the Fermoy Battalion staff, found guilty, and sentenced to death - a sentence confirmed by the Cork No. 2 Brigade staff. He was executed on 16 May 1921… near Glenville.' *Cork's War of Independence Fatality Register* (eds. Borgonovo, J. et al.) which can be accessed at http://theirishrevolution.ie/1921-248/#.Ww_bCsgh00o
149 Tom O'Neill, *The Battle of Clonmult: The IRA's Worst Defeat*. See also 'Major Setback for East Cork IRA at Clonmult' in *Timeline of Cork IRA's No. 1 Brigade*, http://homepage.eircom.net/~corkcounty/Timeline/Clonmult.htm
150 John Borgonovo et al. (eds.), *Cork's War of Independence Fatality Register* at http://theirishrevolution.ie/1921-248/#.Ww_bCsgh00o
151 Florence O'Donoghue, *No Other Law: The Story of Liam Lynch and the Irish Republican Army, 1916-1923*, Irish Press, Dublin, 1954

of contacts… of persons known to be loyal to the British connection'. [152] Vincent was judged to be looking for, and relaying information about, the 'safe houses' that were hiding national IRA leader Liam Lynch. The archives go on: 'Lieutenant Vincent was removed to the Glenville area under guard, and arrangements were being made for his trial. On the morning of the day following his capture, British forces began a round-up of the area, and the prisoner made a desperate attempt to escape. He was shot down and killed'. [153]

Although he was indeed killed on that day, that is not the last that Crow Glen saw of Lieutenant Vincent. During my research, I found that pulling on these threads in Gleann's layers of secrecy and silence constantly revealed new layers underneath. It turned out that the Lieutenant's story in Gleann would twist on further, beyond his own lifetime. And Norma Buckley would later reveal how someone else whom I had lived with in my own household - someone other than my grandmother Nell - had gotten entwined with it.

References

Breen, Dan, *My Fight for Irish Freedom*, Anvil Press, 1993
Buckley, William, testimony at Irish Bureau of Military History, BMH WS1009, available at www.bureauofmilitaryhistory.ie
*Buildings*, Ireland XO, 'The Hermitage, Rathfarnham', available at https://irelandxo.com/ireland-xo/history-and-genealogy/buildings-database/hermitage-rathfarnham
Carroll, Aideen, *Seán Moylan: Rebel Leader*, Mercier Press, Cork, 2010
*Cork Beo*, 'An Interactive Web Map of All IRA Operations in Co. Cork, 1919 -1921', 27-4-2020 at www.corkbeo.ie/news/history/interactive-map-ira-operations-cork-18113200
Cork County Council, *Centenary Timeline for the County of Cork (1920 – 1923): War of Independence and Civil War*, available at www.corkcoco.ie/sites/default/files/2020-02/centenary-timeline-for-the-county-of-cork-1920-to-1924.pdf
Cronin, J., Murphy, M. & Smyth, W.A. (Eds.), *Atlas of the Great Irish Famine*, Cork University Press, Cork, 2012
Crowley, J., O Drisceoil, D., Murphy, M., Borgonovo, J., (Eds.), *Atlas of the Irish Revolution*, Cork University Press, Cork, 2017
Cullen, Fintan, *Sources in Irish Art: A Reader*, Cork University Press, 2000
Dorney, John, 'The Irish Civil War, A Brief Overview', *The Irish Story* website, 2012

152  IRA fighter James Hackett's testimony in Irish Bureau of Military History Archive, BMH WS 1080, p. 6
153  IRA fighter William Buckley's testimony in Irish Bureau of Military History Archive, BMH WS 1009, p. 21

*Encyclopedia Britannica*, 'Young Ireland - Irish Nationalist Movement', available at www.britannica.com/topic/Young-Ireland

English, Richard, *Ernie O' Malley: IRA Intellectual*, Clarendon Press, 1999

Ferriter, Diarmaid, 'From Turmoil to Truce: A Mature Reflection on the War of Independence', *The Irish Times*, 11-1-2020

Hart, Peter, *The IRA and its Enemies: Violence and Community in Cork*, Oxford University Press, Oxford, 1998

House of Lords of Great Britain, *Report from the Commissioners*, Volume 29, Part 1, London, 1842

Keane, Barry, *Cork's Revolutionary Dead*, Mercier Press, Cork, 2017

Leddy, Con, testimony at Irish Bureau of Military History, BMH WS0756, available at www.bureauofmilitaryhistory.ie

Lewis, S., *A Topographical Dictionary of Ireland,* Lewis & Co., London, 1837

Loach, Ken, feature film *The Wind that Strikes the Barley*, Sixteen Films Matador Pictures, 2006

Murray, Daniel, 'The Fog of Certainty: Liam Lynch and the Start of the Civil War, 1922' in *An Irish History Blog*, 2017

Nic Dháibhéid, Caoimhe, 'Portrait of a Revolutionary Afterlife', *The Irish Times*, 12-11-2011

O' Brien, Patrick, testimony at Irish Bureau of Military History, BMH WS0764, available at www.bureauofmilitaryhistory.ie

O' Donoghue, Florence, *No Other Law: The Story of Liam Lynch and the Irish Republican Army, 1916-1923*, Irish Press, Dublin, 1954

O' Malley, Cormac, 'The Publication History of *On Another Man's Wound*', *New Hibernia Review*, Autumn 2003

O' Malley, Ernie, *On Another Man's Wound*, Mercier Press, Cork, 2013

O' Malley, Ernie (author) and Ó Ruairc, P., Borgonovo, J. & Bielenberg, A. (eds.), *The Men Will Talk To Me*, Ernie O'Malley Series, West Cork Brigade, Mercier Press, Cork & London, 2015

O' Neill, Tom, *The Battle of Clonmult: The IRA's Worst Defeat*, THP Ireland, 2019

O' Reilly, Terence, *Rebel Heart: George Lennon, Flying Column Commander*, Mercier Press, Cork, 2005

Power, George, testimony at Irish Bureau of Military History, BMH WS0451, available at www.bureauofmilitaryhistory.ie

Ryan, Meda, *The Real Chief: The Story of Liam Lynch*, Mercier Press, Cork, 2005

*The Cairo Gang* website, 'British soldiers Who Died in Ireland, 1919-1921', www.cairogang.com/soldiers-killed/list-1921.html

*The Cork Examiner* , 'Land Meeting in Glenville', 29-12-1880

*The Evening Echo*, 'Late Mrs K. Hickey, Glenville', 5-6-1978

Townshend, Charles, *The Republic: The Fight for Irish Independence, 1918-1923*,

# Chapter 10

# The Look-out

Images at the start of this chapter:

~ Cork city, burned by the British Army during the War of Independence
~ Tomás Mac Curtain, Lord Mayor of Cork, executed by the British in his
bedroom in Cork in 1921
~ Terence MacSwiney, the next Lord of Mayor of Cork, jailed in England
where he died of starvation on hunger strike in 1921
~ At the centre of the photo in civilian clothes: Captain Denis Hickey,
former Commander of the Crow Glen IRA interned by the British, with
pro-Treaty Free State soldiers during the Civil War

# Days of Fear

While doing this research, I thought a lot about the climate of fear that local people must have lived in during those years. [154] As Cork University's War of Independence historian John Borgonovo puts it, 'the British military were authorised to carry out 'official' reprisals against civilians and to execute republicans captured carrying arms'. [155] In fact, most of the punishment reprisals authorised by senior British Army commanders were in County Cork. [156]

Of all the IRA fighters executed by the British in Ireland in 1920-21, half were in Cork. And as the war's biggest single reprisal, the burning down of Cork city centre in December 1920 by the British forces (pictured at the start of this chapter) brought world attention. As spying and counter-spying intensified across the Cork countryside, it was also the case that 'civilians suspected of providing information to the [British military] were much more likely to face IRA assassination in County Cork than elsewhere in the country'. [157]

In fact, civilians in County Cork had an ascending scale of things to fear from the British forces at that time. The first was routine searches: they stopped, searched and questioned you as you went about your business along roads and streets, in homes and workplaces. The next was targeted raids on specific homes, villages or townlands. These raids were looking for traces of IRA activity or support, or that IRA men had visited or stayed in the house, or that IRA arms or messages were being handled, stored or supplied there. Raids often happened just after IRA men had left a house, or had escaped from the back of the property while the raid began.

The next level up was official British reprisals against civilian homes and livelihoods. In the countryside, this involved burning down their house and farm, destroying their farming equipment and leaving them homeless.

---

154 The phrase 'days of fear' is used by West Cork IRA leader Tom Barry in his memoir *Guerilla Days in Ireland* (Anvil Press, 1993). He describes the moment in 1923 when he felt their 'days of fear were ended, at least for a time', when he heard that a Truce had finally ended the Civil War. Fighters like him may have seemed fearless but they often describe feeling inside the same fear that ordinary people would. After all, they themselves had been just ordinary young civilians a couple of years earlier.
155 John Borgonovo, 'Atlas of the Irish Revolution, The War in Cork and Kerry', 18-9-2017, *www.IrishExaminer.com*
156 John Borgonovo, as in Note 155
157 John Borgonovo, as in Note 155

The next level of punishment was for anyone caught carrying dispatch messages for the IRA: they were taken away and interned indefinitely. And anyone caught carrying arms was executed. [158]

As IRA soldier Con Leddy put it in his testimony to the Irish government's Bureau of Military History, 'on account of the strength and large number of garrisons within a radius of ten or twenty miles of Fermoy (the British military) were active, and big round-ups and searches were of frequent occurrence. Our Column had many lucky escapes and were it not that we only billeted one night in any house we stayed in, we would have been captured, for on two occasions, in Glenville and at Ballynoe, the houses in which we stayed the previous night were raided the following day.' [159] That Glenville is our own Crow Glen.

Beyond raids, the next level that was greatly feared was 'round-ups', where British forces closed in on a whole area, sweeping up large numbers of men to be taken away for interrogation. An example was a round-up against the IRA's Millstreet Battalion, the one to the north-west of Crow Glen. There, 6,000 British troops closed in on and combed an area covering 100 square miles. [91] Local men were taken away for interrogation or internment. The British carried out massive burnings of homes and farms during the round-up.

As Con Leddy puts it in his testimony: 'Fire blazed on the hilltops, not only to the east but north, south and west also. They were searching everywhere, firing on everyone who failed to halt when called upon. Three men had already been shot [during the round-up], one an old man working in the fields.' Historian Aideen Carroll states that 'there were also round-ups in the Boggeragh Mountains, Clare, Glenville and the Dingle Peninsula'. [160] The one in Glenville - that is, the tiny village of Gleann an Phréacháin - must have been quite significant because the three other round-ups that she mentions covered areas nearly the size of a county.

Norma Buckley's parents had told her about one day when the British soldiers rounded up the Village men at gun-point. Apparently one Village woman known to be a simple, innocent person ran out and - losing the little wits that she had - screeched straight out to the British sergeant: 'Sir, are ye shooting today?' Not without straight-faced humour, he answered

---

158  Peter Hart, as in Note 123
159  IRA soldier Con Leddy's testimony at Irish Bureau of Military History, BMH WS756, available at www.bureauofmilitaryhistory.ie
160  Aideen Carroll, *Seán Moylan: Rebel Leader*, Mercier Press, Cork, 2010

'No ma'am, we probably won't be shooting these today.' Instead, the men were requisitioned as forced labour to rebuild their own Keame Bridge down in the Bride River Valley, which their own IRA men had just blown up in order to prevent the British from moving about freely in Gleann.

Norma told me the details that she had managed to get from my grandmother Nell over the years. As a look-out, raids and spies were the two things that Nell had to watch out for and spot coming along the lane to the homestead in Doon. By day, there was an agreed signalling system between the triangle of IRA-supporting houses that could see each other across the Bride Valley. A single bedsheet hanging on a clothesline across the front yard was the alerting signal that IRA men were hiding there, or that British soldiers were in the vicinity.

For illegal night meetings in Nell's house, there was a special hole beside the house for burying the hot coals and embers from the fireplace, if the British were found to be coming down the lane. During raids in the middle of the night, the first thing the British would do was to check the fireplace to see if it was still lighting or hot. If it was, they knew that men had been up talking or sleeping beside it, a sure sign that IRA fugitives were being hidden there.

With the sharp eyes of a child out in the dark, Nell learned to spot the glowing cigarette-ends of the bored British soldiers as they approached Doon at night. She had seen that a cigarette-end would glow red, then white, as a British soldier inhaled on it while coming down the long lane.

But the thing that was feared most of all was being anywhere near the dreaded Black and Tans, a lawless segment of the British forces. Britain's own war records show this command being formally given to the Black and Tans: 'If a police barracks is burnt, then the best house in the locality is to be commandeered, the occupants thrown into the gutter. Let them die there, the more the merrier.' [161] Official British records also show a Black and Tan commander instructing his men 'to shout *Hands up* at civilians and to shoot anyone who did not immediately obey'. He told them: 'Innocent persons may be shot but that cannot be helped, and you are bound to get the right parties sooner or later. The more you shoot, the

---

161 *The Independent* (UK), 'Ireland's War of Independence: The Chilling Story of the Black and Tans', London, 21-4-2006, available at www.independent.co.uk/news/world/europe/irelands-war-of-independence-the-chilling-story-of-the-black-and-tans-5336022.html

better I will like you. And I assure you that none of you will get in trouble for shooting any man.' [162]

I will not give words here to what some Black and Tan interrogators did to some of the Irish activists that they rounded up for questioning.[163] Words can have value and power. A word spoken can change the course of a lifetime. An IRA prisoner muttering the name of a fellow-soldier, a spy or a look-out could spell death, prison or lifelong exile for that individual. Activists prepared themselves as best they could. George Power, one of the IRA leaders near Crow Glen, describes in his memoir how the Battalion's nurse had, at his request, given him a vial containing enough morphine to avoid being taken alive. [164]

In fact, a top figure of the British Army, Field Marshall Sir Henry Wilson visited British Prime Minister Winston Churchill in person to beg him to rein in the Black and Tans' atrocities in Ireland, which were tarnishing the British Empire's reputation around the world. But he wrote of his visit: 'Winston saw very little harm in this, but it horrifies me… He won't listen or agree….' [165]

In fact, the reality is that Britain's whole war effort in Ireland depended entirely on information. All they needed to know was *which* house - of the tens of thousands of houses in north County Cork - was the one where IRA leader Liam Lynch was being hidden. If they could only know that, the Irish independence effort would be consigned to history. All they would have needed were the three words '*Kate Hickey's, Glenville*' and the game would be up in North Cork.

You'd think it would have been relatively easy, for instance, to scare that information out of a young girl. So what incredible trust Nell's family and neighbours had put on her small shoulders, and on many like her. With spies, informers and interrogators everywhere in 1921, you placed your life in the hands of dozens of neighbours, dependent on them never revealing your name or role. Cork historian Diarmuid Grainger who wrote the Foreword for this book, points out in his own book the large 'number of ambushes where the IRA were 'given away', pointing to informers in the

---

162  *The Independent*, as in Note 161
163  If you want, you can read about those horrors for yourself online in the British *Independent* article cited in Note 161 above
164  O' Reilly, Terence, *Rebel Heart: George Lennon, Flying Column Commander*, Mercier Press, Cork, 2005. Page 123 explains that the nurse 'had given him a slim tube of morphine tablets as the idea of wounds and torture filled him with terror'.
165  *The Independent*, as in Note 161

ranks or in the wider community' - a constant danger. [166] Nonetheless, the winning weapon on the Irish side was silence, not telling, *acting as if you didn't know*. The British had countless soldiers and unlimited firepower. And yet relatively quickly, to the surprise of the watching world, *not telling* won the Irish their war against the army of the great British Empire.

The only thing that my grandmother did ever tell me in person about the War of Independence was that both she and everyone else were very much afraid of the Black and Tans. Drunk and unsupervised, you never knew what they were going to do. She told me about one day when she was in the Village with other children and the Black and Tans came rounding up Village men. They were swivelling around on the spot in the middle of the Street, shooting the chimneypots off the Village houses in a circle around them for fun.

Back when she told me that, I could imagine how frightening it must have been for a little girl. But it's all magnified a hundred times by what I know now. The Black and Tans didn't know it, but she did: it was her and her family and friends that they were looking for.

## Friends and good people

In fact, historians know now that women and teenagers played a deep and dangerous role in the success of the Irish War of Independence. Three-quarters of IRA fighting units had a matching District Council of *Cumann na mBan*, the women's branch of the IRA. [167] The archives show that there was indeed a Cumann na mBan Council for the neighbouring villages of Watergrasshill, Glenville and Rathcormac. [168] They record that its Secretary, Cecilia O' Mahoney, was a qualified nurse who gave first aid lectures but also carried dispatches, acted as a scout, lodged and fed IRA men at her house, and helped to make explosives there. [169]

The Irish government archive also describes another local Cumann na mBan girl, Margaret Flood, aged 20: 'She helped her sister with the operation to rescue IRA Volunteer Denis Hegarty - Commanding Officer

166   Diarmuid Grainger, *Witnesses to Freedom: A Day by Day Account of The War of Independence in Cork*, Independent, 2019
167   John Borgonovo, as in Note 155
168   *Military Service Pensions Collection*, available at www.militaryarchives.ie
169   *Military Service Pensions Collection*, record on Cecilia O' Mahoney, available at www.militaryarchives.ie

of Glenville Company - from Fermoy Hospital, by providing the horse-cart and driving him 11 miles.' [170] This Denis Hegarty, wounded and captured by the British, was the son of the IRA house across from Nell's in the Bride River Valley. He took over the leadership of Gleann's IRA fighters when their neighbour, Denis Hickey, who had been leading them, was captured by the British and imprisoned for the rest of the War of Independence. Both men survived the war but Denis Hegarty will make a sad reappearance in our story in the coming chapter, in the year 1949.

Historian Peter Hart points out that 'women's contribution to the revolution differed fundamentally from men's in that many women were active outside of any organisation. Behind the guerrillas was an essential cadre of mothers, sisters, wives, and other domestic revolutionaries - some affiliated to Cumann na mBan but most not - who ran their homes as safe houses. Typical of these was Mrs Hickey of Badger's Hill, Glenville, whose house was a way station and headquarters for the North Cork Brigade. Liam Lynch, George Power, Lar Condon, and others spent months living there, and the Brigade's Flying Column was formed there.[171] Without Mrs Hickey and others like her, there would have been no Column. Every Brigade had its network of Mrs So-and-So's, vital but invisible.' [172]

I was so happy, sitting there in the library archives, to see the young widow Kate Hickey, the courteous neighbour at the other point of Nell's local triangle in the Bride Valley, named in person by an international historian for her incredible risks and bravery. As recent historians of women's role in the War of Independence have put it, 'the crime of harbouring a rebel was punishable by death'. For instance, 'Mrs Tobin provided a safe house at Tincurry, Tipperary (…) Her home was ever open to 'the boys' until it was burned to the ground as an official reprisal.' [173]

I often wonder now, who *were* they really, this network of exceptional individuals that Nell's family risked their lives with and for? We are lucky enough to have the photo of Denis Hickey, Commanding Officer of the Glenville Company, that is shown at the start of this chapter. In the centre of the back row, he wears his civilian clothes as a farmer. John Arnold, the

---

170 *Military Service Pensions Collection*, record on Margaret Flood, available at www.militaryarchives.ie
171 Peter Hart, *The IRA and its Enemies*, as in Note 123
172 Peter Hart, as in Note 123
173 Louise Ryan & Margaret Ward, *Irish Women and Nationalism: Soldiers, New Women and Wicked Hags*, Irish Academic Press, Dublin, 2019

newspaper journalist who recently published this photo, writes: 'In the middle of the back row is Denis Hickey of Badger's Hill, Glenville. One of four children born to Michael Hickey and his wife Abina Dinan, Denis is the oldest in the picture at 38. [His relative, Kate Hickey's] household was a well-known 'safe house' for volunteers 'on the run'. Denis was Commanding Officer of the Glenville Company and was interned for a period also... The Army Census [records him] as Captain Denis Hickey. When the fighting was over, Denis returned to his ancestral acres and bore the name Captain Hickey 'til the day he died.' [174]

As we saw earlier, the Hickey family had households in neighbouring fields on their lands at the western end of the Bride River Valley. One was the home of the young widow Kate. The other was the house of this fighting man Denis Hickey, Commanding Officer of the IRA's Glenville Company before he was captured by the British Army and interned in Northern Ireland.

Liam Lynch was the national IRA leader whom all these local fighters followed and who lived with them at Kate Hickey's house, strategising from there at times to coordinate the whole Southern Irish war effort. This description by one of the local IRA men is typical of how many others also describe him: 'He was a strange young man to be at the head of a rebel army. He was handsome, in a boyish, innocent way. His large blue eyes and open countenance indicated his transparent honesty. His looks, bearing and presence might have belonged to a single-minded, devoted priest.' [175]

Another wrote, fondly and wittily: 'Lynch was one of the few men I ever met whose authority while under command I accepted without question. He was also my friend, or I liked to think so. How can he be a military man but have the appearance of a responsible superior of a religious order? He was by nature most abstemious and never raised his voice, which was gentle. If he ever smiled, I have no recollection of the occasion.' [176]

Engaged to be married once the war was over, Liam survived the War of Independence but not its aftermath. He was felled by a bullet on the

---

174 John Arnold, '97 years on: The Stories behind these Seven Proud, Brave Men', *The Echo*, 4-10-2019, available at www.echolive.ie/nostalgia/John-Arnold-97-years-on-the-stories-behind-these-seven-proud-brave-men-178581d3-4bdd-463f-9e27-4c1f58d75417-ds
175 Daniel Murray, 'The Fog of Certainty: Liam Lynch and the Start of the Civil War, 1922' in *An Irish History Blog*, 2017
176 George Lennon speaking in Terence O' Reilly's *Rebel Heart*, as in Note 132

Knockmealdown Mountains in April, 1923, about 80 miles north east of Gleann an Phréacháin. He shouted orders to his men to leave him and escape. When those who had shot him reached his crumpled, bleeding body, he said to them: 'I am Liam Lynch, Chief of Staff of the IRA. Get me a priest and a doctor. I'm dying.' [177] He was 29.

Even if you disagree with their politics and believe they shouldn't have taken up arms to decolonise Ireland and create a democracy, individuals like Liam Lynch were people who 'cared nothing for material wealth or possessions, and exchanged their lives for the emancipation of their fellow Irishmen and Irishwomen'. [178] It would not seem right to me that his activism in Gleann continue to be covered with a blanket of silence.

There is one partial explanation for that silence. Historian John Borgonovo points out that the IRA had a strict policy of forbidding members to engage in any combat in areas close to a HQ, a 'safe house' where important leaders were hidden, or a place where weapons were stored or strategic meetings happened. Crow Glen was all those things. On the maps of the British surveillance forces who were trying to find them, such places needed to appear quiet, neutral and irrelevant, as part of a strategy 'recognising that the Crown Forces would ignore any areas known to be quiet'. [179]

And in fact, if you drew a circle that stretched a few miles away from Crow Glen in each direction, there were many recorded ambushes, shootings, skirmishes and battles *outside* that circle, in places like Watergrasshill, Carrignavar, Rathcormac, Castletownroche, Killavullen and so on. But *inside* that circle - close around Crow Glen where the IRA were hiding - there were no public combats involving the IRA.

We have seen that the British army did raid and shake up Crow Glen repeatedly, searching unsuccessfully for signs of IRA activity. And the local IRA did blow up the bridge at Keame, just a mile from the Village and from their own Bride Valley HQ, to prevent the British getting through. But the IRA themselves did their best not to engage in any public combat there, to avoid drawing attention. The two trials and executions of

177  Meda Ryan, *The Real Chief: The Story of Liam Lynch*, Mercier Press, Cork, 2005
178  Lorcan Collins, *Ireland's War of Independence 1919-21: The IRA's Guerrilla Campaign*, O' Brien Press, 2019
179  John Borgonovo, 'The Guerrilla Infrastructure: IRA Special Services in the Cork Number One Brigade, 1917-1921', *The Irish Sword*, Vol 27, Military History Society of Ireland, 2010

British spies that happened in Gleann an Phréacháin were of course done in secret and not known about at the time, and the bodies were disposed of in secret places (places we will return to later in this book).

We will also see in a later chapter that there was in fact one public attack by the IRA in Gleann an Phréacháin, and that was on the Manor. But interestingly, it was by the IRA battalion from Cork city, who came out specially to steal badly needed car parts from the Manor's garages (cars being very scarce and useful at the time). Historians show us that the IRA leadership often disagreed internally about these things. And I would wager that, for the reasons we've just seen above, the Gleann branch were not at all pleased at this incursion by their colleagues from the city. The local IRA deliberately never touched the Gleann Manor, no matter how tempting it might have seemed, because it would have been an obvious way to attract unwanted attention onto themselves.

On one of my visits to Norma Buckley, she asked me whether I remembered one particular Sunday drive that she knew my family had gone on when I was a child, to a place 80 miles away in a very remote part of the northeast mountains. I did remember it because it was unusual, in that my granny came with us. She would normally stay at home by the fire when we went out. But I remember that she squashed in with us kids and dogs in the back of the car to make that long journey.

Our destination was a wild, windswept mountaintop with no houses in view. It was raining and bitterly cold by the time we got there. There was a granite monument at the top, like a large gravestone. When Norma prompted me, I remembered now that I'd been told it was a memorial to some man called Liam Lynch who had died there, and I'd thought no more of it.

Now I remembered that my grandmother made the climb all the way from the car up through the rough sloping heather to the monument, and that she put her hand on it. I remember that it looked vaguely odd to me, her standing up there shaking in the wind in her best tweed coat with her handbag on her arm, as if going to Mass.

I cannot imagine how she made the long car-journey to that mountain-top with us without ever mentioning a word of what is written in this chapter, and then made the journey home again equally wordlessly. How I wish she had had someone to talk to about it all, to unburden herself. But those are modern notions, and didn't seem to be what she wanted. My grandparents and their peers had their whole lives in the Glen of the Crow to discuss their War of Independence experiences, at least between themselves. And they all, together, decided not to.

But how I wish that I could go back in time and stand by her side in the rain at that monument and pull on her hand and say: 'Granny, I am *so* sorry. I understand it all now. I know now who this person is. I know that you held each other's lives in the palm of your hands, dozens of times over. I am so sorry that he had to die from a bullet-wound, so young, on this dreary mountainside so far from anywhere. I'm so sorry that you couldn't protect him then, as you did so many times before when you were a little girl.

I am so sorry that he never got to enjoy the country that he gave everything to create. But he succeeded in the mission he had given himself, Granny. And from the start he was happy to give his life in exchange for that. I am so grateful to you all for what you went through to win this free and ordinary future for us. I am so sorry for being an insouciant little brat who didn't know anything about it and took everything for granted. I am so sorry that I didn't know before.'

I would have held my granny's hand and helped her pick her way back down through the knee-high wet heather towards the car. So that she would know that at least I was aware, and that I could begin to imagine how she must feel at that moment beside that monument. But I was unaware, and I said none of that. I just pushed into her hand a little bunch of bog cotton that I'd picked for her, and ran off with the dogs. That I was a child was no excuse: I was the same age as she was, when she was responsible for keeping dozens of men alive and out of prison, as a look-out in Crow Glen.

## Oınnʒ and Nell

During the War of Independence, another thoughtful young man from the Nagle Mountain had also risen to prominence. He was Tomás Mac Curtain (pictured at the start of this chapter), elected Lord Mayor of Cork city in 1920. From his youth in the wild outbacks of Mourne Abbey in the Nagle Mountains, Tomás nurtured a passion for Irish music, poetry, archaeology, history and language, as centuries of people had done in that landscape before him. [180] He studied the culture of the Irish-speaking poets of the Bardic Schools before Cromwell's invasion. He taught Irish language classes in his free time. And he campaigned zealously for the new political party, Sinn Féin, which openly called for a free Irish Republic to be established through peaceful democratic elections.

Historians describe Tomás as a keen cyclist who pedalled tirelessly all over the backroads and mountains of North Cork. 'On his bicycle he would travel rural Munster, establishing branches of the Gaelic League as he went.' [181] As they put it, he 'embodied the multi-stranded nature of Ireland's revolution, his life a cross-over of the Gaelic language revival, the emerging IRA and the ascendant Sinn Féin political party'. [182]

He was the first ever Republican Mayor of Cork city, which the people saw as a great milestone of hope and progress towards an Irish republic. At his election, 'thunderous applause and a rendition of 'The Soldier's Song' at the City Hall' rang out over the city. [183]

In 1920, while trying to motivate himself with positive thoughts about how good things could be if they won the War of Independence, Tomás had a business idea that was born of his intimate knowledge of the North Cork countryside. Over a pint of Murphy's stout, he recommended the idea to a friend of his, JJ Dineen. And it so happens that if Tomás had not had that idea, and if he had not passed it on to JJ, I would never have been born.

JJ came from the remote, Irish-speaking area of Ballyvourney towards West Cork. It was mostly poor but JJ ran a chain of successful grocery shops in in Cork city. He mentioned to Tomás that he'd like to open more there. 'Don't', Tomás said. 'There's too much competition in the city. You'd be a nobody. Listen, I guarantee you that we'll win this war - I can feel it in my bones. And when we do, a whole new market will open up across the countryside. Our farmers will at last be able to develop their farms, grow more, buy more, and trade and sell their produce freely. I've been thinking about it. Bring me a map of the county and I'll show you

---

180  Tomás was born in Mourne Abbey: Liam Lynch moved his HQ over the mountains from Crow Glen to Mourne Abbey in the later part of the War of Independence.
181  Donal Fallon, 'A Tribute to Tomás Mac Curtain, the Martyred Lord Mayor of Cork', *The Journal*, 14-3-2020, at www.thejournal.ie/readme/tomas-mac-curtain-5045854-Mar2020
182  Donal Fallon, as in Note 181
183  Donal Fallon, as in Note 181

where to put your shop. And I guarantee you'll have a thriving business beyond anything you're imagining now.'

JJ dutifully brought a map round to Tomás's house. Tomás smoothed it out on the kitchen table and pointed to a very large triangle of open terrain in North Cork with only one small village in the centre of it - Gleann an Phréacháin. 'See there, I was born out in the back of beyond, way past that village' he said, pointing to the wildest north of the triangle. 'There's nothing out there only isolated farmsteads. But see here: to get down south to Cork city you have to pass through that one village, Gleann. And if you put a food-shop in there, you'll have not only a shop but a trading post.'

'Put a cart on the road with a man to drive it, and run it in and out from Cork city a few times a week to bring produce out to the Gleann shop. But then send your driver out on the country roads the rest of the week delivering groceries out to the country farms, and bringing back in from them all the produce that they'll be only too happy to sell to you. And you bring all that back in to sell on in Cork city every time your man goes in there. So your cart will never do a journey empty, in any direction. And I swear to you, man: our farmers will have their own milk, butter, eggs, meat, chickens and vegetables rolling back and forth along our own roads only seventy years after the Famine!'

Tomás's vision must have seemed outlandishly optimistic at the time. He could not have known that in less than three years, it would be a reality. That they would win their War of Independence and that JJ would implement Tomás's plan in full, exactly as Tomás had described it. In 1923 JJ took the road north out of Cork city and kept going until he found Gleann an Phréacháin. He built a shop there opposite the blacksmith's forge, where farmers from all over the mountains to the north brought their horses to be shod and their tools to be mended. And from its opening day, the little business thrived right through the twentieth century, in exactly the way that Tomás had predicted.

What Tomás did not know, on that day when he and JJ got excited about how life would be in the future, was that the following Tuesday morning, on the 20 of March 1920 (Tomás's thirty-sixth birthday), there would be an early ring on Tomás's doorbell. That his wife would answer the door with the teapot in her hand, their young son standing behind her. And that British militia with their faces blackened would push past her up the stairs and shoot Tomás dead where he stood in his pyjamas. He would be

Cork's first democratically elected Republican Mayor for just forty-nine days.

The *Evening Echo* obituary for Kate Hickey of the Bride River Valley in Gleann explains that as well as the national IRA leaders named already, Tomás too had been lodged in secret hiding by Kate at her house. The article explains that 'Mrs Hickey was a great friend of Tomás Mac Curtain, the late Lord Mayor of Cork. He found safe asylum in her home for some weeks before his election as Lord Mayor of Cork.' [184]

Tomás was succeeded in the role by his close friend Terence Mac Swiney (also pictured at the start of this chapter). Married to one of the Murphy family who made the stout that they all socialised over, Terence was a well-known author and playwright who founded the Celtic Literary Society and the Cork Dramatic Society. A sensitive poet-intellectual, he had a degree in psychology and ethics. He had reflected and written deeply about the ethical dilemmas of opposing an occupying regime.

For instance, his *The Ethics of Revolt: A Discussion from a Catholic Point of View as to When it Becomes Lawful to Rise in Revolt Against the Civil Power* was published in 1918. As soon as he became Lord Mayor of Cork, Terence was captured and illegally imprisoned in England by the British. In protest at his unlawful abduction as an elected Mayor, Terence spent 74 days starving to death on hunger-strike in his English prison cell. A month earlier he had written to a colleague: 'If I die, I know the fruit will exceed the cost a thousand-fold.' [185]

British atrocities in the War of Independence had sparked frequent protests around the world. But this death by hunger-strike of the Lord Mayor of Cork in an English jail 'galvanised protests in the streets of Barcelona and New York city'. [186]

It was in memory of his friend Tomás that JJ implemented so faithfully Tomás's idea of opening a shop in Gleann an Phréacháin once the war was over. To run it, he brought up from Ballyvourney a tall, serious young cousin of his called Dinny who was good at mathematics and card-playing. And that is how my grandfather came to Gleann, where he enjoyed

184 *The Evening Echo*, 'Late Mrs K. Hickey, Glenville', 5-6-1978
185  Diarmaid Ferriter, 'From Turmoil to Truce: A Mature Reflection on the War of Independence', *The Irish Times*, 11-1-2020
186  Donal Fallon, as in Note 181

running *The Shop* for the rest of his life, as cousin JJ later left it to him in his will.

Looking just like a provisions store in a Wild West movie, the Shop provided everything from sides of bacon and hand-filled bags of sugar to six-inch nails and lengths of rope. Dinny developed close relationships with the dozens of farmers who came in there weekly from all over the hills and mountainsides north of the Village. Card-games played no inconsiderable part in his success. When the working day was finished, Dinny hosted in the back of the Shop endless, convivial card-games that lasted long into the night. The War was over and they were free men now. They could do what they liked. There were no curfews, no raids, no round-ups. They could stay up and associate all night if they wanted to, with no need to bury the hot coals out of the fireplace if they heard boot-steps coming along the road.

In that setting, Dinny became especially close to the Sweeney family in Doon. Like their daughter, he too had been a young look-out in Ballyvourney, towards West Cork. But a few years older than her, he had also been a dispatch-carrier for the IRA, a 'runner', as they were called at the time. Within a few years, Dinny was well established and respected in the Village and Nell was a strong and handsome young woman. Nell decided to break with the tradition of marrying across the Bride River Valley, perhaps disappointing one or two young farmers on the opposite slope.

This photo shows Dinny and Nell (in white at the centre) on their wedding day with their family and friends, lazing around contentedly in their own lush fields (formerly Johanna Carney's) in Doon. The picture seems to gather some of the things they value most - friends and neighbours, making their own music with violins and an accordion, with their pets and children around them in their own meadow. On a sunny day, there's nowhere on earth more beautiful than Doon for a party.

But only those in the know would understand the significance of the rifle that Nell's father, the old second-generation gamekeeper, Michael Sweeney, takes care to include in this peaceful family photo, despite it no longer being needed. In his suit, waistcoat and hat, my great-grandfather, the old countryman, stands to attention slightly in front of the young group, as if he is protecting them and the new freedoms they have attained through such recent sacrifices. In a relaxed but almost military stance, he holds the rifle on his shoulder rather than on the ground or at his feet.

Well behind them now is all the pain suffered to achieve this new-found freedom on their own land, in their own country. But it would not have been achieved without the rifle, transformative enough to win its own place in this contented family scene.

It was very unusual indeed that as a wedding present, Nell and Dinny received the gift of a house in the Village. It came from a well-off friend of the gamekeeper. As Elliot Hudson had been, this man too was an upper-class sympathiser with the cause of Irish independence. He used to come down from Dublin to stay at the Manor House, and eventually grew so attached to Gleann that he bought himself a house in the Village as a country retreat. The gamekeeper befriended this likeminded man, perhaps confiding to him some of the secrets of their IRA activities in the area. When the dust had settled after the War of Independence and Nell and Dinny were ready to marry, this man, who had no heirs of his own, bequeathed to the newly-weds his house in the Village, where I grew up beside them decades later.

Hunger has turned out to be one of the themes that twist through this book, from the Famine to Cork's Lord Mayor starving to death in jail. Oddly, I had my own brush with hunger as a toddler in the late 1960s. For the first three years of my life, I had a life-threatening illness that required long, frequent fasts as part of the tests and treatments.

But the memory of starvation still lay close to the skin in Gleann an Phréacháin. One day Denis Riordan, the gruff bachelor farmer who lived next door, couldn't stand it any longer. He came to the door dragging me along by the wrist behind him and roared in agitation: 'For the *love of god* can ye not *feed* the child?!' Apparently, I had been knocking at his back door, little hand out begging for a crust of bread, repeating the word '*Crusty? Crusty?*' as appealingly as I could.

Denis was the nephew of Michael Riordan, who had to take the coffin ship during the Famine. It was Denis's uncle Mike who had put the advertisement in the *Boston Pilot,* searching the American East Coast for the bereaved Johanna Carney so that he could help her, as the two families had been close back in Gleann. Denis's parents had somehow survived the Famine in the Village. And Denis believed those city doctors were wrong: a child should be *fed.*

## The cost of peace

One day when I was leafing through the ornate calligraphy of the teacher Seán Ó Duinnshléibhe's folklore manuscript I read, to my surprise, that at the Mass Rock - just below where he sat writing in Chimneyfield School - 'Mass was celebrated in 1921, when 16,000 attended'. [187] I asked Norma Buckley about this crazy, surely mistaken, attendance figure and she more or less confirmed it with a press clipping and a photograph of the occasion.

What an exceptional occasion that must have been - when thousands from all over the region descended on that ancient place of rebellious worship to celebrate ending 700 years of occupation. One can only imagine the joy of the Hickey family that day, on whose land the Mass Rock stands. They, more than anyone, had risked everything to hide the national IRA leaders in their home. My granny Nell, then aged 12, decided to attend the historic event wearing her ceremonial white Confirmation dress.

A few years later, the newly independent Irish government set about an exhaustive search to locate, acknowledge and thank everyone who had given active service that had contributed to the Irish victory. By 1931, all had been meticulously traced, individually assessed and awarded small but symbolic military pensions for their service to the nation in those few all-important years. The government records include a hand-written document of 187 pages recording the names and contributions of all those

---

187  Seán Ó Duinnshléibhe, *Gleann an Phréacháin - Béaloideas,* as in Note 32

in the local IRA Companies around Crow Glen, including the Glenville Company.

For instance, they record that Timothy Forde of Lepers' Hill, Glenville, aged 18, was badly wounded in an attack on the British barracks near Fermoy in February 1920. The government records attest that during 1921 he searched for spies, did overnight guard duty where IRA officers slept, and 'assisted his first cousin, Denis Hickey of Doon, Glenville, to manufacture ammunitions'. Timmy Forde died peacefully in his seventies in Gleann an Phréacháin, in 1972. [188]

The archives show that Eoin Curtain, aged 23, was also in active military service around Gleann. He was the driver of the car that abducted the British VIP General Lucas from the British Army's Fermoy garrison and drove him 'via Glenville, to Mallow' to be hidden. [189] But seven years later Eoin had fled to Montreal, and a year after that, he was living in New York City. This is a sad motif that I saw repeatedly in the outcomes for Crow Glen's IRA leaders.

The Irish military archive tried to contact him to honour him with a pension but it records: 'He lived in a series of addresses in New York city, Brooklyn and the Bronx. The last communication with him was in 1940. The Irish Department of Defence received back its last letter stamped 'Return to sender' in 1943. It is unclear when and where Eoin Curtain died.' You can read between those emigrant lines and see that Eoin Curtain died alone and unknown in his early forties, somewhere in a back-street on the other side of the world.

As I read the fates of five men who had led the IRA Companies in Gleann an Phréacháin and four surrounding villages, yet another layer of their lost past was surfacing. Denis Hegarty from Ardarow in Glenville was Commanding Officer of the Glenville Company - the man rescued from Fermoy hospital by the brave Margaret Flood in the records cited earlier. Among the triangle of IRA houses in the Bride Valley, he came from the one nearest to Nell's. But suddenly, right after they won the war, he was living in the USA. The Commanding Officer of the Watergrasshill Company was Jeremiah Ahern from Scatbarry, Watergrasshill: he was by then in Australia. Matt Mulcahy was Commanding Officer of the nearby Kildinan Company. He spent the rest of his life in England. And Liam

188 *Military Service Pensions Collection*, record of Timothy Forde, available at www.militaryarchives.ie
189 *Military Service Pensions Collection*, record of Eoin (also spelled Owen) Curtain, available at www.militaryarchives.ie

Dorgan, Commanding Officer of the local Rathcormac Company, saw out the rest of his life in the USA. A commanding officer of the nearby Millstreet IRA ended his life as a homeless person in England, his body found in a street gutter.

It felt so sad to see that scattering of immediate emigrations, as the local leaders seemed thrown to the four winds. After all the terrifying sacrifices that they, their friends and families had made, they, unlike my grandparents, didn't get to sit and live in the country that they had liberated.

'They *escaped*, fortunately', Norma Buckley told me when I asked her about it. I was surprised that she thought a life of anonymous exile in the US, Australia or England was a positive thing. [190] But she reminded me that the alternative was to risk being imprisoned or even executed by the new Irish Free State government in its first year.

In the famous Treaty that concluded the War of Independence, the deal that the British offered was that they would end their 700-year occupation of 26 counties of Ireland, but would retain the 6 counties of the north east. They would withdraw their military and police forces and Ireland would become a 'Free State'. But crucially, they would not accept the fully independent Irish Republic that had been declared by those leading the 1916 Easter Rising. Instead the Irish 'Free State' would be part of the British Commonwealth like Australia or Canada, with the British monarch as its head of state, albeit symbolically

One can imagine the bitterness of this deal for the IRA fighters and activists who had won the War and assumed they now had a 32-county Irish Republic that was fully independent, only to work out the details of the handover.

The dramatic question for them on hearing the details of this Treaty was how to react. Some felt they had to accept the compromise route of ending the War and taking whatever national gains were available now, in order to build on them later. This was what IRA Treaty negotiator, Corkman Michael Collins, called 'the freedom... to win our freedom'. [191]

---

190 I have explored the complex experiences and emotions of later Irish emigrants in 'Saoirse, from the Catholic Republic of Ireland' in my book *Asylum under Dreaming Spires: Refugees' Lives in Cambridge Today* (with University of East London, 2017) and in 'The Irish among the British and the Women among the Irish' in *Location and Dislocation, the New Irish at Home and Abroad* (Cork University Press, 1997).
191 Micheal Collins, *The Path to Freedom*, NuVision Publications, South Dakota, USA, 2005

Others felt that after so much risk and suffering, they just could not accept signing away the Irish Republic that they had fought for, to now become part of the British Commonwealth and subjects of the British Monarchy. They had won the War, for God's sake, not lost it! They felt they should fight on and claim the full prize that was almost within reach now. This was the view of some of the prominent IRA fighters in the Crow Glen area.

Any sensible person can empathise with both viewpoints. Any of us might have gone for either option. But what none of them in their wildest dreams could have imagined was what happened next. No-one could have foreseen that within months, the new Irish 'Free State' would treat so severely any IRA fighters who now opposed the Treaty.

The armed Civil War conflict between the two sides lasted only 11 months, from June 1922 to May 1923. But recent studies suggest that it cost almost 2,000 lives, about the same as the War of Independence.[192] The new Irish Free State imprisoned 12,000 IRA fighters who, just months earlier, had fought shoulder to shoulder with them against the British, but now opposed the compromise that was the Treaty.

The Free State government led out 81 of the most prominent captured leaders and formally executed them. [193] Hundreds more on both sides were killed in pitched battles fought around the country.

Michael Collins, who had had the unenviable task of negotiating the Treaty in London, had been an IRA military leader since the Easter 1916 Rising in Dublin. Just two years earlier, Britain had unsuccessfully offered any member of the Irish public the equivalent of 400,000 euros today for information leading to his capture. Yet in August 1922, he was assassinated by the anti-Treaty forces of his own IRA. Half a million people - almost a fifth of the country's population - attended as mourners at his funeral. [194]

By October 1923, eight thousand of the anti-Treaty IRA prisoners were on a very public hunger strike that lasted for 41 days and cost the lives of three local men from North Cork villages. [195]  Cork City & County

---

192  Gemma Clark, *Everyday Violence in the Irish Civil War*, Cambridge University Press, 2014
193  Timothy Breen Murphy, *The Government's Executions Policy During the Irish Civil War, 1922 - 1923*, PhD thesis, National University of Ireland at Maynooth, 2010
194  Tim Pat Coogan, *Michael Collins*, Random House, Random House, UK, 2016
195  *The Irish Times*, 'The Long History of the Irish Hunger Strike: New Exhibition in Kilmainham Gaol Tells the Story from Thomas Ashe to Bobby Sands', 21-9-2017

Archives hold a touching document from that time. It's a 140-page *Prison Autograph Book*' or personal souvenir album kept by one of those prisoners. He was Seán Puinse (Seán Punch in English) and the Archives describe it as covering 'his time in Gormanstown Camp, County Meath, Jan-Nov 1923 and Mountjoy Prison, Dec 1923-January 1924', with 'sketches, quotations, verse and poetry and signatures, made by friends and fellow inmates'. [196]

I was surprised to find that one of the signatories in it is Arthur O' Leary from Gleann an Phréacháin. As children we used to play at his house, less than a mile south of the Village. I had never previously heard that he had anything to do with - nor had made such sacrifices for - the War of Independence. His niece, Betty, grew up in that house and was a close childhood friend of Norma Buckley. Norma confirmed to me now that Art had been an active IRA man during the War. Near his house there was a cave where he used to stay in hiding when he couldn't safely go home during the War. She and Betty used to play around the cave as kids and they knew it as 'Arthur's cave'.

Another moving signature in the little album, by one Seán Hayes from the village of Kilmallock, specifies that Seán signed his friend's book '*On the 9th day of the big hunger strike*'. They must have been feeling unpleasantly hungry as Seán wrote those words after not eating anything for nine days.

Historians describe how Liam Lynch - the IRA leader that my grandmother had protected as a young look-out in Crow Glen - 'made strenuous attempts to heal the split in Republican forces prior to the Civil War, but was a vigorous opponent of the Treaty'. [197] That bullet that finally felled him on the Knockmealdown Mountains - where my granny went to visit his memorial with us 54 years later, to lay her hand on it so painfully - was not an English bullet. It came from the Irish Free State forces who were hunting him. This high-profile killing of the leader of the anti-Treaty IRA is often considered to be the last bullet of the Civil War, which was finally brought to an end by a truce a few weeks later.

In all, since the Proclamation of Independence at the Easter Rising in 1916, over a hundred of the more visionary, egalitarian and progressive thinkers of the Irish revolution had been formally executed - almost 80%

196   Cork City and County Archives, *Seán Punch Autograph Book 1907-1923*, Archive Ref. IE CCCA/U089

197   *Cork Beo*, 'Who Is Who in the Second Cork Brigade? - Liam Lynch', on *An Interactive Web Map of All IRA Operations in Co. Cork 1919 -1921* at www.corkbeo.ie/news/history/interactive-map-ira-operations-cork-18113200

of them by the new Irish Free State during the Civil War, and 20% by the British.

One theme of this book is the many things that, at certain moments of our lives, *we do not know* about our own future. Johanna Carney didn't know whether or not they would survive the coffin ship. Tomás Mac Curtain didn't know that he'd be shot in his pyjamas on that Tuesday morning. During the War of Independence, the Crow Glenners did not know whether they could ever defeat the might of the occupying British Empire - they were just determined to try.

All those outcomes were unknowns, like the fall of a dice before it is thrown. But they weren't unimaginable. However, that the new Irish Free State would execute 81 of its own recent comrades is the only thing in this book that was genuinely beyond imagining. A few months earlier, people would have bet their lives that that could never happen.

In the government records on the five IRA Companies in and around Gleann an Phréacháin, it is heartbreaking to see that all had Commanding Officers who didn't get to live out their lives in the new country that they had fought to create. The Sweeneys looked on in horror while their friends and colleagues '*escaped*, fortunately', as Norma Buckley rightly put it, to a life of hidden, anonymous exile in the US, Australia or England. Sweeneys, not having a son of fighting age, weren't at risk of interment by the new Free State.

Historian Diarmuid Grainger reminded me that just a few years later in 1927, the anti-Treaty 'side' became an official political party under De Valera, and came to power to govern the country from 1932. Called Fianna Fáil, that government under De Valera sought to finish tracing and honouring all who had contributed to the War of Independence victory, including of course those who had opposed the Treaty. But as Diarmuid explained, 'for many it was too late', as they were already settled abroad. [198] The lonely, unrecorded death of young Crow Glen IRA fighter Owen Curtain in a New York backstreet, which we witnessed earlier in that government's archives, is just one example among many.

The assassinated Michael Collins, before he went to London to negotiate the Treaty, had written of his impatience that Britain should '*give us back our country - to live in, - to grow in, - to love*'. [199] I felt so glad that, unlike so many of their colleagues, Nell and Dinny did get to live out their lives

---

198 In correspondence with the author
199 Michael Collins, *The Path to Freedom*, as in Note 191

peacefully in the country that they had all risked so much to decolonise. As I write these lines today, Ireland's two main political parties, descended from the two 'sides' of the Civil War, have formed a government where for the first time ever, they will govern together, sharing their power with the Green Party. A fitting gesture for the centenary of the Civil War in 2022, it also acknowledges that the environmental crisis looming ahead of us all today will need our united forces to tackle it.

But Norma Buckley had something more to tell me about healing resolutions in Gleann an Phréacháin. Apparently, one day in 1947, a car pulled up outside Nell and Dinny's house in the Village. This was unusual: the only cars on the road in those days were those of the doctor and the priest. Two tall, burly strangers in long dark overcoats got out. They knocked on the door and one said he needed to see Nell, needed to talk to her.

It happened to be the day of her daughter's First Communion, a major festival for the family, full of celebrations around the child in her elaborate white dress, veil and shoes. But going against custom, it turned out that Nell would not be available to participate. She spent the afternoon in private discussion with the stranger, alone in the side room of her house.

No-one will ever know what they said to each other. He was Denis Hegarty from the farm opposite Nells' across the valley. He was the one who as an 18-year-old IRA soldier had been rescued out of Fermoy hospital by Margaret Flood when he'd been wounded in battle, captured and held by the British in the hospital. As Commanding Officer of the Glenville Company, he was one of the leaders of the local villages who, immediately after the Truce, had to flee abroad to escape the new Free State's National Army. And 25 years later, he had now made the long ocean voyage back from America to speak at length with Nell in her side room. *What on earth did they say to each other...?*

Did he feel raked with a sickening envy, that he had to spend his life in anonymous exile while former colleagues like her and Dinny got to enjoy their lives in the Village? Or was he doing okay in America now? Or did he feel a mix of both those things? We will never know. He left that afternoon in the car to start his journey back to America and was not seen in Crow Glen again.

# One Last Thing

During the Irish government's tracing of IRA people in the late 1920s to give them recognition, Dinny was offered a military pension for the service he had given in his own village of Ballyvourney during the War of Independence. [200] He declined the pension offer, feeling that his roles as a teenage look-out and dispatch-carrier didn't merit it compared to the sacrifices he had seen made by so many others. But instead of taking a pension, he did do something else to address a piece of unfinished business that he felt was important.

Remember the second British spy who was captured and executed by the IRA in Gleann an Phréacháin during the War of Independence - the British officer, Lieutenant Vincent? [201] In 1926, a few years after he arrived in Gleann to run the new shop, Dinny intervened to assist the Manor House to get the body of that executed spy exhumed from the Gleann bog where it still lay hidden, and to have it decently buried in the Manor's own Protestant cemetery. Dinny was an ideal intermediary because, as a recent arrival from the west, he had nothing to do with Gleann at the time when the spy was shot there in 1921. But through his new friendships in Gleann (not least with the Sweeneys of Doon whose daughter he would later marry), he had learned enough about the situation to be able to help arrange the exhumation.

Meanwhile, someone else was also thinking about Lieutenant Vincent, though we will never know who. In June 1924, someone who was a supporter of British rule in Ireland posted an anonymous letter to the British Secretary of State for War. The letter denounced Gleann an Phréacháin's IRA activities in the War of Independence and told exactly where the IRA had buried the British Lieutenant's body in a Gleann bog. The letter claimed that Vincent's body and that of 'another poor man' had been secretly buried in a bog at Coome East, at the west end of the Bride River Valley, on a piece of land owned by '*Hickey, the notorious reble* (sic)

---

200 Historian John Borgonovo explains that the area around Ballyvourney was in fact an intense focus of IRA activism as it 'harboured the Cork Number One Brigade flying column, Brigade headquarters, and First Southern Division headquarters'. 'The Volunteers established five permanent mountain top observation posts that were manned 24 hours a day. The sentries used flags during daytime and torches or signal fires at night, to warn of approaching Crown forces.' John Borgonovo, 'The Guerrilla Infrastructure: IRA Special Services in the Cork Number One Brigade, 1917-1921', *The Irish Sword*, Vol 27, Military History Society of Ireland, 2010

201 We saw him meet his death as a prisoner of the Crow Glen IRA in Chapter 9.

*farmer'*. The letter was typed on formal writing paper and posted in Cork city so as not to carry an identifying postmark. [202]

Norma Buckley and I have pondered at length on who could have sent it. She insists that no local Irish person would have had access to a typewriter in 1924, even if you could manage to find among them someone who had been a supporter of the British occupation. I would have assumed that the letter was sent by the colonials at Gleann's Manor House, were it not for the spelling mistake on the hated word *'rebel'*. The residents of the Manor House were educated at England's most elite private schools and at Cambridge or Oxford University. They knew how to spell *rebel*. Norma made the wily suggestion that they might have inserted the spelling mistake on purpose to disguise themselves.

As it happened, the Manor House, with my grandfather's help, did go on to assist the British authorities to exhume Vincent's remains on 18 October 1926 and rebury them in the Manor's Protestant graveyard at the top of the Village, where you can still see his gravestone today.

In a way, this reburial closed a loop. Our side had given them back a body that they wanted. And we had buried with honours in our own family cemetery in Doon their son who had come who came over to the Irish side, whom they did not want in their own cemetery.

With these matters behind them, Dinny went on across the twentieth century to trade in his shop all the rich foodstuffs produced by the local farmers and those around the mountains north of Gleann an Phréacháin. One of my earliest memories is of going into the Shop aged 4, to have my lunch behind the counter on the day when I started school across the road. My illness had cleared up, and as Lord Mayor Tomás Mac Curtain had predicted, hunger has not been known again in Crow Glen to this day.

References

Allen, Kieran, *1916: Ireland's Revolutionary Tradition*, Pluto Press, 2016
Arnold, John, '97 years on: The Stories behind these Seven Proud, Brave Men', *The Evening Echo*, 4-10-2019, available at www.echolive.ie/nostalgia/John-Arnold-

---

202 *The Cairo Gang* website, 'British soldiers Who Died in Ireland, 1919-1921', www.cairogang.com/soldiers-killed/list-1921.html

97-years-on-the-stories-behind-these-seven-proud-brave-men-178581d3-4bdd-463f-9e27-4c1f58d75417-ds

Barry, Tom, *Guerilla Days in Ireland*, Anvil Press, 1993

Borgonovo, John, 'Atlas of the Irish Revolution, The War in Cork and Kerry', 18-9-2017, available at *www.IrishExaminer.com*

Borgonovo, John, 'The Guerrilla Infrastructure: IRA Special Services in the Cork Number One Brigade, 1917-1921', *The Irish Sword*, Vol 27, Military History Society of Ireland, 2010

Breen Murphy, Timothy, *The Government's Executions Policy During the Irish Civil War, 1922 -1923*, PhD thesis, National University of Ireland, Maynooth, 2010

Carroll, Aideen, *Seán Moylan: Rebel Leader*, Mercier Press, Cork, 2010

Clark, Gemma, *Everyday Violence in the Irish Civil War*, Cambridge University Press, 2014

Collins, Lorcan, *Ireland's War of Independence 1919-21: The IRA's Guerrilla Campaign*, O' Brien Press, 2019

Collins, Michael, *The Path to Freedom*, NuVision Publications, South Dakota, USA, 2005

Coppinger, W.A., *History of the Coppinger Family of County Cork*, Sotherton, London, 1884

*Cork Beo*, 'An Interactive Web Map of All IRA Operations in Co. Cork, 1919 -1921', 27-4-2020 at www.corkbeo.ie/news/history/interactive-map-ira-operations-cork-18113200

Fallon, Donal, 'A Tribute to Tomás Mac Curtain, the Martyred Lord Mayor of Cork', *The Journal.ie*, 14-3-2020 at www.thejournal.ie/readme/tomas-mac-curtain-5045854-Mar2020/

Ferriter, Diarmaid, 'From Turmoil to Truce: A Mature Reflection on the War of Independence', *The Irish Times*, 11-1-2020

Foster, Gavin, 'IRA Emigration and the Social Outcomes of the Civil War' in *The Irish Civil War and Society: Politics, Class and Conflict*, Palgrave, London, 2014.

Grainger, Diarmuid, *Witnesses to Freedom: A Day by Day Account of the Irish War of Independence in Cork*, Independent, 2019

Hart, Peter, *The IRA and its Enemies: Violence and Community in Cork*, Oxford University Press, Oxford, 1998

Hoffman, Marella, *Asylum under Dreaming Spires - Refugees' Lives in Cambridge Today,* with the Living Refugee Archive, University of East London, 2017

Hoffman, Marella, 'The Irish among the British and the Women among the Irish' in *Location and Dislocation, the New Irish at Home and Abroad,* Cork University Press, 1997

Leddy, Con, testimony at Irish Bureau of Military History, BMH WS0756, available at www.bureauofmilitaryhistory.ie

*Military Service Pensions Collection*, available at www.militaryarchives.ie

Murray, Daniel, 'The Fog of Certainty: Liam Lynch and the Start of the Civil War, 1922' in *An Irish History Blog*, 2017

Ó Duinnshléibhe, Seán, National Folklore Collection, Roll No. 12542, p. 221-467. *The School Collection, Volume 0382: Áth Dúna, Gleann an Phréacháin, Mainistir Fhearmuighe - Béaloideas,* viewable at www.duchas.ie/en/cbes/4921859/4896737/5190225?ChapterID=4921859

O' Reilly, Terence, *Rebel Heart: George Lennon, Flying Column Commander*, Mercier Press, Cork, 2005

Ryan, Louise & Ward, Margaret, *Irish Women and Nationalism: Soldiers, New Women and Wicked Hags,* Irish Academic Press, Dublin, 2019

Ryan, Meda, *The Real Chief: The Story of Liam Lynch*, Mercier Press, Cork, 2005

*The Cairo Gang* website, 'British soldiers Who Died in Ireland, 1919-1921', www.cairogang.com/soldiers-killed/list-1921.html

*The Independent*, 'Ireland's War of Independence: The Chilling Story of the Black and Tans', London, 21-4-2006

Walsh, Maurice, *Bitter Freedom: Ireland in a Revolutionary World,* Liveright, 2016

Chapter **11**

# Petition the divine beings

Images at the opening of this chapter:

~ Saint Patrick
~ Padre Pio
~ Jesus manifesting as the Divine Mercy
~ Saint Michael the Archangel

I now had one last day alone with Norma Buckley before the Americans would return to take us with them to the Manor House. She had answered my questions last time about how Crow Glenners saw the spirit world. But I wanted to know more now about precisely how they *interacted* with it. What kinds of relationships did they maintain with the spiritual beings in those dimensions? How did they choose which ones to interact with? And what did those encounters do for them?

She received me with her usual even-tempered patience, for what I promised would be my last set of questions to her. Miriam, the black greyhound, looked less pleased and sighed wearily when she saw me, burying her snout under her front paws on her couch.

 Norma...

## Angels, saints and intercession

You know for children especially, their Guardian Angel used to be their starting point really, like trainer wheels if you like! Which was lovely, and good and simple. Only later really, you graduated on to getting to know Jesus.

But for some reason the individual Guardian Angel is quite dropped now. It's not discussed anymore. The Church seem to find the idea almost threatening now. Is it that one's own Guardian Angel could be *too* direct a connection between the individual and the spiritual realms, now that people have gotten more sophisticated and more confident in themselves? You wouldn't want to let them run off with their own Guardian Angel and cut out the middle-man, would you?!

The archangels on the other hand are very regimented and very important and they each has their own *brief*, so to speak. Saint Michael is the best known. There's also Saint Gabriel and Saint Raphael. I'm not mad about this idea of hierarchy but I suppose you need it even in the spiritual world. In the vast dimensions of the Communion of Saints there are all these levels and realms.

Archangels are especially powerful beings. But maybe they don't intercede in human lives as much as ordinary saints do. But there was a prayer to

Saint Michael that we used to always say in our house. And I do believe genuinely in Guardian Angels. Not the whole New Age thing about angels in general that's become so popular now. But I do believe in the traditional idea that an individual Guardian Angel is given to assist each of us throughout our life. I believe there's a protective spirit attached to every human being and we need their guidance and blessing and protection. Every day I name all my children and grandchildren specifically in my prayers and I pray to the personal Guardian Angel of each of them.

But you'll be pumping me for saints next. Well, the canonised saints of the Church are all in Heaven now, obviously. They were people who lived truly saintly lives while on earth, and they are pure enough to be beside the Lord in Heaven. But they are also very much available to us here, to help us as we struggle with our own daily lives and challenges. And that's what we call Intercession. If you petition them, they can intervene to help you with a blessing of their own. Or they could intercede with the higher Heavens on your behalf, to help your situation. It's worth being well in with a few good saints, I can tell you!

One woman here in the Village has a lovely way of putting it. '*I have Heaven stormed for you*', she'd say if she was praying for you for some reason. For instance when she heard that you were finally engaged to be married, she said: 'I had Heaven stormed for her!'

I had a book of saints as a child, of women saints. They were all without exception virgins and martyrs. But I loved it. I used to read it backwards and forwards. These were people from elsewhere in the world. And you didn't really have much means in those days of hearing about the daily lives or the inner lives and feelings of people elsewhere. I loved that book.

The booklets about saints are edited in a very different way today. It's a much lighter, softer version of their life-story, not so heavy and dreary. Most of them still end up being martyred of course, but that isn't the focus of the whole book these days.

So, who was there? Well Saint Anthony, for one - he was huge, for his power in finding things. But I wonder if anyone ever prayed to him for himself, or for divine direction? I think it was only ever because he was so, so good at finding things that were lost.

I never got into Saint Anthony. I suppose when I was young, I just thought: 'There are plenty other saints around that you don't have to pay for'. Because you have to pay Anthony for his favours! People firmly believe that Anthony has to be paid (by giving a donation to the Church, obviously).

No, my particular man is Saint Jude, the Patron Saint of Hopeless Cases. I started praying to him when I was in secondary school, to get a good husband. I thought that was important. And he didn't let me down. I turned to him again when there was a terrible storm one night, not long after we were married. We had our precious new car parked up the Street. And someone called and told us there was a huge tree after falling across it, from inside the Wood Wall.

While my husband was going up there, I prayed like the clappers to Saint Jude, that they'd be safe in getting the car out from under the tree and that the Wood Wall wouldn't fall down on top of them. [203] And I can't say Jude has ever let me down.

Then I started to pray to him too for the court case that we took against the Manor, to compensate for our new car that their tree fell on. And the Manor's lawyers stopped the case at the steps of the courthouse and agreed to settle with us out of court (after first putting us through all that worry and misery to get that far, of course).

A popular saint for young girls when I was a child was Saint Maria Goretti. She was a very young Italian girl who was terribly religious. A man loved her and she loved him but she wouldn't sleep with him until she was of age and married. And he assaulted and abused her. He battered and killed her because she fought him off so hard. And she was considered a martyr. The perpetrator was still alive in jail when she was canonised. So she was quite a modern saint, of modern times. She's a complicated story. I'm very aware that she faded out subsequently, the Church faded her out. Later books of girls' saints, she never featured in them.

Saints recommended to young boys at that time were Saint Don Bosco and Saint Dominic Savio. I think they were South American. Don Bosco was a very saintly man, a teacher. He was a minder and saviour of young boys, street urchins. He housed them and saw after them, fed and clothed them, begging money for that. He's widely written about. Saint Dominic Savio was one of the boys he protected, and he became a saint too and even holier than his protector. He was the one that young boys were

---

203 Seán Ó Duinnshléibhe explains that 'clappers' (called 'clapar' in Irish), were three boards loosely bound with string which were banged together by 'a small boy' (a bit like Spanish castanets) to frighten crows away from the crops. Ó Duinnshléibhe, as in Note 32

encouraged to pray to, when girls were encouraged to pray to Saint Maria Goretti.

These were models for young teenagers, basically, in the 1940s and 50s. They were guides for living - practical instructions for how to live your life. Saint Don Bosco lived his last hour on the street, as it were, among the people, actively helping others. They were actual people of our own era, not just remote mystics or historical characters.

A lot of our saints were very international, but there are a lot of Irish ones too. Here in the Glen of the Crow, people favour most our own three: we have beautiful full-length stained-glass windows to them behind the altar in the Chapel here. There's one to Saint Patrick and one to Saint Brigid, two fine Irish saints. You grew up with them up there in front of you so they always seem readily available, to have a word with them.

People here have great faith too in Saint Joseph, as we have a lovely stained-glass window of him between the other two. My father had immense devotion to Saint Joseph. He prayed to him in two ways. First, so that he himself would be a good father, and then even more importantly, that Saint Joseph would be with him at the hour of his death. When Saint Joseph died, he is supposed to have had at his bedside both Jesus and Our Lady. So who better to do the trick for you on your own deathbed? My father prayed to him every day of his life for a happy death. And I pray to Saint Joseph in that way every day too.

I have a bit of an argument every year with the priest on Joseph's behalf. We're not allowed to put flowers in the Church during Lent, but Saint Joseph's feast day is in Lent and I always put flowers in the Church to him then. He is the patron saint of our Church, after all. It's called Saint Joseph's Church.

My father died at 87, after a brief stay in hospital in the city. My mother and I went to Mass for him one morning while he was in hospital and just as we got in from Mass, the phone rang. It was a nurse from his bedside and by coincidence, she was a local girl whom we knew well. She said 'I'm ringing to tell you your Dad passed away with me ten minutes ago. I stayed with him and he had a lovely, peaceful death. I just wanted to let you know.' So we felt Saint Joseph had answered his prayers, putting that lovely local young nurse that he knew by his side.

Then there was Saint Monica. Most people hadn't heard of her but I always had faith in her and I used to pray to her. I knew that she was the mother of Saint Augustin, and he was an awful playboy - a murderer and a killer. Poor Monica, he kept her on her knees all her life but she made a saint of him in the end, fair dues to her. So she's a good one for mothers, anyone with sons - or daughters either for that matter!

Saints did have specific powers, and I suppose that's why Saint Jude became so popular and widely used. As the Patron Saint of Hopeless Cases, you could apply him to *anything*. I took Saint Teresa, The Little Flower, as my patron saint at my Confirmation. There is a red hawthorn blossom associated with her, but conversely then it's supposed to be very unlucky to bring that flower into the house. People still have all their faith in The Little Flower.

But some saints got strangely demoted around the 1960s. The Church used to talk about them all so much. But then in the 1960s they talked about a lack of proof around the authenticity of some of these saints. Saint Patrick was nearly done for too. That was very much an issue in the 60s, but you don't hear about it now.

Of course, we have hugely too our own Saint John here because our Holy Well is dedicated to his name, as John the Baptist. Padre Pio was huge as well. He was considered very powerful at intercession, for fertility for instance. But think of the short timespan that he was popular for! Loads of young people born between the 1960s and the 80s were called Pio, but none before or after.

Saint Francis was huge everywhere. I think the current Pope Francis has connotations of him - he seems to be a gentle man. Saint Peter is okay too, because he founded the Church, so he is very much prayed to. Saint Oliver Plunkett is another one of our own - he was Irish. He was martyred by the British. I'll never forget my father's joy when he was canonised. It was the only joy I ever saw him get out of the television. He was glued to it, for the canonisation of Oliver Plunkett. And I know he was thanking god every minute for having the television so he could participate a bit in the ceremony.

When I was a child there was a neighbour called Ellie Lenihan up the Village. She was what we called a Chapelwoman, who held the keys for opening and locking up the church. She collected leaflets of all sorts of different saints. Where she got them, I have no idea but when I was small I used to run errands for her because then she might give me a look at her leaflets. She had them inside a prayer book and it was bulging. For instance, she had a Saint Rose of Lima, and that was so exotic! To us they were like celebrities are to people nowadays. It was such an excitement to get a look at these new saints and the lovely coloured pictures of them, and to hear all about their character. Saint Rose of Lima: her name really fired my imagination. You'd sit down at the table and leaf through the saints with her. And she delighted too in showing me her collection. I still feel so grateful to her for that inspiration.

But individual people had devotion to specific saints - that was how it worked. For instance, Saint Martin de Porres was a South American saint. When my sister was ill as a baby, my mother prayed to him and she firmly believed that he cured the baby. A little medal of Saint Martin de Porres was always attached to her baby-clothes. Oh, I knew loads of people who had devotion to him at that time. He was Black, and that gave him some mystique, made him special. But then he faded out in popularity too. You get waves of popularity, with saints. My mother went a small bit with the flow of fashion so she was into Saint Jude for a while too, but her saint was basically Saint Martin de Porres.

We had one neighbour who went all over the world after saints. She has a daughter called Bernadette, and of course she came from a pilgrimage to Lourdes. And she has a daughter Dolores, named after Our Lady of Dolors. Then she wanted a son, and she has Padre Pio to thank for him, and of course she called the son Pio. But she wasn't just faithful to Padre Pio. She named them all after whatever saint she was into at the time.

Then there's Saint Michael. He's Saint Michael the Archangel, and archangels aren't saints technically. They are way up there in the hierarchy. They're something else. You don't want to be knocking on the door to them every day. But I do. I pray to Saint Michael every day of my life. He's lovely.

But of course, the other huge thing in the old days was *to be seen* to be doing all these things. It was a wall to wall religious society, so you have to ask yourself how much of it was about appearances too. For instance, I think I'm looked down on by some because I don't go to the evening Rosaries in the church.

But you know, I'm often sitting in the Church and you'll hear people nipping in just to the back of the Chapel and they'll give money to one of the saints that are there at the back. They'll drop in their money and say their prayers and toddle off again after five minutes. I can never understand that. That they wouldn't first go up to the front and say Hello to Our Lord, who is always present and real, we're told, up there in the tabernacle on the altar. You're in *His* house! But they just go straight to their own saint's niche and that's it.

But then my father was totally different from the rest of us. He didn't think it was necessary to go round by the saints at all. He felt you could go direct. He had a hotline. But he did have that one great saint devotion to Saint Joseph. He had such faith in him.

## Saint Goónaiτ's Measure

One female saint that I had a lot to do with was Saint Gobnait. Now those were very *regional* blessings, because Saint Gobnait was from Ballyvourney, the village to the west that my father came from. But even people who had moved away from there, their descendants would still have great devotion to her and would go back to visit her in Ballyvourney, and they could benefit greatly from her still. As I did myself, I consider.

I had always heard from my father's female relatives in Ballyvourney about something they called 'Gobnait's Measure'. It was a special blessing you could get from Saint Gobnait to help with pregnancy and childbirth, though people used it too for a heart attack or a stroke. The blessing was delivered via a length of ribbon tied around the body. That ribbon was called her 'Measure'.

One day my husband was working back in Ballyvourney and I went with him. I was pregnant with my second child and I wasn't very well, and I just wanted to find out how to approach Gobnait to ask her to pray for me. I had heard that there was a very old priest there who 'had the keys to Gobnait', as it were. He had the keys to a shrine to Saint Gobnait that was inside the sacristy of the church there, and was much guarded. The sacred statue of Gobnait is kept in there. But she's very small and very thin, because she's very ancient, of carved wood. And the wood is very old now and crumbling, very delicate. Nobody is allowed see her now because she's so fragile. They only bring her out on one day of the year.

I was in the church in Ballyvourney and I saw that old priest up on the altar. I approached him, and told him that my father was from there and used to come to that church as a young man. The priest was very elderly but he could see I was pregnant and he said 'I can see you're with child yourself'. I said 'I am. And I'm not terribly well and I'm worried.' 'Well there's no need for that', he said. 'I'll take you into my house. Tell your husband you'll be over there. And I'll bring Gobnait over to the house to you.'

Well! For me to have a private audience with Gobnait, up close in the priest's house, and even to touch her, was just amazing. His housekeeper took me in and gave me tea and scones while the priest went to get the saint. But when he came back he said to the housekeeper 'There's no ribbon. Run out to the shop and get a length of ribbon for us', which she did.

She came back with an almighty length of ribbon. And he did the ceremony there and then in his kitchen. You have to wrap the ribbon around Gobnait's statue lengthways three times. And then he was murmuring away, saying a blessing. I couldn't hear or understand anything he was saying. And then he got the housekeeper to cut the length of ribbon and he handed it to me. I went into their bathroom and you wrap it around your bump and pin it in place with a safety pin. And you wear it all through the pregnancy.

That priest truly believed it would help so much. As if he was giving you the correct medicine, as if *'this is what works'*. And he was delighted of course to be continuing the tradition of Gobnait's powers and blessings.

And it did help me enormously, and it helped my husband enormously. Because he was terrified out of his wits too. But he had such faith in that priest that he felt reassured that things would be okay.

I genuinely believe that it was a minor miracle that helped with the difficult birth of my daughter. But if I hadn't *believed* in Gobnait… It was my belief that enabled me to be helped so much by her. I firmly believe that a blessing can't do you any much good if you don't believe in it. Now I'm not saying that it's only one's own belief that's operating. But if you don't believe, I don't think a saint can help you. You won't get your request answered. You have to buy into it too on your own side and *give* that belief or trust. Genuine spirituality can cause miracles and a saint can be a conduit to arouse that level of spiritual energy in you. If there's going to be spiritual energy coming from the saint, you'll have to be in a spiritual state to receive it, won't you?  He or she can't just send you the favour in the post!

I gave a loan of Gobnait's Measure later to a neighbour who had a heart attack. But I'm not sure where it is now. I have it in an honoured relic-box in my head, up in the front of my mind, but I'm not sure where it is physically.

When I went into hospital for the birth the nuns wanted to tear it off me, take it away from me, and I said: 'No way'. I said, 'I'll wear it around my arm if I have to'. A lot of those nuns were doctors. Becoming nuns enabled them to become doctors in a way that no other ordinary woman could when they were young, in the 1930s and 40s.

But some of the nuns in that maternity hospital were horrible. When I was in labour, I was clasping my Rosary beads and one of them whipped them off me. She said 'Look at this, this really gets to me. Ye come in here grasping Rosary beads. And I say: when did ye ever do that before?' I was very frightened because I was in labour and not well but I said to her: 'Excuse me, I pray with those Rosary beads every day of my life.' What she said was crazy because in those days, everyone in Gleann prayed the Rosary every day of their lives!

But to this day, the ambiance at Gobnait's holy well in Ballyvourney really is incredible. Her place is up a hill overhanging the village. And it is amazing. The atmosphere up there feels so ancient, so pure and clean and very, very deep. And it seems to pour down over the whole village. My grandparents on my father's side are buried up at her well, of course.

Once when I went there, a congregation of laypeople were coming away after saying the Rosary in there together. And I must say the atmosphere that they left behind around Gobnait's well was extraordinary - you could cut it with a knife. I was so struck by it I asked one of them discreetly what their ceremony had been. And she said they had prayed the Rosary for a local person who was seriously ill that evening. There was no priest with them. It was laypeople gathering together for that purpose.

Then, as well as saints, there are the Stations of the Cross - that can be a big personal devotion too. Some people would have specialised in that, as their favourite devotional practice. I remember having to wait in long *queues* to work your way around the Stations of the Cross in the church. We used to do them by ourselves before Mass too, but we've stopped that now.

Our Catholicism in the old days offered this huge, diverse palette of devotions or options as prayers and practices. There was a lot of what I would call these *peripherals,* but it gave people a lot of different things to focus on. The more, the merrier, was the view back then.

# The many 'Our Ladies'

But there was always enormous devotion to Our Lady, as well as to the Sacred Heart. People can have a great personal devotion to either of them. A huge thing, one to one. You'd say: 'She has great devotion to the Sacred Heart' or 'He has great devotion to Our Lady' - in other words they'd have a path beaten to their door. A lot of people who took their religion seriously and prayed a lot, they'd go straight to the top like that with no intermediaries, without passing through the saints. And here in Gleann, the top was the Sacred Heart and Our Lady.

Jesus and the stories of his life and the Gospels - they are something that we have in common with Protestants. But devotion to the Sacred Heart was like an aspect of Jesus that Irish Catholics had wrestled back for themselves. They had intense, personal, one to one devotion to the Sacred Heart, completely independent of the priests. Again, the Sacred Heart was very much a home-based practice, when we all had the big picture of the Sacred Heart at the centre of the home, and the red lamp burning to it perpetually.

But Our Lady, on the other hand, can have so many, many different aspects or manifestations. There's Our Lady of Lourdes, Our Lady of Fatima, of Guatemala, of Medjugore, the Blessed Virgin Mary, Our Lady Queen of Heaven, Our Lady of the Immaculate Conception, Our Lady of Perpetual Succour, and so on and on.

The Rosary in itself is of course a whole set of devotions that some people specialise in. They really meditate on the mysteries of the Rosary as they recite them. And that does make sense because to say the Sorrowful Mysteries at Lent, for instance, it really takes you to the heart of what you're trying to reflect on. And for Christmas, you'd meditate on the Joyful Mysteries. I pray every day of my life and go to Mass as much as I can. But I do put the Mass and Jesus ahead of the Rosary.

As we said, Mary has lots of variants, of course. But are they really different? No, there's only one Mother of God, as far as I'm concerned. And devotion to her was overwhelming in the old days - to the detriment of Jesus, to be honest. My father was one of the few people who always said that - that Jesus' life should be the central thing. Now my father did pray the Rosary every day of his life too. But what he was focusing on was the *Mysteries* of the Rosary, and they are indeed about the phases and events of Jesus' lifetime.

But if you looked at it slantways sometimes in the old days, you could almost think that the whole religion was centred around Our Lady, that she was the main deity or godhead as it were. That it was a religion of devotion to the Rosary. From the people themselves. Not coming from the priest, who was doing a lot of other things in the church and on the altar - the liturgy throughout the year and so on.

For instance, my friend Eily, you couldn't deny that she had the most amazing, amazing, amazing devotion to Our Lady, the strength of it was amazing to watch, and she went to her deathbed with that. My mother's main devotion too was to the Rosary, though my mother is still a bit of an enigma to me about religion, even after her 90 years of life. She was very religious but she never talked about it so I still don't quite know how she saw it in her own mind.

But the people, yes, it was as if the Rosary was their own ceremony and they took that over and they could say or perform that by themselves individually or in groups. There was no need for a priest, yet it was a very complete ceremony in itself. It's both a very inner thing and a group activity, because you have to meditate on the Mysteries in your own heart and mind as you recite the Rosary.

But then you see, remember where the people were coming from in their faith. This was handed down from Penal Times when all practices of Catholicism were illegal and outlawed. The priests were taken away from the people and they had to manage on their own mostly, without priests and without Mass. And the Rosary was perfect for that.

Think of the Mass Rocks. You might get Mass there every six months if you were lucky, and that was deadly dangerous for all concerned. But you could come into your home every night and kneel down in the living room and say the Rosary in secret as a family, with no impediment. And She was a mother anyway so she could mother the lot of them.

It was a spontaneous religion of the people. They could say it by themselves, almost as good as Mass, and they could say it privately in the home as a family as well without fear of detection by the English authorities. There was a very good reason for all that, it was no accident.

We said the family Rosary every night at home until well into the 1980s, when I decided to stop saying it as a group. My parents still said their own individually every night. But it was tough after a hard day at work or school to turn off the television at 9pm and get down on your knees as a family for it.

The gender aspect of it all is interesting too - I mean the gender of the divine beings being prayed to. All the people had absolute devotion to the Virgin Mary, men just as much as women, if not more so. It was what they had to hang onto. The Virgin Mary religion was almost like a self-contained religion in itself.

After all, Jesus was a man and lived a man's life. And God the Father was male, although we rarely took any notice of him. And the priests were men. And they delivered all the ceremonies of the Church in quite an administrative sort of way. It was all very formal, organised and fixed, like school or government or the law.

Whereas the devotion to Our Lady - or as I say, Our Lady's *religion*, almost - felt very different. Much more feminine, human, soft and intimate… It's more private and interior. It can be home-based or anywhere-based, independent of the Chapel. It's more of a direct line to Her, the Blessed Mother, quite removed from all the male divine beings. And no need to go through an 'operator', like the operators on the old telephone lines long ago (the operator being the priest, in this instance).

But I'm afraid that, compared to many around here, devotion to Our Lady is a great lacking point with me personally. I think it was over the decades, having *so much* Marian devotions rammed down your throat, and everyone all around you rattling off countless decades of the Rosary. But privately I started thinking 'Now do I ever stop up to really reflect on all these *Hail Marys* that I'm reciting?' Am I really taking the words to heart or am I just chanting them, basically? I think there will be a certain merit for the effort, time and thought put into it. But how much of it is just engendered and indoctrinated into us, I don't know.

I have friends who have enormous devotion to Our Lady, but at this point of my life I myself pray fervently to the Divine Mercy, and that's it really for me. And I prefer to think of the Blessed Virgin Mary in one simple way, not in terms of all her different manifestations. I think our religious education was wrong back then. I think that the one Our Lady is supreme, and it was too diverse, if anything, back then.

There are really only a few distinctions between Catholicism and Protestantism. One is the Virgin Birth and our level of devotion to Our Lady as the Blessed Virgin Mother. They honour her just as Jesus' ordinary human mother. In the Protestant world, she's just a normal, though saintly, woman. She's the mother of god in the human sense of being a physical mother.

But the Irish Catholic Mary is a vast mystical being with unlimited powers. If the British were out hunting for Irish Catholics during Penal Times, you may as well paint a big 'C' on your face if you were going to go around showing public devotion to the Virgin Mary.

But how many centuries of praise and glory did that come from? I think that the devotions and practices themselves actually help to create the deity in some way too, and make her more available to those doing the devotions to her. A lot of it is mythology in some ways, you might say.

I would say that today, devotion to the Virgin Mary has decreased, but devotion to the Mother of God has increased. There's like an overlap between the two now, and the Mother of God is less seen as a virgin.

But we're wasting a lot of time on this here. The bottom line is that there aren't 180 different Our Ladies, Our Lady of the Sea, of Knock, of Medjugore and so on. All these different manifestations or aspects of her as a divine being - they don't come into it anymore. I can still see those gaps in your education as a Catholic, where you're stuck in those memories of the old days. You haven't moved on like we have, most of us.

I'm not saying it's a lesser practice, all those variations. But I don't like it myself. Because truly, there's only one Our Lady, and she's the Mother of God, and what need is there for any finer details? Though I admit that I do still pray sometimes to Our Lady of Knock at certain times, but not often.

Why they were all ever introduced originally was to strengthen any devotion to Our Lady that we could lay our hands on. If She'd appear anywhere on the side of a mountain, it made the locals feel ownership of Her and it created a huge, huge devotion to Her.

I suppose it's being 'tidied up' now into a more orthodox Christianity where Jesus is the centre, rather than the Blessed Virgin Mary being the centre. At times She was almost like a rival deity who had displaced him from the centre of it all. For instance, the Marian Year was in 1950 and that brought a wave - an onslaught, a *tidal* wave - of devotion to Our Lady. There were special Rosary priests going around - wonderful singers often. They travelled around the country, promoting the Rosary and the Marian devotions. And the Church was really behind that at the time. I think they foresaw the threat of secularisation coming down the track, and the potential decline of religion in the decades ahead.

And they caught up with the fact that the people had their own intense, independent devotions to the Blessed Virgin Mary already. And the Marian Year reclaimed all that back in, to strengthen the Church. That's when the Marian Processions started too, our Procession of Our Lady through the Village in May. People were already by then really into all the foreign apparitions of Our Lady and the pilgrimages abroad to Her. But the vastness of the names and titles and manifestations of Our Lady - I think the Marian Year was a move to tidy all that up a bit and gather Her devotions more into one.

# Simplicity

I think that the biggest change today really, and especially for children, is the Divine Mercy movement. That's Jesus encountered as a spirit of pure divine *love*, compassion and forgiveness. That's what children are introduced to these days - not the 'judge and jury' kind of God condemning them for all their little sins! *Mercy.* There's no more hell and thunder now, and being battered for your sins.

It really is about the forgiveness of sins through the Divine Mercy. And of course, the Church has cottoned on that nobody's been going to Confession, so now before Easter and Christmas we have special ceremonies of *general* absolution. A lovely, calm, loving ceremony. And we put our own sins on the altar there privately in our own minds and that's it. The religion no longer has this huge public emphasis on sins. Before, you were meant to be a sinner so you were wrong from the outset, from original sin. You could never get it right from day one. And then Jesus had to die to try to clear your sins. It was quite a guilt trip really. You had inherited all this sinning from Adam and Eve and there seemed to be no way out of it!

Now it's more about building your connection with that loving, healing force that is the Divine Mercy. It's changed beautifully in that way. It's now a direct pathway you're given so that you can connect directly one to one with total compassion. And when that *Mercy* comes to you, you can then pass it on to others. For me now, that's my world.

But there's no doubt that in our Catholicism there was and still is a great deal of choice, though perhaps more so in the past than now. There was a vast array of practices and spiritual beings you could get involved with. It was down to your personality and your personal inclinations, which practices you felt drawn to. And you were pretty much encouraged to find whatever appealed to you and to run with it. It's more simplified and uniform nowadays, compared to that huge array of options before.

Things have been very much 'tidied up' now. Modernised and streamlined. You're more encouraged to say *'Lets all do one simpler thing together'*, which is quite a different approach. I personally prefer it, to be honest. I don't think of it just as 'modern' but more as *lived through*. Through genuine experience with and learning about the spiritual world, you eventually come to realise that at its core it's quite a simple thing - it's just divine love, underlying everything and all of us.

But one fairly elaborate practice that I admit I have carried on all my life is that, during Lent and coming up to Easter, I still do the Stations of the Cross. Physically in the Church whenever I can, or else I do them mentally in my head, lying on my bed. And I would pause on some of them to really meditate on them. *'Veronica wipes the face of Jesus'*, *'Jesus comforts the women of Jerusalem'*, *'Jesus is stripped of his garments'* and so on, all the way to the 14th Station of the Cross, *'Jesus is laid in the tomb'*. I can recite them all from memory but it's not a feat of memory really. It's no memory at this point - it's just there in my mind, as part of the furniture.

But the actual Sacred Heart, for instance - you don't see those old pictures of the Sacred Heart anymore. Remember, the Heart with a crown of thorns, pierced with a little dagger and bleeding? And there were rays of flames coming out from it, flames of love. But the Sacred Heart is more just used as a term now because that graphic visual image of it is very much gone out of fashion. Now there is this move towards viewing Jesus as the Divine Mercy, and this is an all-encompassing view of Jesus that supercedes other approaches.

He's being depicted now as this one thing from start to finish - the bright, radiant Divine Mercy. I haven't a picture of Him on me this minute to show you, but I have Him in my heart and soul. The image of the Divine Mercy is always of the *Risen* Jesus, white and shining, his full body with hands raised, beaming out warm, positive, healing life and love. A simple Cross might be in the background of the image sometimes, but he's not attached to it in any way. One parish priest that we had here had great devotion to the Divine Mercy, and I'm very grateful to him for putting that at the centre of our devotions here. [204]

---

[204] That was Fr. Cashman, who also brought major financial investment to the Village by getting an impressive Catholic community centre built onto the back of the church. Norma

I have a wonderful, wonderful introduction to Him in one of my modern Prayer Books, and the most beautiful depiction of Him. There are no thorns, no wounds. He's obviously risen as He's in his full white radiant energy, relaxed, hands down by his side turned outwards, and from each of his fingers there's a beautiful, beautiful ray coming out of every fingertip - pure love, pure light.

You must look at the leaflets I have and you'd be amazed at the difference, compared to the old days. Just go into my bedroom please and you'll see a little booklet of the Divine Mercy on the table. Bring that out and you'll see the difference, compared to the imagery that you would have been used to. Make sure you don't drop any of the Mortuary Cards or leaflets out of it.

See? This has replaced the older Sacred Heart devotions now, and this is an example of what I mean about the religion evolving. What you have there is a million miles from what we had before. Remember that what we received in the old days, it started from the year dot and went through *so* many countries and regimes and languages and wars… But this is a lovely stage that it's at now, a really wonderful - I won't say transformation - but *evolution*.

I have great devotion now to this Divine Mercy manifestation of Our Lord. It really connects with me, that pure love, white and radiant, that can heal anything. And I feel that's all you need really. It sums up everything else, all the complicated saints and practices. There's nothing wrong with them if that works for you. But as far as I'm concerned, the bottom line today is this total healing and forgiveness, this power that Our Lord has when manifesting as the Divine Mercy.

You see, with this all-encompassing Love that we focus on nowadays, the Lord seems so much gentler, just full of limitless love and forgiveness. He couldn't have been this cruel mastermind, could he? I think the Church must feel now that the spiritual world under Christ as we see Him today is actually a gentler, kinder place than we had thought. And we just didn't know enough at the time to see it. But now we can see Christ in all his positive power. It's a really serious evolution in the religion, fundamentally. This pinpoints a lot of what's happening in the background, this more loving positivity that's in the religion nowadays.

---

Buckley describes this investment as bringing 'confidence' to local practitioners as a spiritual community, at a time when their faith was perhaps becoming unfashionable.

You know I've lived through the heart of all these changes in the religion across nearly eight decades of practicing it. You left but I've been here all along, negotiating all these changes. So I try to common-sense the whole thing as I go along and to put it through my own filter, filtering out over time any bits that might seem an insult to our intelligence now, or whatever.

But in your mind, the religion here in Gleann an Phréacháin is frozen in time, because you left in the late 1980s. And now you're like a time-traveller coming back and finding it all changed. The priests too of course are after going through huge traumas in their own religious life, with all the dreadful sex abuses committed by their colleagues. I think that those that are still in the priesthood now, they're for the Church unto the death, and rigidly faithful to it. You can't really question them openly about much. But I'm not at all sure what they think in their heart of hearts. They aren't where they would have been before all the abuse cases came out, that's for sure.

But one thing that's incredibly clear from all we've said here is that we're only just scratching the surface of the complexity of practices that ordinary people did. Just here in Gleann alone. What leaps out when I look back over all we've talked about is the incredible diversity of practices done here in the Village. In a single village in a single era in our lifetime there was a vast array of spiritual activities available. And the people knew them, and they selected within them the ones they felt a personal affinity with.

Remember, in the old days, we had little else in our lives. There was no internet, few books or magazines, very little travel, very little television. So that was a whole spiritual universe that we explored, full of colour and personalities and adventures and life-stories, and sufferings too like our own, and ways of coping with sufferings and making the best of things.

But nowadays the world is so different, so chock full of secular information coming at you from every conceivable angle. The internet, social media, films, television and news from all over the world. And people are so busy now! They have to be on the internet and on Facebook and keeping up with Netflix round the clock, and they just haven't time to be fooling around with thirteen different versions of the Virgin Mary.

You have to keep the faith and the religion simpler now, and clearer, so it doesn't get entirely lost under the onslaught of information in the media and online. And this new simplicity that it has can help people to distinguish it as a separate, realm - a distinct spiritual universe. But for that, it has to be fairly loud and clear and simple, to not be drowned out by all the other stuff in the media and the wider world. I think people need that greater simplicity in the religion nowadays, as the world itself gets ever more complicated. It was the opposite in the old days: our religion could be complicated because our world was in other ways so very simple!

You had people who were actually praying every day to most of these deities, like to all thirteen versions of Our Lady or whatever. They had that time on their hands. But I think it's better now, now that everyone focuses more simply on the one Mother of God for who She is and what She is. Not because She landed some day here or there over in Portugal or Yugoslavia. That's hardly the greatest distinction about Her!

It's a part of my wonderings, you know, that question of diverse deities versus core deities. For me now, the thirteen variants of Our Lady and so on are like an actual obstacle to me. You must start somewhere but it's confusing and splintering and I feel it dilutes it and lessens the bloodline of the whole thing for people.

Coming back to the Catholic education for people nowadays… In the old days we had a much more complex religious education because there was a huge amount to learn: deities and images of them and prayers and recitations and visualisations and pilgrimages and the calendar of the religious year and the backstory of every saint, and so on. Whatever you think about it, it was an immense amount of sheer culture that you held in your memory, off by heart. In terms of religious traditions around the world, I'd say that one with all the multiple versions of Our Lady and so on was a very complex one indeed.

But nowadays we're having a different experience of spiritual energy that we seem to be accessing more strongly now, if anything. And I think I got my taste for that from my father. Even in the old days, he was very much into that more direct experience of going straight to the top, without all the fussy, complicated practices. I think if a limousine had pulled up outside the door to take him on free pilgrimages abroad, he wouldn't have bothered going. Sure, he didn't feel the need.

\*

When I listened back later to the recording of this final interview with Norma, I was struck by the sheer ancientness and longevity of so many of the spiritual practices that she had told me about. For instance, Saint Gobnait is a very 'live', real and contemporary presence to so many people around West Cork. While researching this book, I went to visit Gobnait's well in Ballyvourney myself. Like Norma, I felt that the whole place has an extremely intense spiritual energy. It's quite extraordinary. I could see why Gobnait is very much a hands-on, go-to, *intervention* type saint for anyone in trouble right now.

But I wondered whether Norma, or practitioners like her, realise just how far back their practice of praying to Gobnait stretches. In the archives I discovered that Gobnait is documented by historians as a devout spiritual leader who did indeed tend to the poor and sick of Baile Mhúirne, as it was called in the old language, which is still spoken there today. (Baile Mhúirne means 'Town of the Beloved'.) But do her present-day devotees realise that the historical records show she was doing that in the *fifth or sixth century?!* [205]

Reviewing this recording of Norma's interview, I was struck again by the mischievous **humour** with which she teases the Church, as one might an old friend. Probably my favourite remark by Norma, which I put on the opening page of this book, is the idea that 'you're not meant to bother Archangel Saint Michael with day to day stuff, *but I do'*. It is at the same time irreverent and devout.

She jokes too that perhaps the reason the Guardian Angel is less promoted by the Church these days is because it might be *'too'* direct a spiritual connection, making the Church feel side-lined out of its role as 'middle-man'!

This is yet another reversal of what I had expected. Here, the old Guardian Angel practice is not problematic because it is outmoded, fuddy-duddy, irrelevant or unfashionable. Rather, it might be too immediate and powerful a channel, giving too direct an encounter with strong spiritual energies!

I had expected these interviews to be all about the religion waning and fading. But Norma often describes the spiritual experience as actually getting stronger, because it's been simplified to give more direct access to divine beings and energies, with less of the 'middle-man' role by the Church. This is the *blow your socks off* kind of **spiritual energy** that strikes many times across Norma's interviews, experienced by very different sorts

205  Lauren Ward, 'Ireland's Saintly Women and their Healing Holy Wells', *National Geographic*, 10-2-2012, available at https://blog.nationalgeographic.org/2012/02/10/irelands-saintly-women-and-their-healing-holy-wells

of people: atheist Scandinavian anthropologists in the new millennium; the seven-year-old Norma 72 years ago at the First Holy Communion altar; visiting Irish-Americans at the Mass Rock today…

She believes that spiritual energies do lie all around us, if people are open to connecting with them. And that sometimes, it's almost about dodging or avoiding them because they could be too strong and unmediated!

Having listened back to all her interviews together now, it seems to me that she is quite familiar with the full **spectrum of intensity** in spiritual experiences. She can relaxedly assess a given spiritual situation and place it along that spectrum. For instance, at one end there are rather 'empty' practices that she sees as just 'indoctrinated' and performed out of habit, like chanting the Rosary a bit mindlessly at times. Or the children's Confessions that were a bit farcical because they had no genuine sins to confess, and felt they had to make them up. Perhaps around the middle of her spectrum lie the mass congregation experiences at the big liturgical moments like Easter.

But there are also those moments in her accounts when people are 'blown away', as she puts it, by spiritual energies. Like her own sense of the Holy Well as a portal to direct and beautiful spiritual energy. Or her father's 'hotline, direct to the top' without any intermediaries. Or her own gentle, relaxed encounters nowadays, simply bathing in the love of the Divine Mercy anywhere, anytime, using her own pictures and prayers, just lying in bed before her afternoon siesta.

As she says herself, she has made a long and vivid journey, lasting nearly eight decades so far, through the heart of rural Irish Catholicism. But you get the sense of a person who has arrived at her desired spiritual destination on this earth - the ability to make at will that relaxed, familiar, homely **connection** with what she calls 'pure love'. There seems to have been a lot of trial and error along the way as her culture adjusted its religious approaches around her over the decades. But I note that she does credit the Church and her parish priest with introducing her to this specific modern practice of the Divine Mercy that works so well for her. She doesn't claim to have found it by herself.

She is thankful to the local clergy for introducing her directly to that Being and giving her this practice as a very direct access to Him. And we get no sense from her that the Church is trying nowadays to keep power as the 'middle-man' or to limit her access to this very direct, personal, unmediated experience of spirit.

In fact, Gleann's current clergy people - Fr Donal Cotter and the two Sister of Mercy nuns who have ministered to the parish for decades, Sister Lily and Sister Philomena - are formal followers of the Vatican who do stay inside all the boundaries that gives them. But I get the sense that as individuals they are also happy for anyone to experience genuine spirit and wellbeing and happiness, in whatever way they can access it.

As former nurses, the Sisters spend a great deal of time visiting with locals in the many homes where they are welcome. They take the keenest interest in everyone's current state of health, the youngsters' latest romances and so on. But Norma told me that Sister Lily has 'eyes like x-rays'. She can tell at a glance whether you've been eating, resting and exercising properly, and will let you know about it if you haven't!

Meanwhile, Fr Donal pursues and promotes Gleann an Phréacháin's sacred sites with enthusiasm. During the Covid-19 lockdown, I know that he drove over to the Mass Rock to say a private Rosary of his own there on the last day of May, a very ancient date for country rituals. He broadcasts his Masses on Facebook for the housebound, but his account is also 'Followed' by hundreds of locals from the younger generations. They all exchange a continual flow of local news: a young wedding, a beloved dog who's missing, a party coming up, a free service for the elderly, a beautiful sunset over the Nagle Mountains... Donal seems to pitch in and enjoy exchanging these things as much as everyone else. After all, as much as anyone else, he too wants to be happy.

Buddhist leader the Dalai Lama defines happiness as the whole purpose both of life and of religion. [206] That would not have been the case with the old Catholic culture that I grew up in, where happiness in this lifetime seemed actively discouraged, as if it would take from one's chances of happiness in the next. It seems that today's religious culture in the Glen of the Crow no longer sees a contradiction between the two.

References

Dalai Lama, *The Art of Happiness - A Handbook for Living*, Hodder Press, 1999
Ó Duinnshléibhe, Seán, National Folklore Collection, Roll No. 12542, p. 221-467.
*The School Collection, Volume 0382: Áth Dúna, Gleann an Phréacháin, Mainistir Fhearmuighe*

---

[206] Dalai Lama, *The Art of Happiness - A Handbook for Living*, Hodder Press, 1999   The Dalai Lama describes this type of happiness as an inner, lasting resource that can nourish and sustain us regardless of outer difficulties.

- *Béaloideas,* viewable at
www.duchas.ie/en/cbes/4921859/4896737/5190225?ChapterID=4921859
Ward, Lauren, 'Ireland's Saintly Women and their Healing Holy Wells', *National Geographic*, 10-2-2012, available at
https://blog.nationalgeographic.org/2012/02/10/irelands-saintly-women-and-their-healing-holy-wells

.

# Chapter 12

# The dinner-bell at the Manor

Images at the opening of this chapter:

~ The colonial Manor House at Gleann an Phréacháin
~ An ancestral portrait in the dining hall
~ The elegant central staircase
~ Our party's banquet in the dining hall, with Norma Buckley on the left

# Feasting

There is the discreet clink of cutlery. The sound of wine being poured. Waiters' quiet footsteps as they move around us. The luxurious creak of oak floorboards. The polished, wood-panelled walls of the long dining-hall as they stretch away around us. The napkins are starched white, the silverware is heavy.

The big day had finally come and the silver bus had made the journey without incident up the winding driveway to the Manor House. Candles flickered now above the aromas of the food that had just been served to us. Finally, the waiters left us, and we had this indescribable scene to ourselves. What *was* this moment that we were sitting in? We were all about to open our mouths and place into them forkfuls of the fine foods that had been served in this very room relentlessly, while our ancestors had starved to death in agony a few hundred yards away outside the Wood Wall.

We had come here to do this. Keith Carney had brought us together here for this purpose. Until now, no-one had mentioned the import of what we were doing. It seemed too big to squeeze it down into words. Keith had just said that we would all dine together at the Manor, and he left it to each to see whatever meaning in it they wished.

But now - sat there with the food steaming quietly in front of us - no-one seemed able to speak or move. It was as if we were paralysed, or about to do something obscene. But then, at the top of the table, with his elderly mum sitting beside him, Keith raised his glass in a toast and declared: 'We have come here to *enjoy* and relish every moment of this feast on behalf of our ancestors. Because it was on their backs that this place was built.'

Those simple words, naming what hadn't been said, cracked the spell of tension that hung over us and we fell upon the food and fine wines as if it was our solemn duty to consume them with delectation. We ate on *their* behalf, as if willing our starved ancestors to be there sitting on the carved dining-chairs with us, tasting the dishes of warm, fragrant foods. If we could, we would have taken them in our arms and fed them from the table like babies.

Look, gently spoon-feed Pat Carney from Doon a bowl of those buttery roast potatoes. Give a taste of that fine white chicken-breast, meltingly tender, salted and savoury to '*Agnes O' Reilly, 27, found dead curled up in the back room*'. Put that child '*Minnie O'Driscoll, dead aged 4*' up on your knee and let her at the cherry crumble and homemade ice-cream. We ate ceremonially, we ate lavishly, with love and gratitude for every sip and mouthful, on behalf of those who could not.

While the food was being served, the lady of the Manor had walked up to Keith at the head of the table. I heard her say to him 'You can ring this each time you are ready for the next course.' But when I glanced at her, my heart thumped in my chest. What she had placed beside his wineglass was *the bell*. The same horrific old handbell that we had seen in the fist of the cart-driver at Doon, summoning the Carney ancestors to the cart for the coffin ship. Its brass skirt and worn mahogany handle sat in the corner of my vision now, as I chewed my way through our appetisers. Once I saw that everyone had finished their smoked salmon, I could stand it no longer.

'*Ring the bell, Keith! Ring the damn bell!*', I called out to him from along the table. I was burning with the desire to hear our party ring that bell for *them*. But Keith ignored me. The lady of the Manor eventually came back, guessing that we must be ready. 'You never rang the bell', I heard her say to Keith. Sitting at the top of her table, Keith looked up at her and said with dignity: 'I'm not the kind of person who summons people with a bell.'

For me that moment was probably the peak of that surreal banquet evening. I usually think of myself as politically aware, but Keith was reminding me that we can always go further, we can do more. We're not looking for revenge: our job is to ensure that things genuinely change, and that we ourselves always do the opposite of whatever wrong was done to us.

In the gentle light of the candles, our group subsided after the meal into a relaxed pool of coffee-drinking and thoughtful reflection around the table. Keith quietly invited people to speak now whatever was on their hearts. And they did. We were a large party, including the bus driver, at this long, imposing table but the discussion was intimate. People spoke one by one and the group listened.

The Americans seemed to be reviewing their whole lives now through the lens of what they had experienced in the past two days at Gleann an Phréacháin. A shy, good-looking blonde woman sat the end of the table. Keith's sister, she spoke now for the first time. Her voice shaking, she described realising that the hot, strong, smothering sensation that she had felt all her life about her Irish-American identity was actually shame.

She said she had taken inside herself an old view that being Irish was a low thing to be vaguely embarrassed about. That it was a culture that was poor, lazy, uneducated, drank too much, fought a lot and couldn't control how many children they had. A cousin put a hand on her arm as she wept, describing how she had always felt tongue-tied, unable to find anything to say in defence against all those accusations in her head.

'And now, this week, for the first time, I'm seeing it all completely differently', she said. 'I just see *beauty*. And courage. And kindness. Spirituality… And the sense that we're all somehow connected together, and connected to lots of different levels of beauty. Beauty in the land, in the music, in people's hearts… It's unbelievable, how differently I'm seeing it all now. As something special to be a part of, something to cherish, something that will sustain me…', she finished with a little sob, her arm over her eyes.

Somehow this space around this most alien of tables had become a sanctuary. Keith's determination that we would all feast there as equals had transformed enemy ground into a place of healing. Many things were said, dropped into a pool of soulful revelations that flowed as easily as the conversation used to flow between me and my teenage friend when we used to lie hidden in the arms of our tree down along the driveway.

## Books

As a child, I had always heard that Mark Bence-Jones, whose family had bought Crow Glen Manor from the Hudsons in 1949, was a writer. That he sat all day in one or other of the Manor's two libraries writing books as his main activity. At our primary school in the Village there was a shelf of borrowable books that we called 'the library', and I liked it very much. I thought that I too would like to write books someday when I grew up. Much later, I had the chance to research his writings a little. After becoming a university lecturer, I ended up holding an academic position at Cambridge University in England, where Bence-Jones had been a student. There I had some leisure to peruse his life's work - a hymn of praise to the British Empire and the system of British aristocracy that was sustained by the Empire. As one commentator put it, 'the values and way of life of their generation remained his throughout his life'. [207]  What was unusual

---

207 *The Irish Independent*, 'World News', 25-4-2010

about him was that this was in the late twentieth century: he only died in 2010.

Bence-Jones was a professional genealogist of the British aristocracy, especially in their colonies in Ireland and India. He built up a lifetime of expertise in tracing and certifying the bloodlines of the colonies' aristocratic families, and demarcating the degree to which they had been diluted by inter-marriage with commoners. 'A stickler for traditional etiquette', he saw it as his job to 'restore rigour... to genealogical qualifications', as one reviewer tartly put it. [208]  As the *London Review of Books* commented wryly in a review of what they called his 'contentious' work, 'the job [of a genealogist] is, after all, to separate the sheep from the goats'. [209]

When I worked as an academic in the very conservative, pro-British setting of Cambridge University in the 1990s, I noticed that even there, Bence-Jones' belief in the inherent genetic qualities of the British aristocracy was considered extreme. The gentlest way to put it would be that the views that he held right into the late twentieth century, reflected the values of the nineteenth-century British Empire rather than modern English values.

When he died in 2010, *The Telegraph*, the newspaper of right-wing British elites, published an enthusiastic eulogy that did indeed take that tactful route, explaining that 'his admiration for the upper classes and grand houses sometimes made him seem a man born in the wrong century'. [210] *The Telegraph* was not bothered by, and even took some delight in, the fact that he 'inevitably met with strong criticism in' what they called 'egalitarian circles'. [211]  But even they baulked at the views that he expounded - with 'jingling fun', as they put it - in his book *The British Aristocracy*. [212] Published as recently as 1979, it is unlikely to be printed again. As the *London Review of Books* put it, in that book Bence-Jones and his co-author 'are not merely charting the British aristocracy: they are saying it is better, more *virtuous*, than any other model'. [213]

A prime focus of that Bence-Jones book is his dismay that the aristocracy were beginning to be blurred with or even overtaken in status by some of

208  *The Irish Independent*, as in Note 207
209  Gabriele Annan, 'Sheep into goats, *London Review of Books*, 24-1-1980
210  *The Telegraph*, 'Mark Bence-Jones, Obituary', 30-4-2010
211  *The Telegraph*, as in Note 210
212  Bence-Jones, Mark, *The British Aristocracy*, Constable, 1979
213  Gabriele Annan, as in Note 209

the middle classes - people who merely earned their name and fortune through their work and income. His collaborator in writing that book was the editor of *Burke's Landed Gentry,* an index that definitively tracks and authenticates the titles of British aristocrats in Ireland. But even that man, as *The Telegraph* obituary had to acknowledge, 'was uneasy about some of the opinions Bence-Jones expressed'. [214]

One of Bence-Jones' first books, *The Palaces of the Raj: Magnificence and Misery of the Lord Sahibs,* focused on the British occupation of India, where his own family held some of their colonial estates and he had lived as a child. [215] He lamented that 'when, after 1960, the British Empire virtually ceased to exist, the landless aristocracy lost its chief support... the loss of their Imperial birthright'. [216]

A later book, *The Twilight of the Ascendancy,* turns the same attention to the branch of the British aristocracy who occupied Ireland in stately homes like his own. [217] This word *'Ascendancy'* is a term some use to describe the generations of expatriate British colonials who owned and dominated all of Irish life, law, wealth and government for centuries. His most well-known book, *Stately Homes of Ireland,* is considered a definitive and complete guide to their stately manors and estates around the country.

Fortunately, Gleann's twentieth-century Bence-Jones was quite different from his dreaded grandfather. It was as a colonial landlord elsewhere in Cork County that his grandfather had earned the worst of reputations. The infamous William Bence-Jones had the distinction of being one of the most hated colonial landlords in Ireland (and that's saying something). In 1880, the *Cork Examiner* newspaper described him as 'widely reviled here' and 'the most thoroughly disliked man in the county.' [218] Much has been written about his cruelty towards his Irish tenants, his opposition to charitable works during the Famine, and his clashes with the Irish National Land League, led by Charles Stewart Parnell, in their attempts at reform. [219]

---

214 Bence-Jones, Mark, *Twilight of the Ascendancy*, Constable, 1987

215 Bence-Jones, Mark, *The Palaces of the Raj: Magnificence and Misery of the Lord Sahibs*, Allen & Unwin, 1973

216 Bence-Jones, Mark, *The British Aristocracy*, as in Note 212

217 Bence-Jones, Mark, *A Guide to Irish Country Houses,* Constable, 1996

218 Robert O' Byrne, 'A Life's Work in Ireland', available at https://theirishaesthete.com/2014/11/10/a-lifes-work-in-ireland

219 In 1889, *The Southern Star* newspaper printed one of many articles denouncing William Bence-Jones. The article angrily quotes WBJ: "An Irish tenant would not know how to farm this land' said William Bence Jones... to illustrate his attitude to Irish farmers and to the Irish

By contrast, his twentieth-century grandson had the genteel eccentricity and elaborate, affable politeness that is typical of today's English elites and aristocrats. He was scrupulously polite to the Gleann women who worked as his housekeepers and the local men who maintained his grounds. It's a tone I got to know well during my years in Cambridge. As Bence-Jones himself explains in his books, they learn it at Eton and other top private schools, and polish it in the halls of Oxford and Cambridge. [220]  Boris Johnson, populist Prime Minister of Britain as I write, is a classic recent performer of this bumbling, elaborate politeness. What I found unpleasant about such people in Cambridge was that it's only when you read the books and articles that they write *for each other* about society and aristocracy that you understand, behind their appeasing gentility, how they really see human rank and class. [221]

## Unlikely allies

From 1779, the Hudson family held the colonial estate in Gleann an Phréacháin for 170 years. When he put Pat and Johanna Carney on the coffin ship, Henry Hudson (1795-1889) 'owned over 5,000 acres' in Cork. [222] All I can say is that he must have been a most complex and unusual individual. On the one hand, his colonial estate in Gleann showed the usual level of disregard for the Famine starvation of its tenant natives. Yet on the other - in a most unusual move for colonial elites - he and his brother Elliot were lifelong devotees, activists for and lavish funders of traditional Irish culture, music and language! This is yet another of those unexpected twists and contradictory layers in the history of the Village.

The family had a townhouse in Dublin but the brothers spent much of their youth enjoying their huge country estate in Gleann an Phréacháin.

as a race and his low regard for their abilities and intelligence'. Quoted in *The Southern Star Centenary Supplement*, 1889-1989, available at www.failteromhat.com/southernstar  You can read a summary of William Bence-Jones' elaborate conflicts with the Irish in the essay 'The Famous 1881 Debate - Key Issues', available online at www.failteromhat.com/southernstar

220  Bence-Jones, Mark, *The British Aristocracy*, as in Note 212

221  As recently as 1995, Boris Johnson has written about the 'appalling proliferation of single mothers (…) producing a generation of ill-raised, ignorant, aggressive and illegitimate children'; his article describes 'blue-collar', working class men as 'likely to be drunk, criminal, aimless, feckless and hopeless, and perhaps claiming to suffer from low self-esteem brought on by unemployment'. Boris Johnson, 'Politics', *The Spectator*, 19-8-1995

222  National University of Ireland in Galway, 'Landed Estates Database - Estate: Hudson (Glenville)', available at http://landedestates.nuigalway.ie/LandedEstates/jsp/estate-show.jsp?id=2974

Presumably, that is where they first came into close contact with poor native Irish people and Gaelic speakers. (We have seen that Gaelic was still spoken by many around Gleann until the middle of the nineteenth century.) By the age of 14, Henry was avidly collecting traditional rural songs in the native Irish. Being a year older than Elliot, he went on to inherit the estate while Elliot (1796-1853), being interested in politics, law and rights, became a barrister.

One can only conclude that in Henry's mind, his passion for the natives' language and music somehow did not extend to compassion for the starving condition that his colonial class kept them in. But for Elliot, those two poles of Gaelic culture on the one hand, and Gaelic politics on the other, did come together. He is the Manor House son who became a close friend of my great-great-grandfather, their new Irish gamekeeper. And we have seen that Elliot eventually alienated his family by agitating for the cause of Irish independence through the movements of his time, such as Thomas Davis's Young Irelanders. That is why Elliot was buried with the independence-supporting Sweeney natives in Doon, not with his own side.

In 2011, the Irish government department for the Irish language launched an online collection of *Biographies* (*Beathaisnéisí* in Irish) of 1,774 people who, from centuries ago to the present day, made the most important contributions to the Irish language. Amazingly, both of the Hudson brothers from the Gleann Manor House earn substantial places in it. [223]

It is truly bizarre to me to think that, while his tenants starved to death in Gleann, Henry Hudson was off travelling around wildest, Irish-speaking Connaught basically doing the job that I do today, as an ethnographer. Biographers confirm that 'he learned Irish as a boy, and made copies of songs that his Irish teacher had collected from the oral tradition'. [224] He specialised in seeking out poor native Irish speakers and collecting their traditional music, gathering from them and preserving songs and music that had never before been recorded on paper. His Irish government biography explains (in Irish) that 'he gathered a large number of melodies in Connaught between 1840 and 1842, 138 of them from the piper Pádraig Mac Conaola... They are [now] in the Boston Public Library'. [225] Another

---

223 Called *Beathaisnéisí* (*Biographies*, in English), it is published by Cló Iar-Chonnacht for the National Library of Ireland and is available at www.ainm.ie ; as it is only available in Irish, extracts are translated here by Marella Hoffman

224 *Dictionary of Irish Biography*, Royal Irish Academy & Cambridge University Press, available at at https://dib.cambridge.org

225 'Bhailigh sé cuid mhór fonn i gConnachta idir 1840 agus 1842, 138 díobh ón bpíobaire Pádraig Mac Conaola (...) Sa Leabharlann Phoiblí i mBoston atá said', (translated by Marella

historian summarises that 'his manuscripts contain a total of 870 tunes, of which 757 are genuine Irish folk melodies and the remaining 113 were composed by himself after traditional models.' [226]

Meanwhile his brother Elliot, soul-mate of my gamekeeping great-great-grandfather, is described in his Irish government biography as 'the person who most generously, in the first half of the nineteenth century, spent his own wealth on associations and publications for [Irish-language] culture'. [227] Apparently, 'he gave a major donation to the Royal Irish Academy to create an Irish language dictionary and he promised a further £1,000 if they needed it.' [228] In 1841, Elliot Hudson from the Gleann colonial Manor declared uncompromisingly in the *Dublin Monthly Magazine*: 'We bid farewell to all Anglican attempts at expounding Irish words. Irish letters for Irish words and nothing else. If you can't read them - learn! If you can't pronounce them - learn! If you can't understand them - learn!' [229]

During my research for this book, I was amazed to discover this passion and activism for the Irish language in these two colonials at the Crow Glen Manor. I had logically assumed that the area's ancient Gaelic language, literature, poetry and songs were conserved and promoted only by the Bardic Schools in the Nagle Mountains above the Village, until Cromwell's Penal Laws suppressed them. The very last place in the world that I would have expected Gaelic language, literature and songs to be loved and gathered in the nineteenth century would have been at the Manor House!

When Henry died without heirs in 1889, the estate passed to his nephew Sir Edward Hudson-Kinahan (1872-1949). He took a keen interest in the estate and developed its famous 'Glenville Gardens'. It was after his death that the Bence-Jones family bought the estate and Manor.

We have seen that the IRA were fiercely active in the area all around Gleann's colonial Manor during the War of Independence. One would have expected them to order the owners out and burn the place down, as

Hoffman), *Biographies /Beathaisnéisí,* Cló Iar-Chonnacht, 2020, available at www.ainm.ie/Bio.aspx?ID=1088
226 Donal O'Sullivan, *Irish Folk Music and Song,* Three Candles, Dublin,1952
227 'An duine is féile é sa leath tosaigh den 19ú haois a chaith a mhaoin ar mhaithe le cumainn agus foilseacháin chultúrtha' (translated by Marella Hoffman), *Biographies /Beathaisnéisí,* Cló Iar-Chonnacht, 2020, available at www.ainm.ie/Bio.aspx?ID=1089
228 'Thug sé síntiús mór don Acadamh Ríoga chun foclóir Gaeilge a chur le chéile agus gheall £1,000 eile dá mbeadh gá leis', *Biographies /Beathaisnéisí* as in Note 227
229 *Dictionary of Irish Biography,* Royal Irish Academy & Cambridge University Press, as in Note 224

they did with so many other icons of the British Empire around Ireland. Presumably, the facts that the Manor's son Elliot had actively supported the cause of Irish independence right up to his death 67 years earlier, and that he had been such a close friend of the Sweeneys who assisted the War of Independence IRA in Doon, must be the reason why the Gleann Manor survived the War of Independence intact.

However, as we saw in an earlier chapter, the IRA did pay one serious visit to the Manor during the War of Independence. Cork University historian John Borgonovo tells us that Cork city's IRA Brigade came out and raid the Gleann Manor for its car. Cars, regularly confiscated by both sides in the war, were scarce and invaluable. He explains that 'in April 1921, six armed Volunteers raided the home of Sir Edward Kinahan. They dismantled his car, took away numerous parts, then destroyed the engine with pickaxes. On the car door, they chalked the message, 'Don't take our parts. By Order, Transport Commandant, 1st Brigade I.R.A." [230]

## CDanor houses

Would you like a tour of the Crow Glen Manor? Where shall we start? In the chapel? In the armoury? In the walled garden? Perhaps we won't bother with the kitchen, former home of housemaids from the Village, because as *The Irish Times* once put it, 'Bence-Jones is reputed to have told some guests that he did not know where it was'. [231]

A tour of the Manor and gardens was part of the deal that Keith had purchased for our evening. I remember that as we approached the house, one of the young Carney women didn't want to go in: she felt physically sick at the thought of her fore-mother starving to death amidst this glamour. But the lady of the Manor, the heiress daughter of Mark Bence-Jones, received us gracefully on the steps of the house when we arrived, and proceeded to take the group on a guided tour of the property. Having seen it all before on my hands and knees in the mud, I stayed with the driver and with Brian O' Donoghue, the learned *sean-nós* singer who had sung for us earlier in the week at the Mass Rock, and rejoined us now. The

230 John Borgonovo, 'The Guerrilla Infrastructure: IRA Special Services in the Cork Number One Brigade, 1917-1921', *The Irish Sword*, Vol 27, Military History Society of Ireland, 2010. Borgonovo is quoting from *R.I.C. Daily Reports*, 8-14 April, 1921.
231 *The Irish Times*, 'Eminent Historian of Irish Ascendancy', 8-5-2010

owner of the Manor parked us politely in the library with the pre-dinner wines.

You can view a full photo-tour of the house online, and it is quite beautiful. [232] Still furnished and decorated in the style of the nineteenth and even, in parts, eighteenth century, it looks pretty much today as it would have looked under the Hudsons at the time of the Famine. It is still renowned for its antique furniture, ancestral portraits and the vividly bright Georgian colours of its original wallpapers and draperies. One modern visitor described how the house, 'which has remained an archetypical Irish [manor house] in a time warp of the 1950s, is pleasantly decaying with its original nineteenth-century faded lemon and grey wallpaper... and vases of fresh flowers from the garden'. [233] The current chatelaine, who as a teenager spent a lot of her youth at the Manor and socialised with ordinary kids from Gleann, is now opening the House more to the public. She runs occasional cultural events, and you can even go there to stay overnight, or for a holiday. [234]

The armoury is surely the most curious of all its rooms. Like the central hall of an early medieval castle, it's a bare, cavernous, stone-walled space at the Manor's centre, with steps leading down into it and a very large stone fireplace as its only decoration. In the corners stand original suits of battle armour holding their weapons, as if ready to rush out and fight you there and then. *The Irish Times* describes how, in the late twentieth century (while I was growing up outside the Wood Wall), 'Bence-Jones still adhered to the manners and etiquette of a previous generation. Sherry was drunk in the armoury, a hall decorated with suits of armour. After dinner the ladies withdrew, leaving the gentlemen to the port'. [235]

That whole layout of a British colonial stately home would have been pretty much the same in India and Africa, as well as in Ireland and back in their home territory in England itself. But I've always thought of the armoury at the centre of the Manor as somehow its strongest link to those other continents. The armoury seems an acknowledgement that colonisation, class-supremacy and '*Ascendancy*', as Bence-Jones and others liked to call it, has to be built on military force. No-one is going to just hand you the keys of the castle and your place at the head of the banquet-

232 Robert O' Byrne, 'A Life's Work in Ireland' is an attractively illustrated photo-story tour of the house's main rooms, available at https://theirishaesthete.com/2014/11/10/a-lifes-work-in-ireland

233 *The Irish Times*, 'Eminent Historian', as in Note 231

234 Visit www.glenvillepark.com

235 *The Irish Times*, 'Eminent Historian', as in Note 231

table while others starve outside the gate: you'll have to take them and keep them by force.

Bence-Jones took it on as his life's work to document the decay of the colonial regimes both in India and in Ireland - how their wealth, opulence and power slowly slipped away from their grip as local movements for reform and independence rose up against them in the twentieth century. And when you stand in his Manor House today, you do feel like you're standing in the remaining shell or husk of something that is gone. Like the way some insects can walk off and leave their carapace behind them.

Symbolic perhaps of that decay was some news that the lady of the house shared with Keith. She told him that the massive Rhododendron trees for which the estate is famous - giant mountains of them in countless flowering colours - have contracted a disease that is killing them off.

I know that Keith thought a lot later about how he could 'give' something to the Manor. That may seem an odd reaction but I had learned that Keith's way of feeling strong is to feel in a position to be able to give, rather than to take. Within his logic, for him to be able to contribute something positive or meaningful to the Manor estate now would bring a healing closure to his ancestors' terrible story, coming from a Carney clan who have survived to be prosperous, generous people.

It occurred to him that he could use some of his own resources to try to get the Rhododendrons' disease attended to and treated. As a family of trees caught up in this epic tale that is the Manor, they were a beautiful gift from Nature that had done no harm to anybody. Maybe he could help them continue to blossom for another hundred years, while privately remembering his fore-mother Johanna, to whom no-one had ever given flowers. Liaising with the chatelaine, he got an expert to go and assess the Rhododendrons but it was confirmed that nothing could be done for them.

Meanwhile, using the wealth from their economic boom around the time of the millennium, the native Irish themselves have taken on a lot of these stately homes, and taken them in a new direction - one that I think is wonderful. Examples just half an hour's drive from Gleann an Phréacháin include *Castlemartyr Resort* and *Fota House*. [236] Today's Irish architects are gifted at bringing modern restoration to old buildings, from gothic castles to maritime warehouses. They use glowing natural materials in clean lines

---

236  Visit online at www.castlemartyrresort.ie/hotel/gallery and www.fotahouse.com

and modern proportions. They somehow make modern polished timber, marble, glass and slate blend seamlessly in with antique elegance. These buildings offer some of the lushest comfort and luxury I've ever seen, while at the same time feeling *universally* welcoming. You can just walk in there for a single coffee. They have been re-designed to welcome in the human body - any human body who can afford a cup of coffee. Their goal is to seat that body, feed it, massage it and offer it lovely views in the lushest environments.

This sense of welcome is uncanny. They will walk you in person from the door to the armchair with the best view over the grounds, and invite you to spend the afternoon there if you feel like it, reading their newspapers. When my family took me to these places in recent years, this culture of welcome was baffling to me. I had lived for nearly three decades amidst the rigid class-system of Cambridge, where the plush, luxurious University Colleges that I had worked in are actively designed to keep the majority out.

These places in Ireland seem to be actively, deliberately reversing thay old bad magic. Like turning a glove inside out, they are an inversion of Bence-Jones' *Palaces of the Raj*, which were designed to deprive and exclude the vast majority of human beings around them. But these reformed Irish palaces present the luxury of the land to *everybody* equally. The food and drink are not expensive there. You are actively encouraged to stay all day over a pot of tea if you want to, feeling at home for the day as if the place is your own. [237] You can take a tour online of these democratic altars to luxury. But if you can, get there in person for a day's coffee, cakes and sandwiches in the drawing-room overlooking the pool.

One day at the Castlemartyr Resort, I saw a very timid family of humble, farming people inch their way nervously inside the palatial front door, the parents anxiously pushing the children ahead of them by the necks of their clothes. The manager greeted them with the same open ease as he does his wealthiest Americans, and asked what they might like. The father, the group's appointed talker, nervously asked whether the place did ham sandwiches and fizzy orange.

The mention of this feast rang a sweet little bell of recognition in my ears. When I was a child, it was the treat of choice for rural people on the very

---

237 As luxury 5-star hotels and spas, you can also spend an unlimited amount of money being pampered there. But the farming family enjoying their fizzy orange on the velvet sofas won't be kept out for your benefit.

rare occasions when we might go into a pub as a family, for instance after a funeral. The manager kindly said he'd bring the refreshments himself, and led them to a spacious corner where they could spread out comfortably on elaborate velvet sofas with gold-leafed, curling frames. I felt so happy to witness this careful scene of cultural healing and reparation.

Before getting back on the bus that night at Gleann's own Manor, our group lingered around the front of the house in the twilight. I stood on the steps outside the front door, beside the lady of the house. It was my first time meeting her. She was near my age and I was very surprised to feel a liking towards her, sensing that she was probably quite a nice girl. We stood there in an almost companionable moment. I knew she was trying to earn some income for the House by opening it up like this. So I said that the evening had been really enjoyable, and was well done. 'Do you think you'll be able to carry on, to keep the place going?' I asked. I meant this to sound kindly and supportive but it snapped the moment in two. She visibly winced, ignored what I had said and walked away.

Eventually, our silver bus was moving back down the driveway, with all of our group behind its dark windows. As we came level with the tree where my teen self and her friend were reclining, I saw out of the corner of my eye that they were peering at us from behind a bushy branch about ten feet off the ground. They must have thought we were just visiting dignitaries because they shrugged, lay back into the bosom of their tree and went back to dreaming about their futures.

## References

Annan, Gabriele, 'Sheep into Goats', *London Review of Books*, 24-1-1980

Bence-Jones, Mark, *A Guide to Irish Country Houses,* Constable, 1996

Bence-Jones, Mark, *Twilight of the Ascendancy*, Constable, 1987

Bence-Jones, Mark, *The British Aristocracy*, Constable, 1979

Bence-Jones, Mark, *The Palaces of the Raj: Magnificence and Misery of the Lord Sahibs*, Allen & Unwin, 1973

Borgonovo John, 'The Guerrilla Infrastructure: IRA Special Services in the Cork Number One Brigade, 1917-1921', *The Irish Sword*, Vol 27, Military History Society of Ireland, 2010

Cló Iar-Chonnacht for the National Library of Ireland, *Beathaisnéisí,* 2020, available at www.ainm.ie (in Irish only)

Johnson, Boris, 'Politics', *The Spectator*, 19-8-1995

O' Byrne, Robert, 'A Life's Work in Ireland', available at https://theirishaesthete.com/2014/11/10/a-lifes-work-in-ireland

O' Sullivan, Donal, *Irish Folk Music and Song*, Three Candles, Dublin, 1952

Royal Irish Academy & Cambridge University Press, *Dictionary of Irish Biography*, available at https://dib.cambridge.org

*The Irish Independent*, 'World News', 25-4-2010

*The Irish Times*, 'Eminent historian of Irish ascendancy', 8-5-2010

*The Southern Star*, 'The Famous 1881 Debate - Key Issues', available at www.failteromhat.com/southernstar

*The Southern Star Centenary Supplement, 1889-1989*, available at www.failteromhat.com/southernstar

*The Telegraph*, 'Mark Bence-Jones, Obituary', 30-4-2010

FARMING FOR
nature

Chapter **13**

# Crow's view

Images at the opening of this chapter:

~ The ecological challenge facing our world
~ About a billion prayers have been said in Gleann an Phréacháin over the past millennium
~ Logo of Ireland's *Farming for Nature* organisation, recent prize-winners in the United Nations competition 'Act for Biodiversity'
~ A local gun club enjoying a feast of game at Barry Kennedy's pub in Gleann an Phréacháin

Those are all the stories from the Glen of the Crow that this book wanted to tell you about. We've met a lot of characters and seen them do some amazing things, in some spectacular places. If Crow were flying back over the chapters of this book now, what would *he* see as themes running through it, the way the River Bride runs through its Valley or the road from Cork runs through the Village and on up into the Nagle mountains?

Everyone plots their own way through a book, being struck by the things that are most relevant in it for them. So in a way, everyone's reading of a book is different. But there are some features that would probably strike us all (highlighted in bold script below), if we flew back over the book the way Crow flies.

One theme that Crow himself noted from the beginning of the book, in his opening section called *Crow Flies In*, was **Returns**. Thousands of emigrants have left and returned to Gleann an Phréacháin during the centuries overviewed in these chapters. As well as people, objects and ideas return too, as if resurrecting out of the mists of time. Memories can return. One of the missions of this book has been to bring back to Gleann the long-discarded memory of those who fought so hard there to bring us a democratic, decolonised Republic. Extraordinary people like Tomás Mac Curtain, Liam Lynch, Kate Hickey and Ernie O' Malley come walking back towards us out of the pages of this book, fresh from their revolutionary activities in Gleann an Phréacháin.

History too can unfold in circling, non-linear ways. Things fall in and out of fashion, of prominence and memory. Forgetting and abandonment are sometimes followed by remembering and revival, especially in Ireland, where there's such a visceral connection to and respect for the past. And is any past ever fully gone? As long as there is a future, there will always be **Returns**.

Another thread running through the landscape of this book like a lazy river is the theme of **food and hunger**. The book started with a Famine and ended with the feast that Keith Carney had promised to his fore-father Pat, when our group visited Doon and saw Pat and Johanna leaving for the coffin ship. Early chapters held the fatal hungers of the Famine. Later, the handsome young Terence MacSwiney, Lord Mayor of Cork, starved to death on hunger strike under illegal detention in a London jail during Crow Glen's War of Independence. He lasted without food for 74 days - exceptionally long for a hunger strike. His biographers describe how the British used to place fragrant foods beside him to try to tempt him, agonisingly, off his hunger strike. [238] But his tormentors were forgetting that in his inaugural address as Lord Mayor of Cork, Terence had 'made the remark for which he would be best remembered': *'It is not they who can inflict the most, but they who can suffer the most, who will conquer.'* [239]

Not long afterwards, we saw almost 8,000 of the Irish who had fought and won the War of Independence go on another hunger strike that lasted for 41 days, when the country's new government rounded them up and interned them during the Civil War. [240] Forty-one days is a very long time indeed to go entirely without food. It is hard to imagine what it must have been like for ordinary Irish people looking on - to think that 8,000 of their own men were sitting starving in jails a few miles away. For those six weeks, every time people sat down to eat their dinner, every mouthful must have reminded them of the modern mini-Famine going on in the jails nearby.

Norma Buckley's chapters also describe much smaller, voluntary hungers, like the communal two-day fasts that she used to find so revitalising on her pilgrimages to Lough Derg island. [241] But the eternal antidote for hunger is good food. Feasts and parties can remedy and resolve old pains, as they did when Keith Carney took us all to feast in the Manor's dining hall. My own visits to interview Norma at her house were always met with plates of homemade scones and the endless pots of Barry's tea that we both found necessary for the work. And the hearty lunch for fifteen that she laid on for the Americans appeased an old hunger that Pat and Johanna Carneys' descendants didn't even know they had.

Another contented feast had preceded my grandparents' relaxed wedding photo at Nell's farm in Doon. In that photo in Chapter 10, we saw them glowing with their new-found, post-Independence ease. Meanwhile, the *Golden Wonder* potatoes that came rolling down the centre of the table when I worked on my cousins' farm in the 1980s - they helped make the fortune of those well-off farming cousins. And the book is punctuated with hospitable rounds of drinks in Barry Kennedy's pub. It's the beating heart of the Village where thousands have found company, consolation

---

238 Francis Costello, *Enduring the Most: The Life and Death of Terence MacSwiney*, Brandon Press, 1995

239 Jason Perlman, 'Terence MacSwiney: The Triumph and Tragedy of the Hunger Strike', New York State Historical Association and the History Cooperative, 2009

240 *The Irish Times*, 'The Long History of the Irish Hunger Strike: New Exhibition in Kilmainham Gaol Tells the Story from Thomas Ashe to Bobby Sands', 21-9-2017

241 Interestingly, there is only one 'e' of a difference between a feast and a fast.

and sustenance over the past two centuries. For that reason, Barry seemed the right person to write this book's *Afterword*.

Before he was executed by the British in his bedroom, Cork Lord Mayor Tomás Mac Curtain had given Gleann an Phréacháin the vision and reality of a Village Shop where, post-Independence, local farmers from all over the north mountains would at last trade their produce freely and independently. A hundred and fifty years after starving while produce was being exported to the British Empire, Crow Glen farmers are now prosperous, affluent and well educated.

But today, governments are having crisis meetings around the world to try to address the environmental emergency that is upon us. At those summits, the vision that Tomás Mac Curtain had in 1921 for the **sustainable production of local food** is now called 'Agroecology', 'Food Security' and 'Food Sovereignty'. Policymakers are showing how it will be part of the solution to the environment crisis looming ahead. [242] They demonstrate that 'many of the problems in food systems are linked specifically to the uniformity at the heart of industrial agriculture, and its reliance on chemical fertilisers and pesticides.' They show how reviving the wisdom of our traditional mixed farming, local chains of supply and sale, and ecological farming that cares for the soil and biosystem, can solve these problems. [243]

The **'BRIDE' Project** (short for '*Biodiversity Regeneration In a Dairying Environment*') is an amazingly clever and successful project that is paying local farmers to do some profitable ecological farming in the areas that the River Bride flows through, including Gleann an Phréacháin. Their free 85-page book, *Farm Habitat Management Guidelines* (downloadable from the internet) gives down to earth, step by step guidance for anyone to get started on even a small patch of ground, and apply for funding. [244]

242 International Panel of Experts on Sustainable Food Systems, *From Uniformity to Diversity: A Paradigm Shift from Industrial Agriculture to Diversified Agro-Ecological Systems*, Institute of Development Studies, 2016, available at www.ipes-food.org.
243 *Irish Environment* journal, 'Agroecology: Is there a clear green path from monocultures to diversity in agriculture?', Report, 1-7-2016, available at https://www.irishenvironment.com/reports/agroecology-clear-green-path-monocultures-diversity-agriculture
To read about a small ecological farm making 100,000 euros of revenue even on the harsh coast of County Clare, see 'Surfing Farmers in Ireland' by Sonya Cunningham, *The Ecologist*, 31-10-2019, available at https://theecologist.org/2019/oct/31/surfing-farmers-ireland
244 *Farm Habitat Management Guidelines - A Guide to Farming with Nature* by Sinéad Hickey, Donal Sheehan & Tony Nagle, The Bride Project, Castlelyons. Download it at

Local farmers along the Bride River who have taken advantage of the project say: 'It's a great start - it's encouragement for farmers. A lot of farmers have an interest in wildlife anyway, they just need that little push.' Another explains: 'It will become mainstream in a few years, because consumers will more and more want to know where their food comes from and what kind of background it comes from, and they will want to know that we're producing food without injuring the environment.' And another points out: 'We can't deny that we're losing biodiversity but (with this funding and guidance) you can have your intensive farmland and your income from that, and you can *also* have wildlife', and your income from that. [245]

A recent *Irish Times* article celebrated the successes of award-winning dairy farmer Donal Sheehan, who farms in an ecological way along the Bride River Valley, and is the manager of the BRIDE project [246] He's also part of Ireland's excellent *Farming for Nature* organisation that is supporting - and paying - farmers to make these changes in a profitable way. They were prize-winners recently in the prestigious United Nation competition 'Act for Biodiversity'. [247]

Having just lived through the Covid-19 pandemic of 2020, we now once more recognise that local food shops are a cornerstone of civilisation, as important as caring for the sick and educating children. *Food Sovereignty* is the buzzword in all mouths as we come out of the twenty-first century's first brush with a food security crisis in the Western world. Unlike many small villages across western Europe, Gleann an Phréacháin still has the benefit of Barry's grocery store. There the hungry, the lonely, those without cars and those needing to refuel them can get fresh local food, household necessities, petrol and a warm chat with the hardworking

---

https://www.thebrideproject.ie/wp-content/uploads/2020/04/BRIDE-Project-Farm-Habitat-Management-Guidlines.pdf

245 To get involved, phone BRIDE project manager and local farmer Donal Sheehan at landline 025-37519, mobile 087-2292880, email enquiries@thebrideproject.ie or follow *The Bride Project* on Facebook or Twitter. With three staff, they're based in nearby Castlelyons, Co. Cork.

246 Sylvia Thompson, 'Ireland's Eco-Farmers Emerge from the Hedgerows - *Farming for Nature* Awards Celebrate Farmers Who Protect Habitats and Wildlife', *The Irish Times*, 10-11-2018, available at https://www.irishtimes.com/culture/tv-radio-web/ireland-s-eco-farmers-emerge-from-the-hedgerows-1.3689426

247 Visit www.farmingfornature.ie/2020/06/29/farming-for-nature-wins-global-biodiversity-award For another Irish project attracting international admiration, see Ella McSweeney, 'Life Attracts Life: The Irish Farmers Filling their Fields with Bees and Butterflies - Rewarding Positive Environmental Impact has Revitalised an Area of West Ireland. Is this a Solution to the Country's 'Acute' Nature Crisis?', *The Guardian*, 6-6-2020

Teresa Barry at almost any time of the day, the evening or the week. Continuing the legacy of the food-market that was held in the Street of Gleann in previous centuries, local food shops like Teresa's are the way of the future for sustainable societies. [248]

Another theme that has threaded through this book in a minor way has been the subject of Guns. Before this project, I had never thought about the presence of guns in my life. My father had been a keen hunter on the Nagles and other mountains throughout the 1970s and 80s. He raised pedigree hunting dogs, raised game fowl to be released to populate the mountainsides and used to organise big, elaborate gun-dog trials for ordinary people on the mountains, with parties to follow in the Village in Kennedy's pub (like the Gun Club's game feast pictured at the start of this chapter).

We kids disliked the grown-up flavour of wild game but for most Sunday lunches of my teens and childhood, there was wild duck, pheasant, rabbit, snipe or grouse that he'd shot on the Nagle Mountains, or salmon or trout that he'd caught in the Bride or Blackwater rivers. A collection of well-polished rifles - from antique muskets to sleek modern shotguns - always lay casually around our house, beside the sheets and pillows in our linen cupboards or piled behind the television. To me they were as normal as the Sacred Heart lamp, the nightly Rosary, the teapot, toilet paper... I somehow assumed all domestic scenes around the world included them.

But my father, an 'outsider' from the next village, had never had any interest in politics, or in guns for political purposes. It was only Norma Buckley's fateful remark as we left Doon that day with the Americans – when she said 'That's where your people used to keep *the weapons*' - that led me stumbling, as if blindfolded, into Crow Glen's War of Independence. Otherwise, I would still be ignorant of it to this day.

We have seen that it was the gamekeeper's well-paid job to manage an impressive arsenal of guns for the Manor's shooting parties. And that job, inherited later by his son, left the son well qualified to hide and manage the IRA's weapons cache on his farm during the War of Independence. With all that I know now about the Glen of the Crow, I look differently on that photo of my grandparents' wedding party, just a few years after their side had won that war.

---

248 When I was a university researcher home from abroad on holidays, Teresa used to hold my wrist across her shop-counter and marvel fondly that though approaching thirty, I was 'still at school'.

The family are reclined comfortably on the lush grass of their farm in Doon. And I am struck by the look in the old gamekeepers' eyes. There is peace and fulfilment at last. But what strikes me most now is that he took care to include his shotgun in this idyllic nuptial scene. The old man remembers to include a reference to the way that peace had to be won.

Another major theme of this book, looming like the wide Nagle heather-moors to the north of the Village, is **not knowing**. The IRA in the Glen of the Crow had no idea whether their efforts would be successful. For many of the most active individuals, their successes would end up being for others to enjoy, while they sacrificed everything to bring that success about.

Johanna Carney didn't know whether her little brood would live or die when she took their last sliver of a chance on the coffin ship. She certainly could not have imagined that after they got to America, one of her sons would grow up to become Secretary of State for Massachusetts. (*Could she* at any level of her imagination have had such wild dreams? She didn't know this either but a destitute young Irishman called Patrick Kennedy reached America on a similar ship two years after she did - and his great-grandson, John F. Kennedy, became President of the United States.)

During the War of Independence, the three households around the Bride River Valley don't know whether they will be interned or shot for supporting the Irish fighters. (As it happened, Mr Hegarty was shot and seriously wounded but survived, and had to emigrate, while Mr Hickey was interned.) And they definitely could not foresee that their side would defeat the mighty British Empire within just two years. At age 11, Nell doesn't know which way the war will go. She has no idea that she will survive to help raise a granddaughter who, after Nell's death and lifelong silence on the matter, will research and publish their story in this book at the 100th anniversary of their War.

My own stumbling route through this book has also, obviously, been paved with **not knowing**. At the outset, I knew almost none of the historical events related here, and everyone around me in the Glen of the Crow acted as if they didn't know them either. The reality is that some did know them and pretended not to, while most of the younger generations today probably *don't* know about them. This book seeks to remedy that current, collective **not knowing**.

Secrets and silences pepper this book, but I understand much better now how many of them were healthy, productive silences. We saw that the whole community's commitment to keeping secret and silent about IRA activities was the weapon that actually won the War of Independence. And afterwards, communities used the same skill - *not talking* about things and acting as if they *didn't know* them - to heal Civil War rifts and move forward quickly together as a modern democracy. Keith Carney, a much-travelled person who works at a high level with the American government in Washington DC, told me: 'I have never seen a nation so good at keeping secrets as the Irish.'

Keith has a professional passion for the opposite - for openness, visibility and transparency in the political regimes and decisions that run our countries and have sweeping effects on our lives. *FedNet*, the organisation that Keith created, owns and runs, 'began broadcasting (US) Congress on the web in 1996 and has since broadcast thousands of hearings, press conferences and complete, live coverage of Senate and House Floor Debates each day'. [249]

As 'the leading provider of multimedia content of the United States Congress, *FedNet* maintains a robust video network throughout the Capitol complex for use in broadcast and web-based production... Millions [of video] clips currently exist in [its] database and its users have access to over 40,000 hours of archived video. Every spoken word in the [US government] chambers since January 2002 is available through an easy-to-use web-based interface.' [250] You can just click on www.fednet.net to watch the US government broadcast live before your eyes at any time, by a boy descended from the boys who were thrown starving out of Doon in 1847. What would their dad Pat Carney, who died on the coffin ship, have to say about that? [251]

PRAYERS are another big presence in this book, as numerous as the leaves in the densely wooded landscape around the Village of Gleann an Phréacháin. As a researcher I have calculated that at least a billion - one thousand million - prayers have been said in Gleann parish over the past millennium. A population of just a thousand people across the parish saying just three prayers a day for a thousand years yields up 1,095,000,000

249 'About Us', *FedNet* website, available at www.fednet.net
250 *FedNet* website, as in Note 249 above
251 It would be interesting to trace today the descendants of all who have ever emigrated from Crow Glen, especially those forced to leave through poverty or persecution, and to celebrate the contributions they have made to the world, alongside those of Crow Glenners who never left.

prayers. And my research suggests that, in fact, the majority of them probably said more than three per day.

So what is a prayer? Your estimation of what those billion prayers actually were depends on your own beliefs and values. If you're spiritually minded, you may feel they were daily connections and communications with the benign energies of the spiritual world. If you're an atheist, you may think they were wasted nothings. But at the very least, they surely were positive intentions and positive wishes, very often for the good of others. Prayers are active wishes for a better world, hopes for a better world, and specific visions for how the world could be better. At the absolute minimum, those billion prayers by Crow Glenners constitute a lot of focused, deliberate mental activity by one group of human beings.

Whatever you think a billion prayers amount to, modern psychologists have also worked out their own 'Billion Moments' theory about human wisdom. They point out that when we reach 31.7 years of age, we have lived - and hopefully learned - for a billion seconds. And although 'we reach the legal age of adulthood at age 21, we reach a new level of maturity in our 30's', once we have lived through those billion moments of experience. [252]

One of the reasons I wrote this book was just to bring attention to and honour the sheer intensity of that vast hive of prayer generated in the Glen of the Crow over the centuries. As a package of mental, emotional and cultural heritage, it's worth at least pausing to look back at and thinking: *'What do we want to do with that now, if anything?'*

To use Norma Buckley's vocabulary, Crow Glenners today can ask themselves 'How do we want to *'inherit'* that amazing tradition, if we do want to inherit anything about it? And what do we want to do with it now and in the future to *'evolve'* it?' If Crow Glenners decide that the huge tradition of prayer in their area is best discarded now, I will be all the more glad to have written this book just to capture and honour it for what it was.

ḣealɪnᴈ acᴿoss ᴄɪme. One day, in the course of my research, I accidentally happened across a record in the archives that - as soon as I saw it - I sincerely wished I hadn't. It's dated the 15th of December - what we would call *'coming up to Christmas'*. It's a legal document from the  British

252  Thomas Frey, 'Life begins at a billion moments', 23-1-2018, available at
https://futuristspeaker.com/artificial-intelligence/life-begins-at-a-billion-moments

government in 1653 (Cromwell's era) authorising specific colonels of the British Army in Ireland to round up 'such Irish children or other Irish as are in any Hospitalls or Workhouses', plus all Irish men, women and children who had been unemployed for over a year, and to ship them by force - as slaves, basically - to the new American colonies for the use of specific British landowners there. [253]

One little phrase of it is very stirring, where it says that all 'Irish persons *not having articles*' are to be shipped in this way. So having a couple of '*articles*' in your possession - say, a hand-tool, a bowl and a blanket - would have saved you. But being a bare human body and soul - the way we are all born, without possessions in our hands - meant the end of you.

The document continues its meticulous record-keeping: 'Permission is granted to Colonel Fealan to transport 1,000 Irish for the service of the King of Spain'. '3,000 Irish natives transported into Flanders from the Southern Counties by Colonel Treswell.' '1,500 Irish Natives transported for the service of the Prince of Condé by Colonel Treswell.' That Colonel Treswell was a busy man. Wouldn't it be interesting to meet him now and have a word with him, to hear what he thought about his day's work?

The records go on: '4 Priests. 16 men. 19 women and children' shipped to Barbados for use on the new sugar plantations there. And, dated ten days before the document just cited: 'James Cary, the Priest at Waterford, sentenced to death for not transplanting', in other words, for refusing to be shipped away. [254]

Such things are truly breathtaking, and very hard to look at in any era, when done to any population, anywhere in the world. But there can be some redemption, even now. Just to unearth it and name it and *feel sorry* gives back some human dignity to those individuals, as if reaching back through the centuries with a torch to shine some kind of light and healing into that hell-realm that they are otherwise forgotten in.

I reached out for some comfort to Diarmuid Grainger, the War of Independence historian who wrote the Foreword for this book. I wrote to him: 'Diarmuid, I happened across this in the archives - some sort of new hell-realm that doesn't bear thinking about. But I suppose it has to be thought about by someone who can bear to face it, as fortunately you are doing with your own book on the Whiteboys resistance movement in

253 Jane Lyons, 'Transportation of the Irish', *From-Ireland.net*, 2-3-2013, available at www.from-ireland.net/transportation-of-the-irish
254 Jane Lyons, as in Note 253 above

North Cork, and those deported for being part of it. It seems to me that good historical work like you are doing can somehow - at an almost spiritual or mystical level - reach back to bring some healing to those immense packages of injustice and suffering, which would otherwise be forgotten.'

What it would mean to those people if they knew that their story would later at least be *told* - the unfairness of it exposed and apologised for. Caring historical remembrance can play its own little part in Purgatory, releasing those tormented souls from the sense that the injustice done against them was entirely forgotten, never recognised, never accounted for. We can respect and honour those individuals now, even though they weren't respected then.

Meanwhile, my own beloved granny, Nell Sweeney, had left us aged 90 in 1999, leaving us to open the new millennium without her. Last night, after writing the closing pages of this book, I went to bed. And I had a rare dream that enabled me to reach out and make contact with her - across time, across infirmity, across death itself and all its apparent distances.

In that dream, I was able to find my granny - right there, in my arms, last night, and to hang onto her and to communicate with her. She was disabled and couldn't stand and had no voice, but was in a nursing home where she was well cared for. (In her lifetime, she had never been unwell or away from home.) [255] She looked like a pale, white, injured bird but I was able to take her in my arms fully, at length, and spend time with her. I took her out to a café. I held her out in front of me and I said to her emphatically, over and over, with all the strength I have: 'I *love* you. I *love* you. And I *know* you love me. I *know* you love me. I can feel it, across everything.' Because my strength got through to her, she was able to re-access her voice for a moment and I heard in reply a quiet little definite '*I do*'. Then I carried her lightly in my arms and we danced happily with the other old folks in the nursing home.

Once in the late 90s, shortly before she died, Nell and I had sat quietly praying or meditating together in the twilight in our family house in Crow Glen. She had gotten into bed for the night and I was sitting in an old armchair beside her in the near-dark. I was feeling clingy, and I said to her something in the vein of that I believe an aspect of consciousness does

---

255 The image of a nursing home is in my dream because my father was cared for in a nursing home on the other side of his beloved Nagle Mountains, when he was stricken by a paralysing disease.

continue after this human life, and that in certain circumstances people who have been very close may be able to meet up again in the spirit world. There was a distinct pause as she gathered her response to this most unexpected of invitations. Then she answered with a dignified finality and acceptance that, being young and foolish, I hadn't yet got to myself. She said: 'I have no control over that.'

With more experience of life, I understand what she said much better now. But even then I was aware of the spiritual maturity in that answer, like a wise old dog kicking off a clingy pup who should be growing up by now and handling reality. She didn't say 'We have no control over that' or 'You have no control over that'. She just spoke for herself and said, with the insight of those nine decades and all those world-transformations that she had seen pass in front of her: 'I have no control over that'.

Nell was quite familiar with things we have no control over. Unbearably, she had lost her own beloved mum Hanora Martin in Doon, when Nell was just 14 years old. It was 1923: their young friend Liam Lynch, the IRA leader, had just been killed, the Civil War was crawling to a close after four years of wars all around them, and then her mum died. What an era for that child. Yet she never discussed with us either the early loss of her mother, nor her experiences of the Independence and Civil Wars just before that. As both a child and a woman, Nell was someone who took definite action on things she could potentially have some effect on. And she also knew all about surrender, acceptance and letting go, on those things over which we have no control at all.

**Vision and action.** Prayers are wishes for a positive outcome. But this book has also shown us so many characters who had a specific **Vision** that life and society could be better - and took selfless **action** to bring that vision about successfully, even against ridiculous odds. Many individuals in this book had the deepest conviction that things *could and should be better* - and the willingness to stake their lives on taking action to bring about that better world.

They were often characters who had very few resources left, boxed into very tight situations - people who seemed to have nothing. But they spotted a small margin of choice and they took **action** within it. Without knowing whether they will succeed, they give it everything, just in case.

For instance, Gleann an Phréacháin's last hedge-school teacher, Fagan, was a penniless, unemployable relic of the lost world of the free Gaelic clans. But Fagan wished for Ireland to regain its independence and for the colonisers to give up and go home. So he set to work on that task. First, he decided to win over the Manor House's gamekeeper to the cause, and then he convinced him to also work with the son of the Manor for that cause.

After six decades of secret preparations, the second-generation gamekeeper and his 11-year-old daughter and their neighbours then went on to host the Irish Republican Army war effort in their farmyards, and the everyday folk of Crow Glen defeated the British Army in their area. At the thought of it, Fagan must be turning over comfortably in his grave in Doon, nudging his best friends - the gamekeeper on one side of him, and the barrister son of the colonial Manor on the other side.

**CReaTIng The FuTuRe.** Most people in this book did not know what the future outcome of their actions would be. But in fact, there is so much about our own train of existence that none of us ever know. We don't even know when our own life will end. Busy with our affairs of the moment, we don't realise either how much more there is to every one of us, stretching backwards and forwards like the tail of a comet through long time. How past and even future centuries weave through us, shaping and influencing, colouring and flavouring us without us realising it. All our lives involve a lot of **noT knowing**.

Yet we each occupy our own little stretch of time that is ours within the flow of history. And like Fagan and Johanna, we all have some margin of choice and action, however tiny it might sometimes seem. Like the famous butterfly wing flapping on the other side of the world, we saw in these chapters that the actions of small individuals can end up having huge positive effects.

As children, my grandparents inherited a society that was in trouble, occupied by a foreign power. It's very difficult for us to imagine this today but all around them - even before the War of Independence started - their whole country 'was the garrison of the British Army, with about a quarter of the [British] army stationed there'. [256]

Today we too are inheriting a world in trouble - a world colonised and occupied by environmental damage that will make our planet unliveable if we don't put a stop to it. We have the ecological **vision**. We also have the

---

256 Eoghan Fallon, University College Cork, 'Irish Masculinity', available at
https://www.academia.edu/35442829/Irish_masculinity_essay?email_work_card=view-paper

solutions - they don't need to be invented. But will we step up, take action and change the way our world is run, like our ancestors did? We won't be threatened with prison sentences or execution for it, but it will be an effort. Will we make that effort?

Before he died of starvation, Cork Lord Mayor Terence MacSwiney wrote *'It will be worth it a thousand times over if we are successful.'* This was a man with a beautiful, wealthy wife, a young family, a literary career and a sparkling social scene in Cork city. That's what he was giving up. It is almost impossible for us to get our heads around such altruism today - that a person would willingly give up their own lovely life in exchange for Ireland becoming a democratic Republic that he knew he himself would never see or enjoy. In the years ahead, how will our own environmental **vision and action** weigh up against his level of commitment?

We can't know the future. But the paradox is that we are the creators of that future, not just passive recipients of it. By the end of this twenty-first century, my life and your life and the lives of all the adults currently living around the Glen of the Crow will be over. Others out in the future will pick up the threads that we have left behind for them. Will they be good threads? For us today, our future actions are still a big unopened book. But its pages will be clear to read for those who will look back on us, as they have to start their own twenty-second century with whatever **legacies** we will have chosen to leave for them, good or bad.

*'Think globally, act locally'* is the slogan that the United Nations use to remind us that local decisions affect the health of the entire planet. So what **choices** will be made in Gleann and its hinterlands under Crow's watchful eye across this coming century? That's the big fork that he can see ahead of us in the road down below. Like the ones that faced our ancestors at those moments when they took action in this book.

This has been a book of many voices. The last word will go below to a very poor and witty man who lived in Gleann an Phréacháin in the nineteenth century. Records describe Bertie O' Flynn as an 'itinerant labourer', which meant he owned nothing. He survived by going about the area, renting out the strength of his arms to work on others' land wherever they would have him for a few days. So Bertie was a lifelong **Traveller** of the locality by necessity. He clearly knew a lot of emigrants who had left Crow Glen, who used to send or bring back perhaps exaggerated news of the exotic places that they got to see, far from the home ground.

(It is a sad and well-documented fact that emigrants of all nationalities - both out of pride and to prevent those back home from worrying about them - often send back exaggeratedly happy reports of how they are getting on abroad.)

**Travels** both near and far have been a major theme of this book. The book is part of Crow Glen's many forms of dialogue with its emigrant children, of whom I am one. This book would not have been able to tell about Crow Glen's War of Independence if the Carney descendants hadn't returned from America to accidentally trigger the release of those secrets. And in an earlier chapter we heard locals perform the nineteenth-century song of longing for the Bride River that was composed by homesick Crow Glen emigrants when they were far away. We also learned to travel Gleann's own landscapes more deeply on foot ourselves. Back around Lyrenamon and Mullanabowree, we discovered that there is no end to how deeply one can travel into such a rich, historical landscape.

And that is the lesson that the nineteenth-century labourer Bertie was already teaching through his song below. Though penniless in terms of funds, Bertie still retained the ancient gift for spontaneous verse composition, inherited from the famous bards of the Glen of the Crow, the Nagle Mountains and the Blackwater Valley. His rhyming reply to the emigrants' boasts is at once hilarious and profound. There are two types of **Travellers**, he explains in his verses below. According to Bertie, the person who has truly travelled and savoured his own locality is worth more than the globetrotter who just glides over the surface of places, without really *knowing* any of them. Bertie's message, as the United Nations slogan goes, is to *think global, act local.*

In Bertie's poem *The Two Travellers*, the very local Crow Glen placenames get special emphasis in the oral performance. In the 100-year-old manuscript, they are underlined to reflect that. The verses are best enjoyed by reading them aloud, to catch their swinging, playful rhythm. [257]

### The Two Travellers

All over the world, the Traveller said,
in my peregrinations I've been.
And there's nothing remarkable living or dead
that these eyes of mine have not seen,

---

257 Seán Ó Duinnshléibhe, as in Note 32

from the land of the ape to the Maramazet,
to the land of Feragheen.
But said the other: 'I lay you an even bet
you were never in <u>Lower Toureen</u>.'

I have hunted the woods near Sarangapata,
I have sailed the Polar Seas,
I have fished for a week the half of Siam,
I lunched in the Kersenees.

I have lived in the Valley of fair Kashmir
under the Himalayas Ridge.
But the other impatiently said: 'All here!
Were you ever at <u>Patterson's Bridge</u>?'

I've been in the land where tobacco is grown
in the suburbs of Santiago.
I've lived six months in Sierra Leone
and one in Delfuego.

I've walked across Panama all in one day.
Ah, me! But the road was a rock.
And the other remarked: 'Will you tell me, James,
were you ever in <u>Inshannach</u>?

I've hunted the tiger in Ukastan,
in Australia the kangaroo.
I've lived six months as a Medicine Man
to a tribe called the Kaffmandhu.

I've stood at the scenes of Olympic Games
where the Grecians showed their paces.
But the other remarked: 'Will you tell me, James,
were you ever at the <u>Mallow Races</u>?'

I've borne my part in a savage fray
and I've got this wound from Alaska.
We were bound just then from Mandalay
to the island of Madagascar.

The sun never tires of shining out there,
on the trees the canaries sing on.

'What of it?' said the other,
'Sure I've got a pair, and the place they sing best in is <u>Lackan</u>.'

Don't talk of your hunting in Ukastan
or your fishing in St Helena.
I would rather see young fellas hunting the wren
on the hedges of <u>Ardnageeha</u>.

No doubt but the scenes of Swiss Cantons
have a passable sort of charm.
But give me a sunset at <u>Touravaghán</u>
on the road near Twomey's farm.

I would rather be walking along the banks
watching the sweet <u>Bride</u> flow,
than growing tea among Chinese ranks
or mining in Mexico.

I would not care much for Sierra Leone
if I hadn't seen <u>Kinahan's Wall</u>.
And the man who was never at <u>Glenville Cross</u>
should not say he had travelled at all.

## References

Costello, Francis, *Enduring the Most: The Life and Death of Terence MacSwiney*, Brandon Press, 1995

Cunningham, Sonya, 'Surfing Farmers in Ireland', *The Ecologist*, 31-10-2019, available at https://theecologist.org/2019/oct/31/surfing-farmers-ireland

Dalai Lama, *The Art of Happiness - A Handbook for Living*, The Hodder Press, 1999

Fallon, Eoghan, University College Cork, 'Irish Masculinity', available at https://www.academia.edu/35442829/Irish_masculinity_essay?email_work_card=view-paper

*Farming for Nature* website, available at www.farmingfornature.ie/2020/06/29/farming-for-nature-wins-global-biodiversity-award

*FedNet* website, 'About Us', available at www.fednet.net

Frey, Thomas, 'Life begins at a billion moments', 23-1-2018, available at https://futuristspeaker.com/artificial-intelligence/life-begins-at-a-billion-moments

Hickey, Sinéad, Sheehan, Donal & Nagle, Tony, *Farm Habitat Management Guidelines - A Guide to Farming with Nature,* The Bride Project, Castlelyons, downloadable free of charge at https://www.thebrideproject.ie/wp-content/uploads/2020/04/BRIDE-Project-Farm-Habitat-Management-Guidlines.pdf

International Panel of Experts on Sustainable Food Systems, *From Uniformity to Diversity: A Paradigm Shift from Industrial Agriculture to Diversified Agro-Ecological Systems*, Institute of Development Studies, 2016, available at www.ipes-food.org

*Irish Environment* journal, 'Agroecology: Is there a clear green path from monocultures to diversity in agriculture?', Report, 1-7-2016, available at www.irishenvironment.com/reports/agroecology-clear-green-path-monocultures-diversity-agriculture

Lyons, Jane, 'Transportation of the Irish', *From-Ireland.net*, 2-3-2013, available at www.from-ireland.net/transportation-of-the-irish

McSweeney, Ella, 'Life Attracts Life: The Irish Farmers Filling their Fields with Bees and Butterflies - Rewarding Positive Environmental Impact Has Revitalised an Area of West Ireland. Is this a Solution to the Country's 'Acute' Nature Crisis?', *The Guardian*, 6-6-2020

Ó Duinnshléibhe, Seán, National Folklore Collection, Roll No. 12542, *The School Collection, Volume 0382: Áth Dúna, Gleann an Phréacháin, Mainistir Fhearmuighe - Béaloideas,* viewable at www.duchas.ie/en/cbes/4921859/4896737/5190225?ChapterID=4921859

O' Reilly, Séamas, 'Ireland isn't Really a Utopia, It's Just its Neighbour is a Gurning Claptrapocracy - The Country's Mild Competency over Coronavirus Can Appear to be Stone-Cold Genius Compared with the UK's Blundering Mess', *The Guardian*, 29-7-2020

Perlman, Jason, 'Terence MacSwiney: The Triumph and Tragedy of the Hunger Strike', New York state Historical Association and the History Cooperative, 2009.

*The Irish Times*, 'The Long History of the Irish Hunger Strike: New Exhibition in Kilmainham Gaol Tells the Story from Thomas Ashe to Bobby Sands', 21-9-2017

Thompson, Sylvia, 'Ireland's Eco-Farmers Emerge from the Hedgerows - *Farming for Nature* Awards Celebrate Farmers Who Protect Habitats and Wildlife', *The Irish Times*, 10-11-2018, available at https://www.irishtimes.com/culture/tv-radio-web/ireland-s-eco-farmers-emerge-from-the-hedgerows-1.3689426

# CROW FLIES ON

High above Gleann an Phréacháin, Crow circles wide and slow.

Way down below, to the north of the Village, he sees the eighth-century cattle-herder putting the finishing touches to his ringfort on the slopes of Doon.

He spies Seán Ó Duinnshléibhe at his desk up in Chimneyfield School, writing out his field-notes in elegant calligraphy. A flap of Crow's wing surges him on to where a horse is leaping the foaming river at Carraig an Aifrinn, a priest clinging to his back. The horse's hooves imprint the rock with a metallic clang.

Another powerful wing-beat soars Crow forward into the day when thousands gathered at the Mass Rock to celebrate their independence in 1921. Wheeling back south over the Village, Crow notices the chatelaine on the steps of the Manor House, greeting guests out of a silver bus.

And you. You were a starving mother called Johanna Carney, leaving Doon in 1847. Or you're Nell the look-out girl in the ditch in 1921. Or you're the priest on the horse in 1712. Or you're Norma, the folk historian, quietly sorting your papers in your side room in the Village in 2021. It just depends which time-hole you popped through, to come into your life in the Glen of the Crow.

Whichever century you're in, when you look up at the end of each day you see Crow drifting back into the Village, returning from wherever it is he goes. Before settling down he circles lazily way up above. You feel his yellow-ringed eye on you, down below. With an upward thrust of his grey talons Crow soars up, high enough to see way beyond today's Gleann an Phréacháin - back into its past and way out into its far future.

He takes a long, leisurely look both ways before starting his descent, the winds of time rushing past him, to spend the night in the trees with his own kind.

# Afterword

## by Barry Kennedy, Crow Glen's publican

We, the Kennedy family, are very pleased to welcome this book to Glenville. Since the days of our ancestor Essie Cuffe, our family have owned and run our pub here in Gleann an Phréacháin, reaching far back into the histories told in this book.

It is moving to know that Pat Carney from Doon, whom you met in Chapter 3 of this book, would have sat sipping a pint in our snug before he ever knew he'd have to take the coffin ship to America (and to his death on board ship during the journey). It was a special moment when we served a cool pint of Murphy's to his great-great-grandson Keith Carney, when he came back with his relatives to visit what had been Pat's homestead in Doon.

Not every Irish village still has a pub. In the 1960s and 70s, we also ran a major dance-hall at the entrance to the village, called the Pinewood. It was a regular 'ballroom of romance' with bands from all over Ireland. Many people learned to dance there, and many marriages came out of there. Over the years, we extended our pub in the village so that our large hall at the back could host card-games, tea-parties, gatherings for older people, meetings of community groups, private parties… And we moved on to serving meals too, or people can drop in just for a coffee.

Like others, we've always felt it's important to have a 'public house' in the village. It helps prevent isolation and loneliness in country areas, and helps those moving in to integrate with the local community. Young or old, on your own or with others, local or newcomer, everyone has always been welcome at Essie Cuffe's!

Barry Kennedy, Owner of *Essie Cuffe's Public House*, Glenville

www.facebook.com/kades.kounty.52

# Keÿ informant, Norma Buckley

The final revelation of this book, dear reader, is that Norma Buckley is actually my mother. My grandparents Nell Sweeney, the look-out girl, and Dinny O' Donoghue, the shopkeeper, were her parents. We all lived together in the Village, where she cared for Nell and Dinny in the traditional way until they passed on aged around 90.

I am Norma's elder daughter who had a difficult birth under the protection of Saint Gobnait's Measure. I saw the Crow Glen Girl Guides founded so that no girl would lack confidence as I did. And it was I who had '*Heaven stormed*' on my behalf by the kind neighbour whose prayers brought me my husband. I didn't mention our relationship before because I felt Norma's other roles in the book merited their own central position.

The book's associates, the *Avondhu Blackwater Partnership*, explained in their *Preface* that Norma was for many years a community representative on their consultative board. A long-term member of Glenville Community Council, she also founded and led Gleann's branch of the Girl Guides. She holds an Environmental Studies qualification from University College Cork as a mature student, and has helped to run a range of heritage restoration projects in Gleann an Phréacháin.

Her volunteering work has helped preserve the built environment - getting stone walls rebuilt, reopening forgotten roads and paths, renovating and protecting the ancient sites of worship in the landscape, commissioning new heritage signage, and creating a community forest. She also restores intangible heritage by giving public talks, school talks and guided heritage visits in Glenn, many of them now documented on YouTube by the local video-maker, Tony Kennedy. She can be contacted at normabuckley2@gmail.com

# Glossary of spiritual terms used

*Absolution* - the forgiving of sins on God's behalf, that can be done by the priest in *Confession*

*Apparition* - an occasion when Our Lady is believed to have appeared and spoken to humans at a specific place on earth; such locations often become sites of pilgrimage for Marian devotions

*Archangels* - Michael, Gabriel and Raphael, three angels of the highest order; Judaism recognises several others

*Calendar of Saints* - a calendar listing every day of the year as dedicated to a different saint

*Canonisation* - ceremony whereby the Church officially recognises a deceased person as a saint, recognising two miracles as having happened through their *intercession*

*Catechism* - official study of the religion as laid out by the Church in textbooks; it was traditionally taught daily during the eight years of Irish primary school

*Communion* - receiving bread, and optionally wine, that has been *consecrated* by a priest during Mass

*Communion of Saints* - the spiritual community of all who have ever been baptised into the Catholic Church, whether now living or dead

*Confession* - the ceremony of confessing one's sins to the priest and receiving God's forgiveness or *absolution*, along with *penance* to do, to make up for those sins

*Confirmation* - ceremony when youths aged around 12 are 'confirmed' as maturing Catholics by a bishop

*Consecrated* - officially blessed by a priest

*Decades of the Rosary* - ten repetitions of the prayer 'Hail Mary', repeated five times, punctuated by other prayers, while saying the Rosary

*Divine Mercy* - one manifestation or aspect of Jesus, appearing as the Risen God dressed in white and radiating coloured rays symbolising pure love and forgiveness

*Eucharist* - the sacrament of changing bread and wine into the Body and Blood of Christ, as well as the name for that bread and wine once consecrated

*Exposition of the Blessed Sacrament* - a simple ceremony displaying the consecrated *host* in a gold display case or *monstrance* on the altar, for silent contemplation

*Favours granted* - requests made through prayer that are understood to have been granted, yielding the results that the petitioner was praying for

*Feast Days* - each day of the year officially dedicated to a specific saint as listed in the Missal or Calendar of Saints

*First Fridays* - the practice of going to *Confession, Mass* and *Holy Communion* on the First Friday of every month for nine months; often done to petition for a *Special Intention* for the benefit of someone else

*First Saturdays* - the practice of attending a special Mass to Our Lady on the First Saturday of every month for nine months

*Guardian Angel* - individual angels believed to protect and support each human throughout their lifetime; a prayer to their Guardian Angel is the first that small children learn, asking for safety during their night's sleep

*Holy Communion* - a small flat disc of paper-like bread, swallowed by parishioners after being transformed via Transubstantiation into the Body of Christ during the Eucharist ceremony at Mass

*Holy Souls* - the souls of the deceased, generally understood to be still in Purgatory and not having acceded yet to Heaven

*Host* - the *consecrated* bread that has been mystically turned into the body of Christ during the *sacrament* of the *Eucharist*; usually a flat disc of paper-like bread just an inch in diameter, swallowed by parishioners during *Holy Communion*

*Indulgence* - earned through specific religious practices defined by the Church, a reduction in the amount of time one will have to spend in Purgatory being purified before entering Heaven; can also be earned on behalf of someone already deceased

*Intercession* - act whereby either a living saint or a divine being in the spirit world intercedes to assist a living individual, often when the individual had requested this by praying to them

*Legion of Mary* - organisation of laypeople devoted to Our Lady, founded in Dublin in 1921, with millions of members worldwide today

*Mantilla* - a triangle of lace, usually black, worn by women over the hair to symbolise religious respect and modesty

*Marian* - adjective of Mary, Our Lady

*Miraculous Medal* - a devotional medal depicting Our Lady as she appeared in an apparition to Saint Catherine in Paris in 1830

*Missal* - liturgical book giving all the instructions and texts for the celebration of Mass on each day of the year

*Mission* - a communal retreat for parishioners; an annual week of intensive daily practices led in the local church by priests who travelled around the country as 'mission priests'; widely attended by the whole community up to the end of the 1980s

*Missions, the* - evangelical projects delivered by Irish clergy in Third World countries, bringing Catholicism to poor communities there, along with healthcare and education

*Monstrance* - gold display box with radiating rays and a circular glass space at the centre: the consecrated *host* is placed in it to be venerated silently by parishioners in the church during a ceremony called the *Exposition of the Blessed Sacrament*

*Mortuary Card* - small two-sided commemorative card with the photo and dates of a deceased person, kept in one's Prayer Book as a reminder to pray for them

*Mysteries of the Rosary* - four sets of five scenes from the life of Jesus, grouped under themes as Sorrowful, Joyful, Glorious and Luminous; one of these sets is to be contemplated while reciting the five decades of the Rosary

*Novenas* - a wide range of different devotional practices but always done in a series of nine (days, weeks or months); often done as a petition for a specific *Special Intention*

*Patron saint* - a saint dedicated to a particular cause or group, e.g. travellers, sailors, mothers, etc.; at Confirmation a child adopts any saint of their choice as their own 'patron saint' for life

*Penance* - acts of atonement for one's sins, specified by the priest at *Confession*; usually a specific amount of prayers to recite

*Perpetual lamp* - a small red lamp in front of the Sacred Heart picture at the centre of the home, originally lit by oil and later by electricity, which was never allowed to go out, by night or by day

*Pilgrimage* - the act of physically travelling to a specific location - local, national or foreign - for spiritual purposes

*Pioneers* - members of the *Pioneer Total Abstinence Association of the Sacred Heart*, a social and religious association of Catholic teetotallers

*Plenary Indulgence* - full clearance of the time that one would have had to spend in Purgatory being purified before entering Heaven

*Relic* - part of an object, such as a body part of a saint or a piece of Christ's cross, believed to have survived from the original era or event; can also refer to a shred of cloth that has touched the original relic

*Resurrection* - the act of Jesus rising from the dead on Easter Sunday morning

*Retreat* - a period of time dedicated entirely to spiritual practice, which may also include relaxation

*Rosary* - five 'decades' of the prayer Hail Mary, punctuated by other prayers and counted out by hand on a personal set of Rosary beads

*Sacraments* - seven rituals channelling God's grace directly, which Jesus performed and then bequeathed to the Church: Baptism, Confession, the Eucharist; Confirmation, Marriage, Anointing of the Sick, and the Holy Orders received by clergy

*Sacristy* - side room off the altar where ceremonial garments and objects are kept, and the priest prepares himself for ceremonies

*Sanctuary lamp* - the red light always lighting on the altar of a Catholic church where the *consecrated host* is present in the *tabernacle*

*Scapular* - a protective object made of cloth, worn against the skin under clothing

*Special intention* - a specific request made by an individual in prayer; will be recognised by the person as a '*Favour granted*' if their petition is successful

*Stations of the Cross* - 14 images depicting scenes around Jesus' crucifixion, each to be visited and accompanied by prayers and contemplations; usually carved scenes or 3D statues along the interior walls of a church, or occasionally outdoors in a special location

*Stations, at farms* - the practice of the priest offering *Confession* and Mass at specific outlying farms, with all the neighbourhood invited and a hospitable meal to follow

*Tabernacle* - a locked box at the centre of the altar containing the *consecrated* host

*Transubstantiation* - the mystery whereby the priest transforms bread and wine into the Body and Blood of Christ during the *Eucharist* sacrament at Mass

# Irish-Language Originals

## of poems by Bards from around Gleann an Phréacháin

**Gearóid Iarla Mac Gearailt** (1338-1398) was 'the earliest recorded writer of courtly love lyrics in Irish', and worked extensively in the Blackwater Valley. [258] In Chapter 8 we saw the English translation of his most famous poem, written around 1370, called 'Speak Not Ill of Womankind'. Here is his original in Irish:

> Mairg adeir olc ris na mnáibh!
> bheith dá n-éagnach ní dáil chruinn,
> a bhfuaradar do ghuth riamh
> dom aithne ní hiad do thuill.
>
> Binn a mbriathra, gasta a nglór,
> aicme rerab mór mo bháidh;
> a gcáineadh is mairg nár loc;
> mairg adeir olc ris na mnáibh.
>
> Ní dhéanaid fionghal ná feall,
> ná ní ar a mbeith grainc ná gráin;
> ní sháraighid cill ná clog;
> mairg adeir olc ris na mnáibh.
>
> Ní tháinig riamh acht ó mhnaoi
> easbag ná rí (dearbhtha an dáil),
> ná priomhfháidh ar nách biadh locht;
> mairg adeir olc ris na mnáibh. [259]

**Eoghan Ó Caoimh** (1656-1726), one of the greatest Irish-language poets of his time, was born in Gleann an Phréacháin. We saw the English translation of the heart-broken lament that he wrote for his dead wife, Eleanor Nagle. This is his original in Irish:

> Mo chás cumha, mo chumhgach, mo chogadh, mo chreach,
> is m'fháth túirse gan cuntas thug srothach mo dhearc

---

258 Angela Bourke, as in Note 75
259 *CELT: The Corpus of Electronic Texts*, University College Cork, available at https://celt.ucc.ie//published/G402258/index.html

la spiúnta mo dhubhachais, dom' chosnamh i gceas,
a bhláth mhúinte is tú dhluth-churtha ar Bhrosnaigh i bhfeart.

Mo chrá an úir iompaithe ar ghorm do dhearc
is do ráite rúin cúil riom, nar chogair tar cheart,
do bhrá mar chúir dúnta faoi chlocaibh, is feas,
d'fhóg mé ciúin cúthail gan soirbheas seal.

Do lámh gan lúth d'ionsmaigh a hobair go deas,
is do bhánchorp úr ionraic dár bhronnas mo shearc –
ag táintibh dubha dúra da dtochailt i gclais,
d'fhúg mé i bpúir brúite go follas ag meath

O ráining tú i n-dúir curtha, a chogair gan chealt,
i gcáil chúnta nár iompaigh ó bhochtaibh do dhearc
go bráth do ghnúis dlúh liom nach cosmhail do theacht,
lá cúntas an Dúilimh go roichir 'na theach.

Gráin chàige ort, a thrí liosta is duibhe ar bith dath,
a ghráigh giúngaigh glún-fhada is miste mo rath,
a bháis bhrúid-smeartha thúrnas gach nduine go prap,
plá chughat ó dhlúth-scarais mise is mo bhean. [260]

**Eoghan Rua Ó Suilleabháin** (1748-1784), with 'fluency and learning in Gaelic, English, Latin and Greek', was tutor to the Nagles of the Nagle Mountains. In Chapter 8 we saw the English translation of this verse that he composed against the effects of the Penal Laws: [261]

Don tsráid nuair théim mar aon ar cuaird
Ní háil leo mé is ní réidhid lem chluain;
Bíd mná le chéile ag plé dá lua:
'Cé háit, cé hé, cá taobh ór ghluais?' [262]

---

260 Deane, Bourke & Carpenter (eds.), *The Field Day Anthology of Irish Writing,* Vol 4, Cork University Press, 2002

261 Pádraig Ó Cearúill, 'Eoghán Rua Ó Suilleabháin: A True Exponent of the Bardic Legacy' in *Proceedings of the Barra Ó Donnabháin Symposium,* New York University, 2007

262 See Seán Garvey, All-Ireland Sean-Nós Singing Champion, singing this and other verses of Eoghan Rua's 'Slán le Máigh' on Trad TG4 TV, 26-8-2017, available at www.youtube.com/watch?reload=9&v=JliwjO90EjI; the page also gives the original lyrics in Irish

# Bibliography of works cited

**Allen**, Kieran, *1916: Ireland's Revolutionary Tradition*, Pluto Press, 2016

**Annan**, Gabriele, 'Sheep into Goats', *London Review of Books*, 24-1-1980

**Arnold**, John, '97 years on: The Stories behind these Seven Proud, Brave Men', *The Evening Echo*, 4-10-2019, available at www.echolive.ie/nostalgia/John-Arnold-97-years-on-the-stories-behind-these-seven-proud-brave-men-178581d3-4bdd-463f-9e27-4c1f58d75417-ds

**Ballineen** & Enniskeane Area Heritage Group, *Murragh: A Place of Graves*, 2017

**Barry**, Tom, *Guerilla Days in Ireland*, Anvil Press, 1993

**Battersby**, Eileen, 'Going Underground', *Irish Times*, 2-2-2002

**Bence-Jones**, Mark, *A Guide to Irish Country Houses,* Constable, 1996

**Bence-Jones**, Mark, *Twilight of the Ascendancy*, Constable, 1987

**Bence-Jones**, Mark, *The British Aristocracy*, Constable, 1979

**Bence-Jones**, Mark, *The Palaces of the Raj: Magnificence and Misery of the Lord Sahibs*, Allen & Unwin, 1973

**Berkhead**, Sam, 'How the *Charlie Hebdo* attack has changed free speech in France and the US', *International Journalists' Network*, 8-1-2016

**Bishop**, Hilary, 'Classifications of Sacred Space: A New Understanding of Mass Rock Sites in Ireland', *International Journal of History and Archaeology*, 2016

**Bishop**, Hilary, *Sacred Space. A Study of the Mass Rocks of the Diocese of Cork and Ross, County Cork*, PhD Thesis, University of Liverpool, 2013

**Blake** *of Ballyglunin Papers, 1770-1830*, Archive ref. IE JHL/LE007, Archives of National University of Ireland Galway

**Borgonovo**, John, 'Atlas of the Irish Revolution, The War in Cork and Kerry', 18-9-2017, available at *www.IrishExaminer.com*

**Borgonovo**, John, 'The Guerrilla Infrastructure: IRA Special Services in the Cork Number One Brigade, 1917-1921', *The Irish Sword*, Vol 27, Military History Society of Ireland, 2010

**Bourke**, Angela, *The Burning of Bridget Cleary: A True Story*, Pimlico, 1999

**Bourke**, Angela, *The Field Day Anthology of Irish Writing*, Cork University Press, Cork, 2002

**Breen**, Dan, *My Fight for Irish Freedom*, Anvil Press, 1993

**Brenneman**, Walter and Mary, *Crossing the Circle at the Holy Wells of Ireland*, University of Virginia Press, 1995

**Buckley,** William, testimony at Irish Bureau of Military History, BMH WS1009, available at www.bureauofmilitaryhistory.ie

**Buildings**, Ireland XO, 'The Hermitage, Rathfarnham', available at https://irelandxo.com/ireland-xo/history-and-genealogy/buildings-database/hermitage-rathfarnham

**Buttimer**, Anne, 'Home, Reach and the Sense of Place' in *The Human Experience of Space and Place,* Anne Buttimer & David Seamon (eds.), Routeldge, 1980

**Calendar** *to Fiants of the Reign of Henry VIII, 1510-47, & Queen Elizabeth, 1558-1603*, London, 1601

**Carroll**, Aideen, *Seán Moylan: Rebel Leader*, Mercier Press, Cork, 2010

**Carroll**, Michael, *Irish Pilgrimage: Holy Wells and Popular Catholic Devotion*, Johns Hopkins University Press, 1999

**Cló Iar-Chonnacht** for the National Library of Ireland, *Beathaisnéisí,* 2020, available at www.ainm.ie (in Irish only)

**Collins**, Lorcan, *Ireland's War of Independence 1919-21: The IRA's Guerrilla Campaign*, O' Brien Press, 2019

**Collins**, Michael, *The Path to Freedom*, NuVision Publications, South Dakota, USA, 2005

**Coppinger**, W.A., *History of the Coppinger Family of County Cork*, Sotherton, London, 1884

**Cork *Beo***, 'An Interactive Web Map of All IRA Operations in Co. Cork, 1919 - 1921', 27-4-2020 available at www.corkbeo.ie/news/history/interactive-map-ira-operations-cork-18113200

**Cork City** & County Archives, *Seán Punch Autograph Book 1907-1923*, Archive Ref. IE CCCA/U089

**Cork County** Council, *Centenary Timeline for the County of Cork (1920 – 1923): War of Independence and Civil War*, available at www.corkcoco.ie/sites/default/files/2020-02/centenary-timeline-for-the-county-of-cork-1920-to-1924.pdf

**Cork County** Council, *Local Area Plan, Cobh Municipal District,* Vol 1, Section 4, 'Main Policy Material', available at http://corklocalareaplans.com/cobh-municipal-district

**Costello**, Francis, *Enduring the Most: The Life and Death of Terence MacSwiney*, Brandon Press, 1995

**Cronin**, J., Murphy, M. & Smyth, W.A. (eds.), *Atlas of the Great Irish Famine*, Cork University Press, Cork, 2012

**Cronin**, U., 'Speak Not Ill of Womankind', translation at *Get behind the Muse,* available at https://ucronin.wordpress.com/2017/09/17/gearoid-iarla-and-ennis

**Crowley**, J., O Drisceoil, D., Murphy, M., Borgonovo, J., (eds.), *Atlas of the Irish Revolution*, Cork University Press, Cork, 2017

**Cullen**, Fintan, *Sources in Irish Art: A Reader*, Cork University Press, 2000

**Cunningham**, Sonya, 'Surfing Farmers in Ireland', *The Ecologist*, 31-10-2019, available at https://theecologist.org/2019/oct/31/surfing-farmers-ireland

**Dalai** Lama, *The Art of Happiness - A Handbook for Living*, Hodder Press, 1999

**Deane**, Bourke & Carpenter (eds.), *The Field Day Anthology of Irish Writing,* Vol 4, Cork University Press, 2002

**Dorney**, John, 'The Irish Civil War, A Brief Overview', *The Irish Story* website, 2012

**Encyclopedia** Britannica, 'Young Ireland - Irish Nationalist Movement', available at www.britannica.com/topic/Young-Ireland

**English**, Richard, *Ernie O' Malley: IRA Intellectual*, Clarendon Press, 1999

**Fallon**, Donal, 'A Tribute to Tomás Mac Curtain, the Martyred Lord Mayor of Cork', *The Journal.ie*, 14-3-2020, available at www.thejournal.ie/readme/tomas-mac-curtain-5045854-Mar2020/

**Fallon**, Eoghan, University College Cork, 'Irish Masculinity', available at https://www.academia.edu/35442829/Irish_masculinity_essay?email_work_card=view-paper

**Farming** *for Nature* website, available at
www.farmingfornature.ie/2020/06/29/farming-for-nature-wins-global-biodiversity-award

**Feller,** Joseph, *Roots and Wings: Orthodoxy, Tradition, and Creativity in Irish Folk Catholicism*, unpublished PhD thesis, University College Cork, 1998

**Ferriter,** Diarmaid, 'From Turmoil to Truce: A Mature Reflection on the War of Independence', *The Irish Times*, 11-1-2020

**Fifteenth** *Annual Report from the Commissioners of Public Records of Ireland*, 'Abstracts of The Conveyances from the Trustees of the Forfeited Estates and Interests in Ireland in 1688', London, 1825

**Fitzgerald,** John, *Denis Hickey, Life and Times*, private slideshow

**Fleming** / *Mulcahy Family Tree*, 'Glenville at the Turn of the Century', available at https://flemmultree.wordpress.com

**Foster**, Gavin, 'IRA Emigration and the Social Outcomes of the Civil War' in *The Irish Civil War and Society: Politics, Class and Conflict*, Palgrave, London, 2014

**Frey,** Thomas, 'Life begins at a billion moments', 23-1-2018, available at https://futuristspeaker.com/artificial-intelligence/life-begins-at-a-billion-moments

**Gaffin,** Dennis, *Running with the Fairies: Towards a Transpersonal Anthropology of Religion*, Cambridge Scholars, 2013

**Galbally,** Ann*, Redmond Barry: An Anglo-Irish Australian,* Melbourne University Press, Melbourne, 2013

**Grainger,** Diarmuid, *Witnesses to Freedom: A Day by Day Account of the Irish War of Independence in Cork*, Independent, 2019

**Joyce**, P.W., *A Smaller Social History of Ancient Ireland*, Longmans, Green & Company, 1908

**Hart**, Peter, *The IRA and its Enemies: Violence and Community in Cork*, Oxford University Press, Oxford, 1998

**Heritage** Council, 'Significant Unpublished Irish Archaeological Excavations, 1930-1997: Ringforts', available at https://www.heritagecouncil.ie/unpublished_excavations/section13.html

**Hickey,** Sinéad, Sheehan, Donal & Nagle, Tony, *Farm Habitat Management Guidelines - A Guide to Farming with Nature,* The Bride Project, Castlelyons, downloadable free of charge at https://www.thebrideproject.ie/wp-content/uploads/2020/04/BRIDE-Project-Farm-Habitat-Management-Guidlines.pdf

**Hoffman**, Marella, *Asylum under Dreaming Spires: Refugees' Lives in Cambridge Today*, with the Living Refugee Archive, University of East London, 2017

**Hoffman**, Marella (then Buckley), 'The Irish among the British and the Women among the Irish' in *Location and Dislocation: The New Irish at Home and Abroad,* Cork University Press, 1997

**House** of Lords of Great Britain, *Report from the Commissioners*, Volume 29, Part 1, London, 1842

**International** Panel of Experts on Sustainable Food Systems, *From Uniformity to Diversity: A Paradigm Shift from Industrial Agriculture to Diversified Agro-Ecological Systems*, Institute of Development Studies, 2016, available at www.ipes-food.org

**Irish** *Environment* journal, 'Agroecology: Is there a clear green path from monocultures to diversity in agriculture?', Report, 1-7-2016, available at https://www.irishenvironment.com/reports/agroecology-clear-green-path-monocultures-diversity-agriculture

**Johnson**, Boris, 'Politics', *The Spectator*, 19-8-1995

**Keane**, Barry, *Cork's Revolutionary Dead*, Mercier Press, Cork, 2017

**Koch**, John, *The Celts: History, Life and Culture*, Vol 1, ABC-Clio, Oxford, 2012

**Lavenda**, R. & Schultz, E., *Core Concepts in Cultural Anthropology*, Oxford University Press, 2019

**Leddy**, Con, testimony at Irish Bureau of Military History, BMH WS0756, available at www.bureauofmilitaryhistory.ie

**Lewis**, S., *A Topographical Dictionary of Ireland,* Lewis & Co., London, 1837

**Loach**, Ken, feature film *The Wind that Shakes the Barley*, Sixteen Films Matador Pictures, 2006

**Lyons**, Jane, 'Transportation of the Irish', *From-Ireland.net*, 2-3-2013, available at www.from-ireland.net/transportation-of-the-irish

**Mac Giolla Chríost**, Diarmuid, *The Irish Language in Ireland: From Goídel to Globalisation*, Routledge, London, 2004

**Mac Manus**, Seamas*, The Story of the Irish Race*, Devin-Adair, 1983

**Magan,** Manchán, *Thirty-Two Words for Field: Lost Words of the Irish Landscape,* Gill, 2020

**Marks**, Kathy, *The Independent* (UK), 'Blair Issues Apology for Irish Potato Famine', 2-6-1997

**McGarry**, Patsy, 'Cork-born founder of Presentation Sisters declared 'Venerable'', *The Irish Times*, 1-11-2013

**McGrath**, Adrian, 'Coffin Ships and the Great Hunger - An Gorta Mór', *Irish American Journal*, 30-8-2017, available at www.irishamericanjournal.com/2017/08/coffin-ships.html

**McSweeney,** Ella, 'Life Attracts Life: The Irish Farmers Filling their Fields with Bees and Butterflies - Rewarding Positive Environmental Impact Has Revitalised an Area of West Ireland. Is this a Solution to the Country's Acute Nature Crisis?', *The Guardian*, 6-6-2020

**Military** Service Pensions Collection, available at www.militaryarchives.ie

**Morley**, Vincent, *Dictionary of Irish Biography*, Royal Irish Academy with Cambridge University Press, available at https://dib.cambridge.org/viewReadPage.do?articleId=a6289

**Murphy**, Mike, '*An Bothán*, a symbol of Famine misery', *News and Views*, University College Cork, 2018

**Murray**, Daniel, 'The Fog of Certainty: Liam Lynch and the Start of the Civil War, 1922' in *An Irish History Blog*, 2017

**Nic Dhaibhéid**, Caoimhe, 'Portrait of a Revolutionary Afterlife', *The Irish Times*, 12-11-2011

**O' Brien**, Patrick, testimony at Irish Bureau of Military History, BMH WS0764, available at www.bureauofmilitaryhistory.ie

**O' Byrne**, Robert, 'A Life's Work in Ireland', available at https://theirishaesthete.com/2014/11/10/a-lifes-work-in-ireland

**Ó Cadhla**, Stiofán, *The Holy Well Tradition: The Pattern of St Declan, Ardmore, County Waterford, 1800-2000*, Maynooth Studies in Local History, Four Courts Press, Dublin, 2002

**Ó Cearúill**, Pádraig, 'Eoghán Rua Ó Suilleabháin: A True Exponent of the Bardic Legacy' in *Proceedings of the Barra Ó Donnabháin Symposium*, New York University, 2007

**Ó Domhnaill**, 'Séamas Eoghan Ruadh Ó Súilleabháin: Aspects of his Life and Work' in *Church and State, Fourth Quarter, Lux Occulta* website, 2010

**O' Donnell**, Katherine, 'Edmund Burke's Political Poetics' in *Anáil an Bhéil Bheo: Orality and Modern Irish Culture*, Cambridge Scholars, Newcastle, 2009

**O' Donoghue**, Florence, *No Other Law: The Story of Liam Lynch and the Irish Republican Army, 1916-1923*, Irish Press, Dublin, 1954

**Ó Duinnshléibhe**, Seán, National Folklore Collection, Roll No. 12542, p. 221-467. *The School Collection, Volume 0382: Áth Dúna, Gleann an Phréacháin, Mainistir Fhearmuighe - Béaloideas,* viewable at www.duchas.ie/en/cbes/4921859/4896737/5190225?ChapterID=4921859

**O' Keeffe** *Clan Gathering and Rally,* 2016, available at http://okeeffeclans.com/fathereoghanokeeffe.html

**O' Leary**, Brendan, Glenville National School at www.glenvillens.wordpress.com

**O' Malley**, Cormac, 'The Publication History of *On Another Man's Wound'*, *New Hibernia Review*, Autumn 2003

**O' Malley**, Ernie, (author) and Ó Ruairc, P., Borgonovo, J. & Bielenberg, A. (eds.), *The Men Will Talk to Me*, Ernie O'Malley Series, West Cork Brigade, Mercier Press, Cork, 2015

**O' Malley**, Ernie, *On Another Man's Wound*, Mercier Press, Cork, 2013

**O' Neill**, Tom, *The Battle of Clonmult: The IRA's Worst Defeat*, THP Ireland, 2019

**O' Reilly**, Séamas, 'Ireland isn't Really a Utopia, It's Just its Neighbour is a Gurning Claptrapocracy - The Country's Mild Competency over Coronavirus Can Appear to be Stone-Cold Genius Compared with the UK's Blundering Mess', *The Guardian*, 29-7-2020

**O' Reilly**, Terence, *Rebel Heart: George Lennon, Flying Column Commander*, Mercier Press, Cork, 2005

**O' Riordan**, Michelle, *The Gaelic Mind and the Collapse of the Gaelic World*, Cork University Press, 1990

**Ó Súilleabháin**, D., National Folklore Collection, Gleann an Phréacháin, Roll No. 450, p. 148, available at https://www.duchas.ie/en/cbes/4921858/4896707

**O' Sullivan**, Donal, *Irish Folk Music and Song*, Three Candles, Dublin, 1952

**Perlman**, Jason, 'Terence MacSwiney: The Triumph and Tragedy of the Hunger Strike', New York state Historical Association and the History Cooperative, 2009.

**Petrie**, George (ed.), *The Petrie Collection of the Ancient Music of Ireland,* Gill, Dublin, 1855

**Placenames** *Database of Ireland*, 'Glossary and Distribution Maps', available at www.logainm.ie

**Power**, George, testimony at Irish Bureau of Military History, BMH WS0451, available at www.bureauofmilitaryhistory.ie

**Quinlan**, Ailín, 'Burial site of legendary Diarmuid found, says historian', *The Cork Examiner,* 10-7-2017

**Real** *Cork* Youtube channel, *Burials at Doonpeter, Glenville, Co Cork, Ireland,* 30-9-2018, available at www.youtube.com/watch?v=mNuNv67Z_T8

**Real** *Cork* Youtube channel, *Doonpeter Well, Glenville, Co Cork,* 23-6-2017, available at www.youtube.com/watch?v=-z0MIRwd69g

**Real** *Cork* Youtube channel, *The Mass Rock in the Glen, Glenville, Co. Cork,* 9-11-2014, available at www.youtube.com/watch?v=o0nsKdcWpnw

**Royal Irish Academy**, *The Book of Fermoy*, RIA MS 23 E 29, Cat. no. 1134

**Royal Irish Academy**, 'Cultural Artefacts from Sixteenth-Century Ireland', available at www.ria.ie/another-view-gaelic-manuscript-culture-edmund-spensers-ireland

**Royal Irish Academy** and Cambridge University Press, *Dictionary of Irish Biography*, available at https://dib.cambridge.org

**Ryan**, Louise & Ward, Margaret, *Irish Women and Nationalism: Soldiers, New Women and Wicked Hags,* Irish Academic Press, Dublin, 2019

**Ryan**, Meda, *The Real Chief: The Story of Liam Lynch*, Mercier Press, Cork, 2005

**Ryan,** Salvador, 'The Quest for Tangible Religion', *The Furrow*, Vol 55, 2004

**Smyth**, Daragh, *Cú Chulainn: An Iron Age Hero*, Irish Academic Press, 2005

**Smyth**, Daragh, *A Guide to Irish Mythology*, Irish Academic Press, 1998

**Stout**, Mathew, *The Irish Ringfort*, Four Courts Press, Dublin, 1997

**Taylor**, Lawrence, *Occasions of Faith: An Anthropology of Irish Catholics,* University of Pennsylvania Press, 1995

**The** *Cairo Gang* website, 'British soldiers who Died in Ireland, 1919-1921', available at www.cairogang.com/soldiers-killed/list-1921.html

**The** *Cork Examiner*, 'Is Fionn MacCumhail's wingman buried in West Cork?', 10-9-2015

**The** *Cork Examiner*, 'Land Meeting in Glenville', 29-12-1880

**The** *Evening Echo*, 'Late Mrs K. Hickey, Glenville', 5-6-1978

**The** *Independent* (UK), 'Ireland's War of Independence: The Chilling Story of the Black and Tans', London, 21-4-2006

**The** *Irish Independent*, *'World News', 25-4-2010*

**The** *Irish Times*, 'The Long History of the Irish Hunger Strike: New Exhibition in Kilmainham Gaol Tells the Story from Thomas Ashe to Bobby Sands', 21-9-2017

**The** *Irish Times*, 'Eminent historian of Irish ascendancy', 8-5-2010

**The** *New Scientist*, 'Vatican Admits Galileo was Right', 7-11-1992

**The** *Southern Star*, 'The Famous 1881 Debate - Key Issues', available at www.failteromhat.com/southernstar

**The** *Southern Star Centenary Supplement, 1889-1989*, available at www.failteromhat.com/southernstar

**The** *Telegraph*, 'Mark Bence-Jones, Obituary', 30-4-2010

**Thompson**, Sylvia, 'Ireland's Eco-Farmers Emerge from the Hedgerows - *Farming for Nature* Awards Celebrate Farmers Who Protect Habitats and Wildlife', *The Irish Times*, 10-11-2018, available at https://www.irishtimes.com/culture/tv-radio-web/ireland-s-eco-farmers-emerge-from-the-hedgerows-1.3689426

**Townshend**, Charles, *The Republic: The Fight for Irish Independence, 1918-1923*, Penguin, London, 2014

**Wallace**, David, *Twenty-Two Turbulent Years, 1639 -1661*, Fastprint, Southgate, 2013

**Walsh,** Maurice, *Bitter Freedom: Ireland in a Revolutionary World,* Liveright, 2016

**Ward**, Lauren, 'Ireland's Saintly Women and their Healing Holy Wells', *National Geographic*, 10-2-2012, available at https://blog.nationalgeographic.org/2012/02/10/irelands-saintly-women-and-their-healing-holy-wells

**Wilson**, *Directory of Ireland, 1834*, 'Fair Towns of Ireland', available at www.from-ireland.net/category/miscellaneous/cork-miscellaneous/page/3

# About the author

Marella Hoffman (née Buckley) was raised in Glenville, the Irish village featured in this, her ninth book.

Hoffman wrote a PhD thesis on literature that has been published as a trilogy, and she lectured at University College Cork. She has held research awards or positions at universities in France, Switzerland, the US and at the University of Cambridge, where she was based for almost a decade. She has also worked extensively for governments, designing systems that boost democracy and social justice among excluded communities. Her tools for assisting dialogue between refugees and host communities were published recently as part of a toolkit for the United Nations.

A Fellow of the Royal Anthropological Institute, her books have studied topics like the attitudes of the permanently unemployed White underclass in an English town; refugees' experiences of nationality and identity in their adopted homeland; or the ecological practices and lifestyle of an 87-year-old hermit shepherd in the French Mediterranean hills. Her work has been published by Routledge, the Sorbonne University in Paris, other academic presses, regional publishers and as journalism.

She is married to the author and medical scientist Dr Richard Hoffman. Though working in Cambridge, they also have a writers' retreat near the Bordeaux vineyards in southern France, where they are rewilding several acres as an ecological nature reserve. From 2021, they will accommodate visiting writers and families on holiday there. For information or to get in touch, visit www.marellahoffman.com or email contact@marellahoffman.com

Printed in Great Britain
by Amazon